UNIVERSITY OF NORTH CAROLINA
STUDIES IN THE ROMANCE LANGUAGES AND LITERATURES
Number 109

FRANCISCO RODRIGUES LOBO

DIALOGUE AND COURTLY LORE IN
RENAISSANCE PORTUGAL

FRANCISCO RODRIGUES LOBO
DIALOGUE AND COURTLY LORE
IN
RENAISSANCE PORTUGAL

BY

RICHARD A. PRETO-RODAS

CHAPEL HILL

THE UNIVERSITY OF NORTH CAROLINA PRESS

depósito legal: v. 4.516 - 1971

artes gráficas soler, s. a. - jávea, 28 - valencia (8) - 1971

TABLE OF CONTENTS

	Page
PREFACE ...	13
CHAPTER I. INTRODUCTION ...	19
— II. THE DIALOGUE IN CLASSICAL AND RENAISSANCE TRADITION ...	27
— III. THE DIALOGUE IN SPAIN AND PORTUGAL ...	37
— IV. THE FICTIONAL AND DIALECTICAL ELEMENTS OF *Corte na Aldeia e Noites de Inverno* ...	61
— V. COURTIER AND COURTESY IN *Corte na Aldeia* ...	86
— VI. THE SOCIAL USES OF LANGUAGE IN *Corte na Aldeia*.	116
— VII. THE TYPES OF LITERATURE IN *Corte na Aldeia* ...	144
— VIII. CONCLUSION ...	175
BIBLIOGRAPHY ...	181

To Edward Glaser

ACKNOWLEDGMENTS

A grant given in 1965 by the Horace H. Rackham School of Graduate Studies at the University of Michigan allowed me to do the major portion of the research for this book, which began as a doctoral dissertation. The publication of the study in its final form was made possible by a grant from the Research Board of the Graduate College of the University of Illinois. Thanks are also due to the Department of Spanish, Italian, and Portuguese at the University of Illinois for sponsoring the revision of the manuscript and to Miss Maria do Carmo Ferreira for her careful reading and typing. I am especially grateful to Professor Edward Glaser of the University of Michigan who originally suggested the topic and provided the encouragement, advice, and criticism necessary for its subsequent development.

PREFACE

Some students of Lusitania literature tend to consider the Phillipine domination of the entire Peninsula (1580-1640) as a Dark Age not only for Portugal's destiny but also for the nation's creative writers.[1] As a result of this view, the artistic endeavors of Portuguese authors of the first half of the seventeenth century are largely ignored by modern critics who occasionally scan the works of the period to unearth a spark of political protest. One of the major victims of this literary neglect has been Francisco Rodrigues Lobo (1580-1621) about whom the following observation was made in 1918: "Monografia ou sequer estudo crítico de algum fôlego ninguém consagrou ao quase olvidado mestre; apenas os historiadores da literatura se detiveram por um momento no exame da sua figura artística...".[2] A recent study of Lobo's poetic development has altered the situation considerably;[3] however, the present state of critical bibliography devoted exclusively to Lobo, particularly with regard to his prose works, remains extremely sparse.[4]

---

[1] As an example we may cite Hernâni Cidade who sees the period as a cultural wasteland. See Hernâni Cidade, *A literatura autonomista sob os Felipes* (Lisboa, n.d.). For a judicious criticism of Cidade's book, see Eugenio Asensio, "España en la época filipina," *RFE*, XXXIII (1949), 66-109.

[2] Ricardo Jorge, "Francisco Rodrigues Lobo, ensaio biográfico e crítico," *Revista da Universidade de Coimbra*, VIII (1919), 116-117. Jorge's study was first published in a piecemeal fashion in the *Revista* from 1913 through 1919.

[3] Maria de Lurdes Belchior Pontes, *Itinerario poético de Rodrigues Lobo* (Lisboa, 1959).

[4] See the article referring to Lobo in *Dicionário de Literatura*, ed. Jacinto do Prado Coelho, Vol. I (Lisboa, 1969), pp. 572-573. The sparse

The short shrift which Lobo has received from modern criticism stands in marked contrast to his popularity during the seventeenth century when Lisbon publishers circulated a combined total of eighteen editions of his three pastoral novels and of *Corte na aldeia e noites de inverno*.[5] In view of the relatively few Spanish translations of Portuguese works, it is equally noteworthy that a Spanish translation of *Corte na aldeia*, generally considered the *chef d'œuvre* of Lobo's corpus, was published in Montilla within three years of its appearance in Portugal in 1619.[6] The translation was obviously well received in Spain, since a second edition was published a year later (1623) in Córdoba, and a third was issued in Valencia as late as 1793.[7]

The subject of the present study, *Corte na aldeia* comprises sixteen dialogues concerning a variety of topics which, in the estimation of the Spanish translator, are designed to provide a curriculum for "una escuela universal donde puede aprender uno a ser hombre y merecer el nombre."[8] Less subject to the charge of partiality is Gracián's optimistic prediction that "Este [libro]... será eterno... miradle y leedle que es la corte en aldea del portugués Lobo..."[9] Equally significant an appraisal comes from

---

bibliography is hardly enhanced by a few omissions and by erroneously entering the name of a recent significant contributor to the bibliography regarding Lobo (Carlos Alberto Silva for Carlos Alberto Ferreira). See below, Chapter I, Note 1.

[5] The following editions all appeared in Lisbon: *Primavera*, 1600, 1608, 1619, 1635, 1651, 1670; *Pastor Peregrino*, 1608, 1618, 1651, 1670; *Desenganado*, 1614, 1615, 1670; *Corte na aldeia e noites de inverno*, 1619, 1630, 1649, 1670, 1695. A complete bibliography concerning Lobo's work in Portugal up to 1918 is found in Jorge's article in Volume VI of the *Revista da Universidade de Coimbra* (1917), pp. 420-421.

[6] Lobo figures prominently among the few Portuguese writers sharing the distinction of translation into Spanish. cf. Edward Glaser, *Estudios Hispano-Portugueses, Relaciones literarias del Siglo de Oro* (Valencia, 1957), p. viii. Lobo's Spanish translation was the work of Juan Baptista de Morales. See his *Corte en aldea y noches de invierno* (Montilla, 1622).

[7] A purloined edition attributed to the Spanish "reviser," Don Alejandro Ponce de León, appeared with the title *Discreción en el retiro y política en la aldea en diálogos historiados* (Madrid, 1755). For a comparison of the Portuguese edition and the pirated Spanish version see Monroe Z. Hafter (who first noted the literary fraud), "Lobo's *Corte na aldeia* (1619) in a Spanish Disguise (1755)", *Romanische Forschungen*, LXXXI (1969), 565-570.

[8] See "Al Lector" in Morales' translation.

[9] Baltasar Gracián, *El Criticón* (Madrid, 1957), p. 412.

Francisco Manuel de Melo who describes the author of *Corte na aldeia* as "claro, engenhoso, elegante" and confers upon him the accolade "grande cortesano e não menor jardineiro da língua portuguêsa que tosou, poliu, e cultivou..." [10] Well over a century after its publication *Corte na aldeia* still aroused enough interest to merit a humorous continuation by António Bento who gave his sequel the formidable title *Aldeia na corte e noites de verão seguidas às noites de inverno de Francisco Rodrigues Lobo* (Lisbon, 1750). [11]

In the nineteenth century, critics were quick to stress that, in an era when prose was couched in the tersely epigrammatic style of the Latin Silver Age, *Corte na aldeia* represented a "kind of Ciceronian style in Portuguese prose" and consequently hailed it as the "first book in classical prose produced in Portugal." [12] More recent critics have continued to emphasize the debt which Portuguese owes to Lobo's development of a clear, direct style, while not precluding the influence which Lobo's penchant for "ditos agudos" may have had on less classically pristine writers such as Gracián. [13]

In the following pages my purpose has been to examine Lobo's prose masterpiece in the light of the dialogue traditions of seventeenth-century Portugal. Three major considerations shaped my approach. First, since Lobo was convinced that "o

---

[10] Francisco Manuel de Melo, *Apólogos dialogais* (Lisboa, 1959), II, 165. For an indication of Melo's importance as a literary critic, see Hernâni Cidade, *Lições de cultura e literatura portuguesas* (Coimbra, 1959), II, 375-391.

[11] In the opening pages the censor is careful to describe the work as an "honesto divertimento" in which "o autor pretende imitar o grande Francisco Rodrigues Lobo."

[12] Frederick Bouterwek, *History of Spanish and Portuguese Literatures,* Vol. II: *Portuguese Literature,* tr. Thomasina Ross (London, 1823), p. 229. Cf. the favorable views of another foreign —albeit anonymous— critic: M. E. M., "Leaves from the Portuguese Olive, No. VI," *Dublin University Magazine,* LVI (1856), 64-78.

[13] Other subsequent writers whose works were possibly influenced by Lobo are Martim Afonso de Miranda in his *Tempo de agora em diálogos,* I (Lisboa, 1622) and II (Lisboa, 1624), and Manuel Faria e Sousa in his *Noches Claras* (Madrid, 1624).

melhor modo de escrever são diálogos escritos em prosa," [14] it was necessary to review the theories regarding the role of the dialogue in didactic literature as seen in Lobo's most likely models. This involved studying paradigms of the dialogue form in Portugal as well as in Spain. Furthermore, as we shall see, Lobo was no less conscious than any other Renaissance writer of following a Graeco-Roman tradition; therefore, consideration was also due to the conspicuous role of the dialogue in classical literature. [15] Still other sources for Lobo are suggested in the very title of *Corte na aldeia* or are mentioned within the work itself.

The second major concern of the study concerned a structural analysis of *Corte na aldeia* seen as a concatenation of sixteen dialogues often involving as many as eight interlocutors. I have pointed out that Lobo's motives for choosing the dialogue form were dictated not only by historical precedent, but also, and perhaps even more importantly, by the dialectical nature of the genre which was admirably suited to his didactic and artistic ends. Throughout *Corte na aldeia* there is a close relation between dialogue and discursive thought, and all the interlocutors contribute to the work's general structure as well as to the individual topics with analyses which reflect the perspective each represents as they mutually confirm, refute, and quality one another's statements.

Only after reviewing the traditional place of the dialogue to which Lobo fell heir and examining his use of the genre's dialectical possibilities with stress on the function of the interlocutors was it possible to turn to the third part of the study, an examination of the major topics which Lobo found practical to include as a means to acquiring a courtly formation. I have pointed out that Lobo often departs significantly from his predecessors in his treatment of such traditionally honored concepts as *cortesia* and *cortesão*. [16] Another recurrent theme in *Corte na aldeia* is Lobo's

---

[14] Francisco Rodrigues Lobo, *Corte na aldeia e noites de inverno* (Lisboa, 1959), p. 29. Future references to this edition are incorporated into the text.

[15] Lobo cites the combited authority of "Platão, Xenofonte, Túlio..." (p. 22).

[16] See Walter J. Schneer, "Two Courtiers: Castiglione and Rodrigues Lobo," *CL*, XIII (1961), 153; and José Herculano de Carvalho, "Um tipo

linguistic nationalism which situates him squarely in the main stream of a long line of theoreticians regarding the use of the vernacular in Portugal.[17] Also, since Lobo devotes no fewer than six of his dialogues to literary problems, I found it necessary to devote a chapter to his theories concerning such questions as the validity of the chivalric novel and its place in the wider realm of fictional as opposed to factual literature. Also in conjunction with a study of Lobo's literary views arises the relevance which he attaches to rhetorical figures in poetry as a consequence of his neo-Platonic basis for a philosophy of love. Throughout it has been my intention to underline Lobo's importance to humane studies in seventeenth-century Portugal.

---

literário e humano do barroco, o cortesano discreto," *Boletim da Biblioteca da Universidade de Coimbra*, XXVI (1963), 1-27.

[17] See Albin Eduard Beau, *Die Entwicklung des Portugiesischen Nationalbewusstseins* (Hamburg, 1945), pp. 36-40 and 81-84; Albin Eduard Beau, "A valorização do idioma nacional no pensamento do humanismo português," *Estudos, I* Coimbra, 1959), pp. 349-370; Edward Glasser, "On Portuguese *Sprachbetrachtung* of the Seventeenth Century," *Homenaje a Dámaso Alonso* (Madrid, 1961), II, 115-126.

CHAPTER I

INTRODUCTION

In any study regarding Francisco Rodrigues Lobo, one is hindered from the start by a total lack of such basic biographical sources as a baptismal certificate, a will, and virtually any other kind of official document. Aside from the entries afforded by the registrar's rolls at the University of Coimbra, the investigator must content himself with fourteen letters bearing Lobo's signature, some autobiographical allusions gleaned from his writings, and a few references to the poet in the works of contemporaries. Since even this meager store of data is the product of recent research,[1] it is little wonder that traditional criticism has been uninformative and generally hesitant even in sketching a biography of one of the major literary figures of seventeenth-century Portugal, the author of *Corte na aldeia*.[2]

---

[1] The most comprehensive study of Lobo's life and work is Ricardo Jorge's *Francisco Rodrigues Lobo, ensaio biográfico e crítico* (Coimbra, 1920). Regarding the general lack of documents, see p. 5; for the discovery of the University records, see 29-33. A more recent contribution which reproduces such unedited material as fourteen letters by Lobo and the Inquisitorial proceedings concerning Lobo's brother and sister is found in Carlos Alberto Ferreira's "Francisco Rodrigues Lobo— Fontes inéditas para o estudo de sua vida e obra," *Biblos*, XIX (1943), 229-317.

[2] The first account of Lobo's life is found in Diogo Machado Barbosa, *Biblioteca lusitana, histórica, crítica, e cronológica* (Lisbon, 1752), II, 242. Subsequent critics repeated Machado's findings. Thus, Innocêncio Francisco da Silva, *Diccionario bibliográphico portuguez* (Lisbon, 1859), III, 45-48, acknowledges his source: "Segundo diz Barbosa..." To be sure he rectifies Barbosa' erroneous rendering of the publication date of *Corte na aldeia* from 1630 to 1619, but he repeats the erroneous date for the publication of the

In postulating the year of Lobo's birth, the biographer receives unexpected aid from the author himself who provides an approximate *terminus a quo*. In the dedicatory letter to *Corte na aldeia*, Lobo anticipates the charge that "...nascendo em idade em que já a [i.e., corte] de Portugal era acabada..." he may therefore be accused of being "atrevido em tratar de cousas de corte..." [3] However, he hastens to add that the non-existence of a royal retinue following the demise of national independence in no way precludes the presence of a genteel milieu at the palace of Bragança where he gained a practical knowledge of courtliness as a guest of his noble patrons, the brothers Duke Teodósio and Dom Duarte. Of particular value is Lobo's admission that he first saw the light of day when Lisbon's royal court had disappeared, either in the wake of national mourning following the debacle of Alcacer-Quibir in 1578 or the death of the Cardinal-king Henry in 1580. [4] Lobo's birth could not have occured long after the latter date, since he was admitted in 1594 to the University of Coimbra and

---

first Spanish translation by assigning it to 1632 rather than to 1622. Innocêncio arbitrarily discounts the possibility of further discoveries regarding Lobo's life and, apparently unaware of the possibility of posthumous publication, categorically assigns the poet's death to no earlier than 1623 on the grounds that *La jornada* was published in that year. Less dogmatic is the earlier version found in José Maria Costa e Silva, *Ensaio biográfico-crítico sobre os melhores poetas portugueses* (Lisbon, 1853), V, 5-112. All three reiterate Lobo's provenance ("Natural de Leiria"") and give his parents' names as André Lázaro Lobo and Joana Brito Gavião. The recently discovered University records show André Luis Lobo to be the correct name of the poet's father. See Jorge, p. 29, while the Inquisition's findings give Izabel Lopes as the mother's name. See Ferreira, p. 231.

[3] Francisco Rodrigues Lobo, *Corte na aldeia e noites de inverno*, (Lisbon, 1619). See edition of Afonso Lopes Vieira (Lisbon, 1959), p. 2. All future references are to this easily accessible edition. Lobo was not the only poet impressed by the fame of Bragança, for we find a poem by Lope de Vega praising the ducal gardens. See "Descripción de la Tapada" in *BAE*, XXXVIII. 455-459. However, it would be erroneous to think Lope de Vega an unqualified admirer of the Braganças and of Portugal in general. See Edward Glaser, "El lusitanismo de Lope de Vega," *BRAE*, XXXIV (1954), 387-412.

[4] Although Ferreira is unconvinced of 1580 as the year of Lobo's birth ("Se é que nasceu — já na época do domínio estrangeiro..." p. 229), Jorge would admit no earlier date: "Ora a corte portuguesa sumiu-se após os desastres sucessivos da morte de D. Sebastião em 1578 e do Cardinal D. Henrique em 1580. Logo, o nascimento de Lobo não é anterior a 1580..." p. 22.

published the *Romances* two years later in 1596. The conjecture, then, that Lobo was born during the period 1578-80 follows from the author's reference to his birth as occurring after 1578 and is further corroborated by the assumption that a student could hardly have matriculated at a university before the age of fourteen.

More definite is the date of Lobo's death, since it has been recently ascertained that the poet's brother, Miguel Lobo, spent the month preceding Christmas of 1621 in mourning for him.[5] However, far from being the public calamity that it has been called,[6] Lobo's death in 1621 went largely unnoticed. Almost a year later the Spanish translator of *Corte na aldeia*, Juan Baptista Morales, still expressed the hope that Lobo would compose a sequel to the work.[7] Just before the actual publication of the translation on 8 November 1622, however, Morales added a prefatory sonnet whose concluding tercet is a *requiescat:*[8]

> Y hasta que el cielo (donde está), dé al mundo
> Para alabarte, suficientes labios
> Reposa en paz, y alábete el silencio.

It would appear, therefore, that Lobo died late in 1621. His death was a violent one and occurred when a barge on which he was traveling down the Tagus overturned in a sudden squall.[9] His final resting place is unknown, since his body, recovered and later deposited in the monastery of São Francisco in Lisbon, disappeared in a fire which totally destroyed the monastery in 1708.[10]

---

[5] The Holy Office states that Miguel Lobo lapsed into Judaic practices "...no ano 1621 e por lhe morrer seu irmão Francisco Roiz Lobo no mesmo ano em Novembro... Miguel Lobo se anojou... não comendo com pessoa nenhuma por espaço de oito ou dez dias." See Ferreira, pp. 245-246.

[6] See Costa e Silva, p. 7.

[7] Francisco Rodrigues Lobo, *Corte en aldea y noches de invierno*, tr. Juan Baptista Morales (Montilla, 1622). See Jorge, p. 9.

[8] Morales' translation, p. 2. Jorge had not allowed for the possibility of a year's lapse between the poet's death and the transmission of the news to Montilla; accordingly, he suggested November of 1622 as a possible date. See Jorge, p. 9.

[9] See Jorge, p. 10.

[10] The date of the fire has also been set in 1741. See Innocêncio, p. 45. An anonymous sonnet recently unearthed mentions that our poet was temporarily laid to rest in Santarém. See Ferreira, p. 246.

In contrast to the conjectures and assumptions required to ascribe at best probable dates for Lobo's life is the abundance of data referring to his birthplace and permanent residence in Leiria, "doce, alegre, desejada" [11] and watered by the often-invoked Lis and Lena. [12] Lobo's financial independence enabled him to enjoy to the full Leiria's natural charms, for he never had to make professional use of the law degree after his graduation in 1602, but simply lived the life of a bachelor country-squire collecting the revenues of a productive family manor. [13] That he probably found such an existence quite satisfactory is suggested by the fact that all his letters and dedications composed after 1604 are dated from Leiria. [14]

However, all was not bucolic retirement for Lobo. He was well-known to the most prominent families of Phillipine Portugal, enjoying a measure of familiarity with the local nobility of Vila Real whom he praised in the *Romances*. [15] Later, in 1598-1599, while still a student at Coimbra, Lobo took refuge from Portugal's last plague at the country estate of the sister of the Marquis of Vila Real, the Countess of Odemira. [16] Shortly after graduation in 1602, Lobo joined the elegant circle of retainers at the palace of the Duke of Bragança in Vila Real where, for two years, he took part in the life of a regal court later described in *Corte na aldeia*. [17] Throughout his subsequent years in rural retirement, our

---

[11] See Lobo's *O Condestabre*, in *Obras políticas, morais, e métricas do insigne português Francisco Rodrigues Lobo, natural da cidade de Leiria* (Lisbon, 1723), p. 537.

[12] See *Primavera* in *Obras políticas...*, pp. 127-129.

[13] See Costa e Silva, p. 6; Jorge, p. 76; Ferreira, pp. 240-243.

[14] Jorge, p. 77. Jorge adduces an additional "argument" by appealing to the engraving of the "...fidalgo camponês..." ruddy with "...os ares da aldeia..." which appears in the frontispiece of *Corte na aldeia*. However, it is far more likely that the engraving represents D. Duarte to whom Lobo dedicated the dialogues. See Ferreira, pp. 252-255.

[15] See *Romances*, *Obras políticas...*, pp. 717-718, Lobo's relations with nobility were probably to be expected, since his father is mentioned in the Inquisitorial proceedings as a member of the retinue of the Princess D. Isabel. See Ferreira, p. 237.

[16] In gratitude for the hospitality showed him, Lobo dedicated the first part of *Primavera* (Lisbon, 1610) to the noble lady.

[17] In Lobo's fourth eclogue we read: "Atravessei a terra e monte avaro / té ver aquela mais ditosa / Por campos, nomes, e árvores viçosa."

INTRODUCTION 23

author continued to enjoy the protection of the House of Bragança, dedicating his epic poem *O Condestabre* (Lisbon, 1610) to Duke Teodósio and *Corte na aldeia* (Lisbon, 1619) to the Duke's brother, D. Duarte.

In reflecting upon Lobo's early acquaintance with the Marquis of Vila Real and his later dedications to leading families, it may appear strange that he should not have composed a work in honor of his noble neighbors. For some critics this literary slight has assumed the proportions of a palace intrigue, which, coupled with the poet's celibacy, has invited speculations concerning a supposed amorous rebuff or opposition to matrimonial pretensions which Lobo is supposed to have expressed cathartically in the figure of Lereno, the hero of his pastoral trilogy. More than a century after our author's death, the Bishop of Grão Pará, Dom João de Queirós, hinted darkly in his *Memórias* that Lobo had been a victim of "Loucos amores... com aia ou dama... se não foram mais altos os seus pensamentos." [18] Subsequent students of Portuguese letters have underscored Lereno's repenting "...atrevidos pensamentos..." and the generally grieved tone of the pastoral novels. [19]

Basic to these conjectures is a disregard for the fact that expressions of amorous temerity such as "...atrevidos pensamentos..." had become a poetic commonplace especially after Camões. [20] The numerous grieving, lovestruck shepherds exist in the pastoral novels of the Iberian Renaissance independently of

---

See Francisco Rodrigues Lobo, *Églogas*, ed., José Pereira Tavares (Coimbra, 1928), p. 228.

[18] The *Memórias* were edited by Camilo Castelo Branco in 1868. See Jorge, p. 42.

[19] See *Primavera, Obras políticas...*, pp. 190-191.

[20] See Maria de Lurdes Belchior Pontes, *Itinerário poético de Rodrigues Lobo* (Lisbon, 1959), p. 163. See also Jorge, p. 44. The same expressions are found even earlier than Camões in Garcilaso de la Vega, ed. T. Navarro Tomás (Madrid, 1958), pp. 50, 186, 216. As in the case of Lobo, Camões has also been credited for the same reason with an impossible love. See *Lírica de Camões*, ed. José Maria Rodrigues and Afonso Lopes Vieira (Coimbra, 1932), pp. xvi-xxii. A refutation is found in Afrânio Peixoto, "A paixão de Camões," *Arquivo camoniano* (Rio de Janeiro, 1943), pp. 232-267. Vieira shows remarkable perseverance as he advances the same theory with regard to Lobo. See Francisco Rodrigues Lobo, *Poesias*, ed. Afonso Lopes Vieira (Lisbon, 1955), pp. xxi-xxxiii.

the personal fortunes of their poetic creators.[21] Since there is not a shred of evidence of an aborted life-long love such an hypothesis should be considered as an unsuccessful attempt to "...tapar o vazio das deficiências biográficas..."[22]

The same biographical lacunae have given rise to a controversy regarding Lobo's patriotism. Some critics point to the epic poem *O Condestabre Dom Nuno Álvares Pereira* as a deliberate exaltation of Portuguese sovereignty during the country's political eclipse.[23] In keeping with such a view, Lobo is supposed to have intended his portrayal of the forurteenth-century hero of national autonomy as a symbol of resistance against the minions of the House of Austria. In defending their position the proponents of this theory single out such ringing verses as:

> Antes se perca a vida em mãos de Marte
> Que a minha pátria e reino ver sujeito.[24]

However, also unmistakably a product of Lobo's pen is our author's encomiastic welcome in verse to Philip III on the occasion of the latter's state visit to Lisbon in 1619. Published posthumously in 1623, *La jornada que la Majestad Catolica del Rey Felipe III hizo al reino de Portugal* is for nationalistic critics an expression of a traitor's loyalty to a foreign occupying power. Nonetheless, both *O Condestabre* and *La jornada* can be reconciled when it is recalled that seventeenth-century Portuguese were generally no less proud of their country's history than they were prepared to accept the claims of the Philips to the throne of their country as direct descendents of Portuguese kings.[25] One's understanding

---

[21] See Hugo A. Rennert, *The Spanish Pastoral Romance* (Philadelphia, 1912), pp. 58, 204.

[22] It also generally escapes notice that it would have been not only temerarious but actually dangerous for our prudent country squire to engage in romantic pursuits at the Marquis' palace, since such a dalliance would have constituted a stain on the Fidalgo's honor as head of his household. See Jorge, p. 43. Ferreira prefers not even to consider the theory; see p. 230.

[23] The foremost exponent of this theory is Hernâni Cidade, *A literatura autonomista sob os Filipes* (Lisbon, n.d.), pp. 72-77.

[24] *O Condestabre, Obras políticas...*, p. 546.

[25] See J. O. Oliveira Martins, *História de Portugal* (Lisbon, 1908), II, 109-120. Jorge points out that there exists an impressive roster of names of authors who composed panegyrics in honor of both the Philips and,

INTRODUCTION 25

of Lobo's relevance to Portuguese literature is accordingly not enhanced by attributing hidden political motives to eulogies of a national hero or to ovations in honor of the recognized monarch of the time.

More significant than apocryphal love affairs and debatable political loyalties is the question of Lobo's status as a *cristão novo*. The accusing finger was first pointed in his direction by Tomás de Noronha in a consummately heartless sonnet addressed as a mock elegy to the recently deceased poet in the name of the latter's pastoral hero: [26]

> Fação as Musas de tristes e enfadadas
> Da fonte cabalina um mijadeiro,
> E Bacco, aquelle grande taverneiro
> Quebre as pipas que tem mais atestadas.
>
> Apollo rache as gaitas afinadas
> E jure não tornar a ser gaiteiro,
> Meta-se Venus em Chipre num mosteiro,
> Desfaça o rapaz setas hervadas.
>
> Sinta o Tejo o que fez, e de orelhado
> Faça um capuz e chore eternamente
> A morte do Lereno desastrado.
>
> Pastor Lereno, a morte injustamente
> Te acometeu, mas dizem que queimado
> Havias de morrer naturalmente.

No less intrigued than dismayed by Noronha's malice, Ricardo Jorge found further reasons to accept the full implications of the charge in our writer's kinship to the older poet and compiler of Camões' lyrics, Fernão Rodrigues Lobo Soropita. While never officially denounced to the Inquisition, the elder Lobo had a niece who was convicted of lapsing into Judaic practices. [27] But such indirect corroborations of Noronha's accusation have been superceded by the recent discovery of inquisitorial proceedings formulated against the brother and sister of Rodrigues Lobo,

---

later, of João IV. See Jorge, p. 132. For a study regarding such a poet, see Edward Glaser, "Miguel da Silveira's *El Macabeo*," *Bulletin des Études Portugaises*, XIX (1955), 5-49. Note especially 31-34.
[26] See Jorge, pp. 13-14.
[27] See Jorge, p. 28.

Miguel and Joana.[28] The Holy Office attributed their purported judaizing to the family background "...três quartos da nação...": i.e., their father, André Luis Lobo, was the son of Jewish parents, and their mother, Isabela Lopes, was the daughter of a Jewish father and a Christian mother.

A spate of speculation has followed the disclosures regarding Lobo's Jewish ancestry in a period when publication of such an origin often invited delations before an inquisitorial tribunal.[29] Thus, it has been remarked that the occasional misanthropy in Lobo's eclogues and pastoral novels, a familiar theme in sixteenth and seventeenth-century Portugal, might also be a consequence of the poet's awareness of his precarious position as a close relative of suspected Judaizers.[30] It has also been suggested that Lobo's maginal place in post-Tridentine Portugal may have colored his literary productions with a distinctly secular hue which some commentators have underscored as characteristic of his writings.[31] However, to attempt a demonstration of such speculations would be rash especially insofar as they are prompted by Lobo's Jewish ancestry. One can only say that a study of his *Corte na aldeia* reveals a significant departure from the dialogue tradition of his time largely owing to Lobo's indifference to ascetism in his writings.

---

[28] Miguel Lobo was arraigned for trial by the Inquisition in April of 1626 while Joana Lobo appeared before the Tribunal in July of 1630. See Ferreira, pp. 231-237.

[29] See I. S. Révah, "Les Marranes," *Bulletin des Études Juives*, CXVII (1958), 29-77. Note especially 39, 44-45. Ferreira is convinced that "Se Rodrigues Lobo tivesse vivido mais uns anos, não deixaria de acompanhar os irmãos aos cárceres... ." See p. 239.

[30] For studies of Lobo's penchant toward melancholy themes, see Belchior Pontes, pp. 25-45. J. A. Saraiva and Oscar Lopes, *História da literatura portuguesa* (Porto, n.d.), pp. 378-379. For the theory relating the plight of *cristãos novos* and the somber tone of their writings, see Marcel Bataillon, "Melancolía renacentista o melancolía judía?" *Estudios hispánicos, homenaje a Archer M. Huntington* (Wellesley, Mass., 1952), pp. 39-50.

[31] Belchior Pontes (p. 326) tentatively describes Lobo as an agnostic; cf. p. 162 and Jorge, p. 354. For an analysis of the tension between faith and religious skepticism in Camões and other sixteenth and seventeenth-century figures see Jorge de Sena, *Uma Canção de Camões* (Lisbon, 1966), pp. 297-317. More recently Belchior Pontes characterizes the writer of *Corte na aldeia* as "um espírito amadurecido, racionalista e quase [sic] céptico." V. *Dicionário de Literatura*, ed. Jacinto do Prado Coelho (Porto, 1969), I. 572.

Chapter II

THE DIALOGUE IN CLASSICAL AND RENAISSANCE TRADITION

In the first dialogue of *Corte na aldeia* the author explains his choice of an interlocutory framework for his work by alluding to a rich tradition comprising "...Platão, Xenofonte, Túlio e outros infinitos...".[1] Although this allusion may smack of the Renaissance writer's dutiful acceptance of classical precedents, the recurrence of references to Plato and Cicero throughout *Corte na aldeia* indicates a firsthand acquaintance with the masters of Lobo's chosen genre. To be sure, some of Lobo's citations of Plato and Cicero are merely casual, as when he describes an orator as "...Túlio no falar..." (p. 98) or glorifies the dignity of a slave by citing "Fedão" in whose honor "...ouvi dizer que Platão escrevera um livro de imortalidade..." (p. 96). However, less superficial are such references as an appeal to "...número um de *Divinatione*..." (p. 275) where Cicero discusses the criterion for choosing a king among the Persians or a quotation from Socrates' definition of politics as "... a ciência dos príncipes..." (p. 317, cf. *Politicus*, 293 E).[2] Accordingly, an understanding of the dialogic technique

---

[1] Francisco Rodrigues Lobo, *Corte na aldeia...*, p. 22. The works of Plato and Cicero in Latin and Portuguese were plentiful from the latter half of the sixteenth century. See António Joaquim Anselmo, *Bibliografia das obras impressas em Portugal no século XVI* (Lisbon, 1926), nos. 328, 583, 595, 811, 1058. The works of Xenophon were available in a Spanish translation by Diego Gracián de Alderete (Salamanca, 1552). See Theodore S. Beardsley, "The First Catalogue of Hispano-Classical Translations: Tomas Tamayo de Vargas' *A los aficionados a la lengua española*," *HR*, XXXII (1964), 295-297.

[2] For other references to the authority of Plato and Cicero, see pp. 15, 20, 158, 236, 293, 313, 314, 316, 318.

of *Corte na aldeia* will doubtlessly benefit from a summary review of the formation of the dialogue as a literary genre developed by Plato, Cicero, and other Classical and Renaissance models.

To its Greek inventors "dialogue" ultimately derived from the rational process and the mind's discursive parrying with itself.[3] The Platonic Socrates describes the operation as "...the conversation which the soul holds with herself in considering about any subject... the soul when thinking appears to be just talking-asking questions of herself and answering them..."[4] The goal of such a process is twofold: "...the comprehension of scattered particulars into one idea..." and a division of previously accepted abstractions into their component parts.[5] Thus, by probing into the nature of virtue, for example, Socrates attempts both to determine the "particulars" of the notion, thereby providing a more solid basis for ethical behavior, and also to expose the inadequacies of traditionally accepted values.[6]

More significant for our present purpose than the philosophical import of the dialectical process is Plato's remarkable success in transforming what is primitively a psychological operation into social repartee. As the central figure of Plato's dialogues, Socrates endeavors to arouse the sluggish minds of his listeners into activity by presenting them with provocative ideas: "...the principles of justice, goodness, and nobility are taught and communicated orally for the sake of instruction and planted in the soul."[7] Socrates goes on to describe his method as a maieutic with himself, the mind as the midwife delivering the thoughts of others: "The highest point of my art is the power to prove by every

---

[3] The etimon is διαλέγεσθαι. For a discussion of the root meaning, see Mortimer J. Adler, *Dialectic* (New York, 1927), pp. 6-8.

[4] *Theaetetus*, 189 E. All quotes from the Platonic dialogues are taken from the third edition of *The Dialogues of Plato*, tr. B. Jowett (Oxford, 1892).

[5] See *Phaedrus*, 278 B. Also *Protagoras*, 333 A-B.

[6] Lobo was fully aware of the nature and the importance of the dialectic in Plato's quest for satisfactory definitions: "... a lógica... insina [sic] a distinguir e fazer diferença do falso ao verdadeiro... é o peso, a balança em que se conhecem todas as coisas leves e pesadas... é esta arte tão celebrada que Platão, e depois dele Santo Agostinho, a fizeram parte da Filosofia..." (p. 313).

[7] *Phaedrus*, 278 B.

test whether the offspring of a young man's thougt is a false phantom or in conformity with life and truth." [8] Thus concentrating on the maieutic process, Plato develops the question-and-answer aspect of the mind "conversing with itself" into the philosophical conversations which are the substance of his dialogues.

Despite the central role of Socrates in most of the dialogues, the other interlocutors "delivered" of their thoughts are rarely mere "yes men," for Socrates himself invites his listeners to join in an active participation: "Let us try the mettle of one another and make proof of the truth in conversation...." [9] By accepting his invitation the participants of a Platonic dialogue often assume a definite personality in modifying if not actually attacking the analysis of a given topic. Plato accordingly must transcend the demands of philosophical exposition and become a creative dramatist as well as if he is to delineate a credible personality as a foil to the central figure of Socrates. [10] It is therefore not surprising that he is fully cognizant of the theatrical element in his dialogues and explicitly refers to his efforts to convey an actual confrontation between speakers by "...omitting the intermediate passages and leaving only the interchange of talk." [11] As a consequence, his dialogues present varying degrees of dramatic immediacy ranging from a narrated report such as the *Protagoras*, where Socrates relates the conversation to his friends, to a direct dramatic presentation in the *Theaetetus*, where Eucleides eschews "...for the sake of convenience the interlocutory words 'I said' or 'and I remarked' ... lest the repetition of them

---

[8] *Theaetetus*, 157 C.

[9] *Protagoras*, 348 A.

[10] The presence of such a dramatic preoccupation in Plato was early recognized by Aristotle who considered his master's writings as essentially the same in poetic intention as the mimes of the first playwrights. See *Poetics*, I, ii. For studies of the elements of drama in Plato, see G. Lowes Dickinson, *Plato and his Dialogues* (London, 1931), pp. 57 f. and Dorothy Tarrant, "Plato as Dramatist," *Journal of Hellenic Studies*, LV (1955), 82-89.

[11] *Republic*, 394 A. For a discussion of the dramatic (direct) as opposed to the narrative (indirect) presentation of dialogue, see L. Andrieu, *Le dialogue antique, structure et présentation* (Paris, 1954), pp. 284-287.

should be troublesome..." and decides to write his report "...as though actually conversing with the persons..." [12]

Since they entail a dramatic relationship between individualized characters, the Platonic dialogues are situated in specific settings which sometimes assume all the details of an elaborate backdrop. Thus, a conversation between Socrates and Phaedrus is held under the shade of a planetree on the banks of a rippling brook with the drone of insects and the lowing of cattle heard in the distance. Other settings range from a littered table following a banquet [13] to a bare cell crowded with the philosopher's grief-stricken friends. [14] While many dialogues unfold in less detailed locales, Plato's pains to reproduce an actual conversation entail at least the possibility of visualizing a scene such as the sandy plot where Socrates draws figures in eliciting *a priori* geometrical axioms from Meno's slave boy. [15]

Character and setting in Plato's dialogues do not exhaust their dramatic essence; there is plot also. However, it is precisely in dealing with their plot that the hybrid nature of the dialogue becomes apparent, for one can point only to the philosophical dialectic itself as the cohesive μῦθος which gives each dialogue its specific form; i.e., a Platonic dialogue is "about" the disputations of the interlocutors as they engage in the analysis and formation of conceptual entities. [16] Hence, an attempt to judge the dialogue as essentially dramatic or substantially expositional does violence to the dual character of the genre as a philosophical inquiry in dramatic form. For Plato, the interplay of personalities in specific settings is no less essential than the desire to discuss the nature of virtue. On the other hand, it is equally clear that he would consider a philosophical analysis of a given problem

---

[12] *Theaetetus*, 143 C. Not all the dialogues are equally dramatic. See Dickinson, 57; A. E. Taylor, *Plato, the Man and his Work* (New York, 1958), p. 19.

[13] *Symposium*, 175 D.

[14] *Phaedo*, 59 C.

[15] For the relevance of setting to dramatic tension in Plato, see Paul Friedlander, *Plato, I: An Introduction* (New York, 1958), p. 160.

[16] See Friedlander, p. 165. Also see Victor Goldschmidt, *Les dialogues de Platon— structure et méthode dialectique* (Paris, 1958), pp. 2-3; Albert W. Levi, *Literature, Philosophy, and the Imagination* (Bloomington, 1962), pp. 125-127.

as an adequate framework for a cohesive literary creation, since he himself insisted that "...each discourse ought to be a living creature, having its own body and head and feet; there ought to be a beginning, a middle, and end with accord with one another and the whole..." [17]

Plato's insistence on formal unity notwithstanding, the bulk of his dialogues contains discussions which often bury the unifying dialectic under a welter of digressions as now one interlocutor now another offers a suggestion or invalidates an opponent's view with an anecdote. However, to attempt greater unity by means of an undeviating analysis of an issue would defeat his efforts to portray realistic individuals freely participating in a discussion. Thus, Socrates and his friends "...wander at will from one subject to another... if fancy occurs... begin again, caring not whether the words are few or many... the only aim is to attain the truth..." [18]

To be sure, Plato does not deny that artistic variety may sometimes hinder the less imaginative aims of the dialectic as Socrates ruefully admits regarding his discussions: "...they were felt to be too long; and I reproached myself with this, fearing that they might be not only tedious but irrelevant..." [19] And yet, in view of Plato's general theory regarding the degrees of certitude, [20] the meandering course of his dialogues sometimes terminates in equally uncertain conclusions, which are all that can be attained through the limited means afforded by conversation. [21]

Fundamental, then, to the spirit of the Platonic dialogues is an absence of practical requirements which manifests itself in rambling, inconclusive debates in which each interlocutor is a "...free man who can command his leisure [and] have his talk in peace... ." [22] As a preliminary exercise for the purely philosophical task of contemplation, in Plato's estimation a goal for

---

[17] *Phaedrus*, 264 D.
[18] *Theaetetus*, 172 D.
[19] *Politicus*, 286 C.
[20] See Francis M. Cornford, *Plato's Theory of Knowledge* (New York, 1957), pp. 140-142.
[21] See Dickinson, pp. 73-75.
[22] *Theaetetus*, 172 D.

the very few, the dialogue is "...a garden of letters..." where the philosopher will "...sow and plant [his thoughts] ...while others are refreshing their souls with banqueting and the like." [23]

To impute to Plato a frivolous intent, however, would be a grievous misinterpretation of the very nature of the dialogue. As social inquiries into the nature of truth, such conversations "...while having no truth nor honesty in them nevertheless pretend to be something hoping to succeed in deceiving the manikins of earth and gain celebrity among them..." [24]

Although there are doubts regarding Plato's chronological priority in the development of the dialogues, [25] there is no question that he stands alone with respect to the excellence which the genre acquired in the ancient world. One need only compare the Platonic dialogues with those of a contemporary such as Xenophon to reveal the latter's inability to maintain successfully the dramatic aspects of the hybrid genre. For Plato's colleague in the Academy, the dialogue is limited in practice to being "...an effective means for eliciting answers; there is no trace of the dialectic in which ideas take shape...none of the wit and much more grim utilitarianism than any [dialogues] of Plato show." [26] As a consequence, Xenophon's interlocutors, unlike Plato's well-defined characters, are personified abstractions who all sound alike in reflecting the views of their creator. [27]

More basically, the very structure of the dialogue in Xenophon is weakened by his failure to provide a μῦθος in the form of an underlying idea combining to unify the loosely joined arguments and observations. The result is a general "...unevenness of style, an awkardness [which] is the mark of so many of Xenophon's

---

[23] *Phaedrus*, 276 D. For a theory which expands this view of the dialogue, see Johannes Huizinga, *Homo ludens: A Study of the Play-Element in Culture*, tr. R. F. C. Hull (London, 1949), pp. 113, 148. Also see Friedlander, p. 118 and Adler, pp. 131-139.

[24] *Phaedrus*, 243 A.

[25] Thomas Alan Sinclair, *A History of Classical Greek Literature* (New York, 1935), p. 341.

[26] Moses Hadas, *A History of Greek Literature* (New York, 1950), p. 127.

[27] See Alfred and Maurice Croiset, *Histoire de la littérature greque* (Paris, 1895), IV, 360-411.

writings..." [28] For Lobo, therefore, Xenophon's importance was probably due less to the form than to his treatment of such well-worn Renaissance subjects as the *speculum principis* and the praise of domestic bliss and plenty. [29]

More important to the history of the dialogue is the role played by the third of Lobo's triumvirate of classical models, "...Túlio...," for, like Lobo, Cicero was also conscious of the artistic challenge of the dialogue. Thus, as would later be the case in the Renaissance, Cicero's admiration for the masters of the genre [30] prompted him to acknowledge his debt to Plato's example: "Cur non imitamur, Crasse, Socratum illum, qui est in Phaedro Platonis?" [31] Moreover, Cicero did not consider the dialogue form merely as a literary exercise but also as a vehicle for philosophical exposition: "Et tamquam in scholia, prope ad graecorum consuetudinem, disputasse... ." [32] The author of the *De Oratore* also echoed Plato in claiming for the writer of dialogues a disengaged motivation free from practical concerns: "...de rebus aut difficillimis aut non necesariis argumentissime disputare... ." [33] With regard to dramatic technique, there is even an implied pretense in Cicero at discovering the direct dramatic presentation which Plato mentions in the *Theaetetus:* "Quasi enim ipsos induxi loquentes, ne 'inquam' et 'inquit' saepius interponeretur atque ut tamquam a praesentibus

---

[28] *The Works of Xenophon,* tr. H. G. Dokyns (London, 1892), III, lxxii. Also see Édouard Delebecque, *Essai sur la vie de Xénophon* (Paris, 1957), p. 503.

[29] These motifs were especially developed in the *Cyropaedia* and the *Economica* respectively. Also attractive to the Renaissance neo-Platonists was the sympathetic portrayal of Socrates in the *Memorabilia*. See Dokyns, pp. xliv-lxix; Moses Hadas, *Ancilla to Classical Reading* (New York, 1954), p. 223. Independent of the thematic considerations is Xenophon's traditional prominence as a master of classical oratorical style, a perennial goal for the Renaissance writer. See Sinclair, p. 341; Hannah H. Gray, "Renaissance Humanism: The Pursuit of Eloquence, "*Journal of the History of Ideas,* XXIV (1961), 497-514. Rodrigues Lobo refers to the *Cyropaedia* on p. 18: "Xenofontes, querendo pintar uma república perfeita e regimento político, por modo de história, fingiu o governo de Ciro, Rei dos Persas... ."

[30] See Cicero, *De Oratore,* III 5: "Quisquam nostrum qui libros Platonis mirabiliter scriptos legit... ."

[31] Cicero, I. 8.

[32] Cicero, II, 3.

[33] Cicero, II, 4.

coram habere sermo videbitur." [34] Lastly, and here Cicero is perhaps more explicit than Plato, there is a clear realization that the dialogue demands considerable skill from the writer if he is to compose a unified literary work with all the air of a spontaneous conversation: "Quamvis subito, magnum opus est egetque exercitatione non parva." [35]

Granted, then, Cicero's conscious imitation of Plato in writing his dialogues, it would nonetheless be erroneous to assume that the Roman simply reduplicated in Latin what the Athenian had done in Greek. Indeed, Cicero's forensic training and consequent interest in oratorical form resulted in dialogues which are markedly different from Plato's recreation of the dialectic. [36] The Socratic concern for pure speculation is often replaced in Cicero by such problems dear to prominent Roman barristers as the art of eloquence: "...ut ex pristino sermone relaxaretur animum omnium solebat Cato narrare Crassum sermonem... de studio dicendi intulisse... ." [37] Again, in Cicero's dialogues Socrates' questions and answers yield to lengthy disquisitions on the fruits of philosophical speculation such as Laelius' lecture on friendship prompted by Favonius' request that "de amicitia disputares... quae precepta des... ." [38] Cicero's interlocutors tend to be proper gentlemen who rarely interrupt one another, nor do they indulge in the lively debate which is characteristic of most of Plato's friendly colloquies. [39]

In light of Cicero's important modification of the dialogue by emphasizing its didactic function at the expense of the genre's dramatic impact as seen in Plato, Lobo's reference to his classical models indicates a variety of perspectives which contributed to the dialogic technique of *Corte na aldeia*. Indeed, that this is the

---

[34] Cicero, *De Amicitia*, 3.
[35] *De Amicitia*, 18.
[36] See Alain Michel, *Le 'Dialogue des orateurs' de Tacite et la philosophie de Cicéron* (Paris, 1962), pp. 14-19.
[37] *De Oratore*, 8.
[38] *De Amicitia*, 13.
[39] Although Cicero minimizes the importance of the combined efforts of the interlocutors in presenting his views, the dramatic immediacy with regard to the speakers is not seriously impaired. See Moses Hadas, *A History of Latin Literature* (New York, 1952), p. 121.

case follows from our author's advertence to "...outros infinitos..." who continued to add to the dialogue tradition to which Lobo fell heir. Thus, subsequent to Cicero, the ancient world provided a final major contribution to the genre in the guise of a novelistic elaboration of characterization such as can be detected in the interlocutors of Lucian of Samosata.[40] However, with the advent of the Christian era the genre was cultivated for more apologetic purposes with a consequent shift of emphasis from philosophical inquiries and oratorical disquisitions to theological arguments and the propagation of faith.

It is not surprising, therefore, that the interlocutors of Medieval dialogues tend to give vent to orthodox positions rather than to individual ideas and are developed not as specific personalities but as types such as Dives and Pauper, Clericus and Miles or even as allegorical figures symbolizing seasons and religious motifs.[41] Moreover, the setting is correspondingly altered from the concrete locations found in Plato and Cicero to the vague surroundings befitting impersonal speakers. However, even these attempts at dialogue do not represent the primary use of the dialectic during the Medieval period which saw the contrast of opinion essential to dialogue gradually limited to the contentions of Scholastic disputation.[42] Thus, although it remained as important for the medieval curriculum as it had been for Plato's philosopher-king and Cicero's orator, dialectic no longer provided a plot for conversation, since all pretensions to literary creation were discarded in the *disputatio*. Rambling discussions were transformed into less imaginative but no less intricate sorites, and the very integrity of the dialogue as a balance between didactic content and dramatic form was jeopardized with the text-book reproductions of the *Questiones Quodlibetales*.[43]

---

[40] See Rudolf Hirzel, *Der Dialog, ein literar-historisher Versuch* (Hildersheim, 1963), II, 288.

[41] See Hirzel, pp. 382-384.

[42] See Adler, p. 7.

[43] Hirzel's tendency to equate "dialogue" with "Platonic Dialogue" and therefore to talk in terms of the decadence of the dialogue whenever its early dramatic aspects are overshadowed by later didactic concerns leads him to question the existence of a "true" dialogue form during the Middle Ages: "... hat es das Mittelalter zu keinem rechten Dialoge gebracht." See p. 384. For an answer to Hirzel's position as stated in the first edition of

The gradual re-integration of the dialectic in a literary tradition was effected by the rise of the Platonic Academies in Italy during the Renaissance.[44] The Scholastic method, however, its importance somewhat diminished, was often incorporated into the imitations of classical dialogue.[45] Indeed, the years comprising the transition to the modern period were especially fruitful for the dialogue in that the elaboration of the genre's various stages of historical development were now concomitantly combined in varying degrees. The humanistic concern for eloquence resulted in assigning Ciceronian discourses on a wide range of topics to carefully conceived characters whose varied backgrounds pointed to an origin in the dialogues of Plato. Also, interlocutors of the Renaissance dialogues frequently couched their views in the language of the Schoolmen while striving for variety by occasionally inserting an Italianate novela into the course of their conversation.[46] As a culmination of previous tendencies, therefore, the dialogue at the time of Rodrigues Lobo presented a Protean means for providing the reader with the combination of didacticism and imaginative diversion which had always figured in the very constitution of the dialogue[47] and which had become the avidly sought goal of the Renaissance writer especially in Spain and Portugal.[48]

---

his study (Leipzig, 1895), see Benedetto Croce, "La teoria del dialogo segundo il Tasso," *La Critica*, III (1943), 144-145.

[44] Croce, 147. Croce attributes the resurgence of dialogue exclusively to the work of the Platonic academies. For dissenting views which trace the persistence of Scholasticism throughout the reappearance of the dialogue in the Renaissance period, see Paul Oskar Kristeller, "Humanism and Scholasticism in the Italian Renaissance," *Humanitas*, (1950), 988-1015; Richard McKeon, "Renaissance and Method," *Columbia University Studies in the History of Ideas* (New York, 1935), II, 36-114. For a theory which sees the popularity of the dialogue at this time as "...largely due to the passion for conversation which is one of the most distinctive marks of Italian society in the sixteenth century...," see Thomas F. Crane, *Italian Social Customs of the Sixteenth Century* (New Haven, 1920), p. 122.

[45] See Giovanna Wyss Morigi, *Contributo allo studio del dialogo all' epoca del' Umanesimo e de Rinascimento* (Monza, 1950), p. 127.

[46] See Morigi, 154.

[47] The dual nature of the dialogue was constantly stressed during the Renaissance; see Sforza Pallavicino, S. J. *Trattato dello stile e del dialogo* (Venezza, 1698), pp. 248-252; Morigi, pp. 13-17; Croce, pp. 145-148.

[48] See Bernard Weinberg, *A History of Literary Criticism in the Italian Renaissance* (Chicago, 1961), I, 72: 250-296.

Chapter III

THE DIALOGUE IN SPAIN AND PORTUGAL

For Spanish authors of dialogues in the fifteenth century, the possibility of combining didactic content with imaginative structure was less attractive than the genre's novelty as a written conversation. As a consequence, a conversational form was often employed for funeral laments and denunciations of luxury simply because "... así parecen al vulgo probable más que en otra manera..." [1] It was only in the following century that authors of dialogues rediscovered the literary-pedagogic function of the form which had been ignored by their predecessors. However, a tendency of the later writers to stress one aspect at the expense of the other resulted in a gradual weakening of dialectical opposition. Our discussion of the genre in the Iberian Golden Age will be limited to some commonly accepted examples of the trend toward a use of the interlocutory form as a means for instructing and entertaining. [2] Such dialogically structured works as the *Celestina* and the *Comédia de Eufrosina,* which have been variously classified with regard to genre, are beyond the limits of our purview. [3] On the

---

[1] The reference is to Juan de Lucena's *Libro de vida beata* (Zaragoza, 1489). See Luis André Murillo's unpublished dissertation, "The Spanish Prose Dialogue of the Sixteenth Century" (Harvard, 1953), pp. 34-41. For another view of Lucena's dialogue as being essentially medieval, see Margherita Morreale, "El tratado de Juan de Lucena sobre la felicidad," *NRFH*, IX (1955), 1-21.

[2] See Murillo, p. 85.

[3] For the difficulty in classifying these works, see Jorge Ferreira de Vasconcelos, *Comédia de Eufrosina,* ed. Eugenio Asensio (Madrid, 1951), pp. lvi-lxiv; Stephen Gilman, *The Art of the Celestina* (Madison, Wisconsin,

other hand, certainly to be included in any survey of the dialogue in Spain and Portugal is the Italian import, *Il Cortegiano*, which provided an admirable model for subsequent Peninsular dialogue writers. [4]

Despite the vicissitudes which befell the dialogue form throughout the sixteenth century, there persisted an awareness of the genre's affinity to natural speech. [5] It is therefore not entirely coincidental that it came of age in Spain in 1536 in the guise of a lively discussion of the vernacular, Juan de Valdés' *El diálogo de la lengua*. [6] Directly presented, the colloquy takes place in the house of one of the interlocutors where a dinner has been given to celebrate Valdés' return to Naples after a two-year visit to his native Spain. The host, an Italian called Marcio, assumes responsibility as director of the conversation by arranging the topics to be discussed; while the two guests, Pacheco and Coriolano, are, respectively, a native speaker of Spanish and an Italian student of the language. All three have accumulated a host of linguistic and literary problems from Valdés' letters, and they now propose to resolve their doubts in a series of questions which provide the substance of the dialogue.

From the very beginning a dramatic situation is provided by Valdés' unwillingness to acquiesce to their demands, and the interlocutors are thus divided into a reluctant master and three

---

1956), pp. 116-118; Marcel Bataillon, *La Celestina selon Fernando de Rojas* (Paris, 1961), pp. 77-107; María Rosa Lida de Malkiel, *La originalidad artística de la Celestina* (Buenos Aires, 1962), pp. 29-78.

[4] See Marcelino Menéndez y Pelayo, *Historia de las ideas estéticas en España*, ed. D. Enrique Sánchez Reyes (Santander, 1947), II, 440. For similar estimations of the influence of *Il Cortegiano* upon Peninsular culture in the sixteenth century, see Ernest Krebs, "El Cortesano en España," *BAAL*, VIII (1940), 95-108; Hernâni Cidade, *O conceito da poesia como expressão da cultura* (Coimbra, 1957), pp. 80-83; Margherita Morreale, *Castiglione y Boscán: El ideal cortesano en el renacimiento español*, BRAE, Anejo I (1959), 12. For a study of the Spanish influences in *Il Cortegiano*, see A. Gianni, "Cárcel de amor y *Il Cortegiano*," *RH*, XLVI (1919), 547-568.

[5] See Murillo, pp. 81-83.

[6] The dialogue was first published as "Diálogo de las lenguas" in D. Gregorio Mayáns y Siscar's *Orígenes de la lengua española*, II (Madrid, 1737). However, it was written "...en papeles entre 1535 y 1536..." See Juan de Valdés, *Diálogo de la lengua*, ed. José F. Montesinos (Madrid, 1928), p. lii. Future references to this work are incorporated into the text.

determined interrogators.[7] Added tension and a mesure of dramatic irony are made possible when the author-interlocutor leaves the house for a breath of air, whereupon the three form a plot: "...meter escondido en algún lugar secreto un buen escribano para que notasse los puntos principales que aquí se dijesen" (pp. 17-18). The result is a complicity throughout the dialogue between the reader and the three students, especially when Valdés senses an undercurrent of excitement and suspiciously asks, "De qué os reís?" (p. 49) or when Coriolano, the instigator of the plot, encourages Valdés with "Aquí estamos solos y todo puede passar" (p. 158). The dialogue proceeds to work up to a climax as Marcio calls the hidden scribe "on stage" to the surprise of the unsuspecting master: "Agora...veréis; Aurelio, da ca lo que has escrito. Veis aquí todo lo que habeís dicho..." (p. 187).

The author skillfully unites both the dramatic and the pedagogic aspects of the dialogue form in presenting an engaging discussion of a problem which was later to figure prominently in Lobo's *Corte na aldeia;* i.e., how to provide a standard for the use of an evolving vernacular. For Valdés, who wrote almost a century before Lobo, the task seemed especially formidable, for he held "... la lengua castellana nunca ha tenido quien escriba en ella con tanto cuidado...para que hombre...se pudiese aprovechar de su autoridad..." (p. 8). The author's criticism of existing Spanish classics consequently provides a major part of the dialogue's content.[8] In overcoming what he considers a serious academic lack, Valdés has recourse to adages ("lo más puro castellano que tenemos...," p. 181), anecdotes, and poems thereby providing the necessary linguistic examples of a standard Castilian speech while simultaneously varying the pace of the conversation

---

[7] "Haveisos por ventura concertado todos tres para el mohín?" Valdés asks as the three insist that he comply "...respondiendo y satisfaciéndonos a las preguntas que os propondremos..." (p. 2).

[8] For a study of Valdés' criticism of *Amadís* and Nebrija's *Gramática* see Amado Alonso, *Español, idioma nacional* (Buenos Aires, 1938), pp. 63-65; Eugenio Asensio, "Juan de Valdés contra Delicado, fondo de una polémica," *Studia philologica; Homenaje ofrecido a Dámaso Alonso...* (Madrid, 1960), I, 101-113. Both authors point out Valdés' insistence that the Castillian of Toledo was to be preferred to the Andalusian dialect of Nebrija and of the *Amadis* as edited by Francisco Delicado (Delgado) in Venice, 1533.

and eliciting the reader's interest.⁹ Further adding to the charm of *Diálogo de la lengua* is Valdés' liberal attitude regarding the truth of his statements which are remarkably free of the dogmatic tone of many later Luso-Hispanic dialogues: "Me contento que vosotros a lo que dijere deis el crédito que quisiéredes..." (p. 41). The spirited "...contienda..." (p. 190) is provisionally ended as the author-interlocutor leaves to attend to business in the city hinting at a resumption within a week (p. 197).

Generally considered, later Spanish dialogues seldom equaled Valdés' sharp delineation of character and able fusion of wit and wisdom.¹⁰ Moreover, it is unlikely that as a circulated manuscript *Diálogo de la lengua* could have exercised the influence of an enormously popular work such as Baltasar Castiglione's *Il Cortegiano* (Venice, 1528).¹¹ Re-created for the Spanish reader in Juan Boscán's translation, *El Cortesano* (Barcelona, 1534), the work saw no fewer than thirteen publications during the half century following its appearance on the Spanish literary scene.¹² Combining literary diversion with the rules of social protocol, *El Cortesano*'s elaborate setting ("... una casa... la más hermosa que en toda Italia se hallase...," p. 31)¹³ and its interlocutors chosen from the Florentine *beau monde* ("...una dulce y amada compañía...," p. 34) provided the ideal milieu for a courtly society concerned with the formation of "... un perfecto cortesano... todas las condiciones y calidades que se requieren para merecer este título..." (p. 47).¹⁴

The major topic is suggested as a game (p. 38) designed to entertain the guests of the Duchess de Urbino. To ensure a semblance of order throughout the following discussions, the hostess appoints her companion, Emilia Pia, as a moderator whose task it is to confer the elaboration of pertinent sub-topics to

---

⁹ The numerous asides are explicitly defended by the author: "Ya sabéis que estos paréntesis no son malos a ratos" (p. 44).

¹⁰ See Murillo, p. 73.

¹¹ See Cidade, *O conceito...*, p. 81.

¹² See Morreale, *Castiglione y Boscán...*, p. 12.

¹³ Baltasar Castiglione, *El Cortesano*, tr. Juan Boscán (Madrid, 1873), p. 31. Future references to this text are incorporated into the text.

¹⁴ Such questions were a common academic exercise as well as a social diversion in Renaissance society. See T. F. Crane, p. 143.

specific individuals. Thus, as the speakers fall into the spirit of the "game," each contributes to the mosaic of an ideal courtier whose qualities, the author tells us, "son muchas y diversas, [y] así son muchas y diversas las materias que se tratan en este libro" (p. 4). *El Cortesano* accordingly contains a wealth of anecdotes, puns, and convivial banter befitting an atmosphere of genteel entertainment. However, the author's didactic purpose is obvious throughout in the dominant role played by one or more interlocutors in each dialogue. Thus, the first two *soirées* are spent in developing the general character of the courtier in accordance with the views of Count Ludovico, Micer Frederico, and Bernardo Bibiena. The third night is devoted to discussing the nature of the courtier's feminine counterpart in the form of a spirited debate between the misogynist Gaspar Pallavicino and the Paladin Julian. The fourth and final evening marks the completion of the courtly paradigm with Octaviano Fregoso's analysis of the virtues necessary for establishing an ideal relation with a prince and with Pietro Bembo's rhapsody on Platonic love.[15] Despite the historical origin of these interlocutors, all members of the author's social circle, the topics discussed are in themselves academic treatises little modified by a dialectical progression. Indeed, Castiglione simply employed real figures as convenient vehicles for expressing his own views.[16]

A far cry from *El Cortesano*'s elaborate setting, characterization, and sophisticated conversation are Pero Mexía's *Diálogos* (Seville, 1547) which substitute the glittering company at the ducal palace of Urbino with bookish clerics and contentious Andalusian *caballeros* in scenes never invaded by a feminine presence.[17] Also,

---

[15] In each discussion the author attributes "...il compito di discutere... di una materia a persone di provata competenza...". See Morigi, p. 135.

[16] See Eric Loos, *Baltassare Castigliones Libro del Cortesano*, Analecta Romana, II (1955-56), 1-235. See especially pp. 73-74.

[17] The references are to the eighth edition (Seville, 1747) and are incorporated into the text. The *Diálogos* have found little favor among modern critics. Menéndez y Pelayo finds him "... tan plúmbeo como Erasmo, a quien parece que se propone por modelo..." (p. 173). His collection has also been described as "...la plus banale miscellanée sous forme de dialogue..." See Marcel Bataillon, *Érasme en Espagne* (Paris, 1937), p. 491. However, his influence in the Golden Age was considerable. See Carlos Castillo, "Cervantes y Pero Mexía," *MP*, XLII (1944), 94-106. Also see Murillo, pp. 182-194.

Mexía's less skillful use of the dialogic technique results in interlocutors completely definable in terms of their arguments. Thus, little more can be said of Gaspar and Bernardo in "Coloquio de los médicos," except that the former attacks doctors while the latter defends them. Of the remaining characters, the ill Nuno whom the others visit, is the moderator of the discussion while the Maestro Velásquez evaluates the cogency of the arguments and offers a compromise. [18] An even more extreme instance of Mexía's anemic characterization is found in "Coloquio del porfiado" where the major character, el Bachiller Navarraez, is totally definable as "...un amigo de ajeno parecer..." (p. 151) "...espíritu de contradicción..." (p. 152) and plays his role by automatically contradicting whatever is said by the three cavaliers who are the other speakers.

Because of the polarity underlying Mexía's interlocutors, the abundance of material found in his dialogues is directly presented with little evidence of Valdés' practical relativism or Castiglione's variety of perspectives. The Sevillian is simply not as interested in a dialectical progression as he is in a display of rhetorical prowess or giving proof of his multifaceted erudition. Nor does he always combine rhetoric and learning such as when Velásquez decides an issue with "la fuerza de la verdad, y ... elocuencia y auctoridad..." (p. 42). Indeed, except for two dialogues concerning cosmology, the discourse invariably involves only a contest and consists of little more than the exercise in sophistry which provides the nucleus of "Coloquio del Porfiado." The latter dialogue is explicitly undertaken to "...hacer muestra de ingenios..." (p. 17) in the belief that "...no hay cosa tan dudosa, que, bien diciendo... no se haga probable..." (p. 191). The author exemplifies his sophistic view with a feat of rhetorical virtuosity as Bernardes proposes to "...probar que el asno es el mejor y más útil animal..." (p. 173). [19] His "proof" is in rigorous form complete with marginal

---

[18] The same polarity is found in the third dialogue ("Del convite") where Arnaldo is simply the defender of a variety of foods and Antonio the champion of "...un manjar..." as opposed to many (p. 111). Here too Velásquez settles the dispute with a compromise; "La templanza en el comer y beber, sea de un solo, o de diversos manjares..." (p. 126).

[19] Professor Edward Glaser has called my attention to an article on classical works which contain praise for unlikely objects, in themselves

notes identifying the parts of the delivery and the arguments used.[20]

Certainly the greatest hindrance to dialectical inquiry is Mexía's persistent use of the argument from authority. Whether deciding a "porfía" or providing information about the antipodes (p. 143), the author invariably relies upon an impressive array of authorities invoked by his speakers. Furthermore, when an issue impinges upon the realm of religious doctrine, the authorities marshalled are such that no disagreement is possible.[21] Thus, a problem regarding the affect of tropical heat on life is settled dogmatically: "Que nos atengamos a lo más verdadero y cierto, que es la verdad de la sagrada escritura" (p. 197). It would seem, therefore, that for Mexía, the conversational form of the dialogue is less important than its doctrinal content: "He procurado... hacer participante a nuestra lengua castellana de algunas de las cosas de erudición y doctrina que la latina... tiene de escondido y secreto... ."[22]

The same desire to instruct motivated Antonio de Torquemada to write his voluminous *Jardín de flores curiosas* (Salamanca, 1570).[23] Composed of six dramatic dialogues taking place on as many consecutive days, the work is intended to aid the inquisitive

---

completely unworthy. See Arthur Stanley Place, "Things without Honor," *CP*, XXI (1926), 27-42. On p. 29 Place mentions the ass as an object for rhetorical praise and traces the topic to *Phaedrus*, 260 B. For a similar panegyric of pigs, see Lorenzo Palmireno, *El Estudioso cortesano* (Valencia, 1573), pp. 104-106.

[20] For the relation of dialogue to rhetoric in general, see Chaim Perelman and L. Olbrechts-Tyteca, "Logique et Rhétorique," in *Rhétorique et philosophie* (Paris, 1952), pp. 1-43. See especially pp. 19-21. See also Myron Gilmore, *Humanists and Jurists* (Cambridge, 1963), p. 136.

[21] In the dialogue on the sun and the earth, the cosmographer Antonio lectures to two friends, Petronio and Paulo. When the latter states "No os porfiaré ni argüiré... que aun dudar no sé..." (p. 134), the possibility of a dialectic through mutual qualifications and discord is precluded from the start. The result of such didacticism converts the dialogue into a "...moyen d'exposition...". See Perelman and Olbrechts-Tyteca, p. 40.

[22] Mexía's didactic purpose led not only to primitive characterization but also to settings bereft of detail.

[23] Modern editions include one in the *Sociedad de bibliófilos españoles*, Series II, XIII (Madrid, 1943) and a facsimile edition published by the Real Academia Española in Madrid in 1955. For a study of Torquemada's dialogues which describes Antonio's speeches as sermons, see Alfonso Reyes, "De un autor censurado en el *Quijote*," *CA*, VI (1947), 188-224.—

reader who is hindered in his search for knowledge by "...la brevedad de la vida y de la grandeza del mundo, de los secretos de naturaleza, y de la flaqueza de nuestro entendimiento... ." As a means to this end, Torquemada limits his interlocutors to the learned Antonio, and his two friends, Bernardo and Luis, who are intent upon gaining Antonio's consent to preside "...en alguna buena plática..." (p. 1). Aside from thus reproducing the traditional Platonic relationship of master and pupil, the author expends very little efforts in creating individual personalities. Antonio, who is the most important interlocutor, is simply described as an "...hombre curioso..." with an interest in the more bizarre realms of scientific oddities. Since the latter were largely the fruits of recent discoveries, the author is forced to look to contemporary sources as well as to Pero Mexía (p. 48), João de Barros (p. 56), and Scandinavian chronicles (pp. 53-54) along with the more traditional authorities such as Pliny, Aristotle, and Solino. [24]

A consequence of Torquemada's preference for such topics as freaks, ghosts, and fate is that he can rarely state his views with the assurance of Mexía's cosmographer, whence his frequent expressions of tolerance for dissenting opinions. [25] However, that

---

[24] João de Barros, *Asia:* Década I (Lisbon, 1552); II (Lisbon, 1553); III (Lisbon, 1563); IV (Lisbon, 1615). This work was more relevant to authors of Barros' time than were his moralistic treatises which are mentioned below. Torquemada frequently mentions the failure of tradition in providing satisfactory interpretations for "modern" situations. Thus, regarding geography, he says "Cierto la ignorancia de los antiguos debió ser muy grande..." (p. 184). Also see pp. 187, 255. Similarly, de Barros says in his *Ropica Pnefma* "Lisbon, 1532) "...se agora cá viesse [sic] Potolomeu, Strabo, Pompónio, Plínio, ou Solino ... a todos [a nova geometria] meteria em confusão e vergonha...". See edition of I. S. Révah (Lisbon, 1955), II, 42. This attitude is in contrast to Mexía who silences a speaker simply because he is about to cite a source "...que es moderno..." See *Diálogos*, p. 77.

[25] See Torquemada, pp. 19, 31, 53-54, 56, 180, 216, 221, 240. Also, see James H. Eisdon, "On the Life and Works of the Spanish Humanist, Antonio de Torquemada," *University of California Studies in Lang. and Lit.*, XX (1937), 127-183. For a discussion regarding the interest of the period in "...lo oculto y extraordinario del mundo..." see José Antonio Maravall, "Sobre naturaleza e historia en el humanismo español," *Arbor*, XVIII (1951), 469-493. Torquemada's interest in scientific curiosities for their own sake contrasts with the traditional view regarding the vanity of wordly knowledge such as is found in Heitor Pinto's "Diálogo da discreta ignorância," *Imagem da vida cristã* (Lisbon, 1572); "Bom é ler bons livros e ter nisso curiosidade; mas há tudo de ser dirigido ao serviço de Deus e proveito de almas... ." See

there is a clear distinction between what is possibly spurious and what is irrefutably certain is implied by Antonio's qualification regarding the existence of Amazons: "Yo no afirmo estas cosas por verdaderas, que tengan por pecado el no creerlas..." (p. 31). An example of "...cosas verdaderas..." and the authority for their veracity is contained in the master's explanation of the origins of rivers as he builds his case for a common source in the sea starting with the "opinión" of Aristotle and Anaximander and culminates with "...la más verdadera opinión, o por mejor decir, la verdad... lo que dice el Ecclesiástico en el capítulo primero." [26]

Jardín de flores curiosas differs from earlier dialogues not only with respect to the quantity and type of material discussed but also with regard to more poetic descriptions of the settings as the author discards the roughly hewn outlines of Valdés and Mexía in favor of detailed, bucolic scenes. Thus, the speakers stroll "...debajo de estos árboles gozando del frescor del aire y del río... listening to "...el regocijado sonido de la agua [sic] deslizándose con su corriente tan clara como un cristal por las blancas arenas ..." (p. 1). Another day sees them seated in a shady grove, with a bubbling fountain at hand (p. 60). [27] Still other days find the trio in a garden (p. 96) or reclining "...a la sombra de estos rosales y jazmines... [gozando] la suavidade del olor que de sí dan y del canto de los rueseñores..." (p. 216). The improbably long discussions — the third lasts a whole day and part of the night — are usually interrupted to go to supper (pp. 96, 214, 257) or to accompany the weary Antonio to his home (p. 179).

---

edition of Lisbon, 1957, Vol. III, p. 11. For a traditional discussion of the futility of curiosity see Pierre Blanchard, "Studiosité et curiosité, le vrai savoir d'après Saint Thomas d'Aquin," *Revue Thomiste*, LIII (1953), 551-562. For the classical precedents of Torquemada's humanistic curiosity see Hans Joaquim Mette, "Curiositas," *Festschrift Bruno Snell* (Munchen, 1956), pp. 227-235.

[26] See Elsdon, p. 137. For a discussion regarding the traditional view on the degrees of assent and the types of proofs from authority, see Perelman and Olbrechts-Tyteca, p. 13.

[27] One is reminded of the setting of the *Phaedrus* while the language recalls the eclogues of Garcilaso. See Garcilaso de la Vega, pp. 28, 124, 126. The actual setting was a garden in Venavente, Zamora, the scene of the author's later years. See Elsdon, pp. 130-131.

Even more encyclopedic than Torquemada's *Jardín* is Fray Juan de Pineda's *Agricultura Cristiana* (Salamanca, 1589). [28] Dedicated to "...la soberana majestad de la gloriosísima Virgen María Madre de Dios..." the thirty-five directly presented dialogues contain neither the humor of Valdés and Mexía nor the idle curiosity which motivates the three interlocutors of Torquemada's dialogues. A promise to create pleasant conversations ("...pláticas recreativas...") and a naturalness of expression is merely a concession to "...condiciones necesarias en la buena conversación y por las leyes de los diálogos familiares..." [29] The laws presuppose the need for occasional disagreements among the interlocutors, but for Pineda such demurs, far from constituting the conflicts of a dialectic, are apologetic strategems, "...para dar entrada a los demás por que descubran nuevas doctrinas..." His dialogues, therefore, should be viewed as the result of a zealous dogmatism tempered by the awareness that an effort must be made if one is to avoid the fatigue which follows from "...hablar siempre en cosas de mucho seso y de dificultosa inteligencia..." [30]

Eloquent proof of Pineda's didactic aims is the abstract quality of his interlocutors, whose allegorical function is explained by their names. The main speaker is Philalethes, "...el maestro /que/ ama la verdad..." A scholarly friar like the author, Philalethes attracts several disciples to his home where he explains the motives for their meetings: "...no tanto por ser enseñado en letras como por su doctrina, condición de los buenos maestros y predicadores." The other interlocutors, all of whom bow before the master's authority, [31] are equally symbolic. Thus, to add further credibility to Philalethes' pronouncements is the voice of one chastened by long experience: "...Polycronio, hombre de mucho tiempo y muy viejo... se ha comenzado a dar a las letras,

---

[28] References are to the modern edition in three volumes of Juan Meseguer Fernández in the *BAE*, CLXI-CLXIII.

[29] The claim to reproduce a natural form of speech ("...como lo sienten así lo dicen ...") is a common one rarely honored in the dialogues of the period. See Pineda, I, 5. See Morreale, *Castiglione y Boscán...*, pp. 24-25.

[30] See Pineda, I, 5. A similar attitude regarding the ancillary place of diversion in the dialogue is found in Pallavicino, p. 252.

[31] The foreword describes their relation to Philalethes with "...todos se le rinden...". See Pineda, I, 5.

y al exercicio de la virtud..." As a contrast providing both opportunity for emendation by Philalethes as well as interpretation of scientific facts is Philotimo who is described as "...ambicioso... médico... liviano..." The final major speaker is the eager disciple, Pamphilo, "todo... amable... mancebo de diez y ocho a veinte anos... hermoso... virtuoso... rico... generoso... amigo de saber letras." [32]

Although the subjects discussed in *Agricultura cristiana* synthesize the curriculum of the Renaissance scholar in a catholic "...mezcla de sagrado y profano..." the conversations are scrupulously designed to be first and foremost "...provechosas para nuestras almas...". Consequently, the plethora of authorities regarding such secular studies as ancient history, mythology, and fictional literature are only conditionally allowed as "...gentílica erudición acristianizada". [33] So pronounced is Pineda's moralistic intention that he often dispenses even with the pretense of a conversational style to insert passages reminiscent of pulpit oratory such as in Philalethes' denunciation of Ignorancia which begins with the thundering apostrophe: "O Ignorancia, hija del pecado y madre de pecadores, alcahueta de sacrilegios y partera de abominaciones. O lagaña espiritual de entendimiento, infernal salpresadora del dulzor del pecar, espuela de los que corren al mal... O con gran razón exclamó S. Agustín que no hay mayor pobreza en el mundo que carecer de sabiduría." [34] To be sure, Pineda's concern is not for the "wisdom" of Torquemada's "hombre curioso". Rather, in a universe where everything is "an alphabet spelling out the proof of God's existence," the inference

---

[32] In the second dialogue there appear two soldiers, Pherencio and Andronico. They are a dissolute pair ("malas hierbas en el jardín...") who stand to profit from the host's homilies (I, 92). In the fifth dialogue an occasion on Christian marriage is provided in the appearance of Polygamo, "...dos veces bígamo..." (I, 303).

[33] See Pineda, I, 73. The one-hundred-thirty page "tabla" lists seven hundred "autores de la obra presente." See I, 8-14.

[34] See Pineda, I, 236-237. The wealth of Pineda's vocabulary has been studied by Iver N. Nelson, "The Contribution of Pineda's *Agricultura Christiana* to the *Diccionario Histórico*," *HR*, XII (1944), 158-167; XVII (1949), 146-158. For a general survey of Pineda's use of language see Jole Scudieri Ruggieri, "Premessa allo studio linguistico del *Agricultura Cristiana* di Fr. Juan de Pineda," *Cultura Neolatina*, XX (1960), 253-259.

is "...cuantas más cosas se sacaren en pláticas tanto mejor cultivada será nuestra agricultura cristiana..." (I, 46).

The trajectory leading from Juan de Valdés' *Diálogo de la lengua* to Juan de Pineda's *Agricultura Cristiana* would seem to indicate that the dialogue in sixeenth-century Spain was gradually divested of its more imaginative elements as a hybrid genre and adapted exclusively for didactic and moralistic aims. However, at no time was the dual character of the dialogic technique explicitly repudiated, and even the stern Pineda allowed for pleasant conversations. [35] Indeed, parallel to the didactic and theological dialogues, there were dialogues which showed a contrary tendency: i.e., an emphasis upon the genre's place in the literature of entertainment. Thus, in the tradition of Castiglione's *Il Cortegiano*, Luis Milán composed a *Cortesano* (Valencia, 1551) permeated with a *joie de vivre* not equaled even by his Italian inspiration. Presented in narrative form, the dialogue provides a convenient framework for puns, anecdotes, *coplas*, and debates in settings which include a hunt, a masque, and a party, all celebrated at the estate of the Duque de Calabria in Valencia. As the author-interlocutor rallies his cronies for an evening's festivities with the cry "...el divertir hace vivir..." the reader senses that, with regard to basic attitudes, Milán and Pineda are at opposite poles. [36]

Near the middle of the sixteenth century the spirit of Milán's hedonism found a more bourgeois echo with Gaspar Luis Hidalgo's *Diálogos de apacible entretenimiento* (Salamanca, n.d.). As implied by the title, the dialogues are a "game" and take place during the three nights preceding Ash Wednesday in an atmosphere of ribald levity. [37] However, the scene is not the pre-Lenten

---

[35] See Pineda's foreword.
[36] See Luis Milan, *El Cortesano* (Madrid, 1874), p. 135.
[37] See *BAE*, XXXVI, 279-316. The date of the dialogues has been set around 1600. See Ludwig Pfandl, *Historia de la literatura nacional española en la Edad de Oro*, tr. Jorge Rubio Balaguer (Barcelona, 1952), p. 142. The three nights preceding Ash Wednesday provided the background for a work very similar in other aspects as well as by the Italian Anton Francesco Grazzini, *Cene* (Firenze). The date has been set around 1540. See Francesco Flora, *Storia della letteratura italiana* (Verona, 1947), II, 362. Nocturnal gatherings for light conversations and story-telling also provide the setting for Gianfrancesco Straparola's *Le piacevoli notti* (Venice, 1553).

ball but a blazing hearth in the home of a professor of Salamanca where the host and his wife entertain a neighboring couple. To add to the festive spirit, a buffoon called Castañeda is included as an interlocutor. [38] The structure of the three dialogues consists of a *pot pourri* of poems, romances, and anecdotes almost all of which are in questionable taste. The final session ends with a plan to meet again during the nights preceding Christmas. [39]

A similar setting suggested a later example of a dialogue of pastime in Antonio de Eslava's *Noches de invierno* (Barcelona, 1609). [40] Like Hidalgo's *Diálogos*, *Noches de invierno* also takes place on three successive nights. However, there is none of the license of the earlier work in Eslava's portrayal of four elderly Venetians who while away the hours with "...pláticas gustosas..." which include Italianate novelas interspersed with comments on a variety of topics. Despite the traditional character of the subjects discussed, the author succeeds in creating an air of spontaneity by such devices as introducing the wife of the host for the third night to provide a garrulous defense of her sex against a misogynist member of the gathering. [41] Also, thoughout the dialogues there is a realistic note as the speakers interrupt their chats to savor their host's malmsey and pass about trays of roasted pear, crab apples, and chestnuts, or feast on bread and quince preserves. [42]

As was the case in Spain with Juan de Valdés, the dialogue tradition in Portugal was also given a promising start by a writer whose career is especially auspicious for his studies regarding the vernacular. [43] João de Barros wrote his *Diálogo da viciosa vergonha* in the same year which saw the publication of his *Gramática da língua portuguesa* (Lisbon, 1540) and explicitly mentions

---

[38] Hidalgo, p. 279.
[39] Hidalgo, p. 316.
[40] Antonio de Eslava, *Noches de invierno* (Barcelona, 1609), p. 4.
[41] For a study regarding such debates between male misogynists and female champions of women, see Barbara Matulka, *The Novels of Juan de Flores and their European Diffusion* (N. Y., 1931), pp. 88-137. See also J. O. Ornstein, "La misogenía y el profeminismo en la literatura castellana," *RFE*, III (1941), 219-276.
[42] See Eslava, pp. 55, 68, 92, 129, 205.
[43] See Hernâni Cidade, "João de Barros, o que pensa da língua portuguesa, como a escreve," *BF*, XI (1950), 281-303.

the latter work in the former.[44] Within the dialogue itself the linguist is apparent in the author's concern for an exact delimitation of semantic areas as the interlocutors distinguish the etymological meanings of terms (p. 3) and lament the absence in Portuguese of the lexical wealth of Latin and Greek (p. 4).[45] There is also a literary aura permeating *Diálogo da viciosa vergonha* in the author's allusion to his earlier, more primitive dialogue, *Ropica Pnefma* (Lisbon, 1532),[46] as well as to his expressed intention to convert what appears to be a deceptively artless conversation with his son into "...um diálogo inocente para inocentes..." (p. 12).

The dialogue opens with the father sending his son to his study ("livraria") to fetch certain notebooks which contain the topic of their discussion: an analysis of mortification which will distinguish the salutary shame which follows from a failure to comply with ethical prescriptions from the culpable, gratuitous shame ("...sobeja e escusada vergonha...") which one may suffer for shortcomings for which he is not responsible ("...que nos vêm por natureleza..."). A convenient touchstone for evaluating motivations provides the basis of the author's counsel: "Olha... a que fim vai dirigida [a obra]: e se o fim é amor de Deus, descansa na tal obra" (p. 18).[47] The father adds weight to his counsel by

---

[44] João de Barros, *Diálogo de viciosa vergonha* (Lisbon, 1540), p. 1. Future references are incorporated into the text.

[45] However, as will be shown in Chapter VI, this does not prevent de Barros from assigning an over-all linguistic superiority to Portuguese.

[46] See I. S. Révah, "João de Barros," *Revista do Livro*, III (1958), 64. Indeed, the author explicitly alludes to his technique: "A maior parte desta obra vai em metáfora..." and situates the dialogue between Reason, Will, Judgment and Time in Reason's "fortaleza... [onde tem] a melhor e mais forte torre de castelo...". See de Barros, *Ropica...*, II, 12.

[47] This moral premise is a paraphrase of St. Augustine's "Ama et fac quod vis." See F.-J. Thonnard, *A Short History of Philosophy*, tr. E. A. Maziarz (N. Y., 1955), pp. 260-261. In de Barros' simple conversation between a father and his son there is a similarity to St. Augustine's *De Magistro* which also involves a dramatically portrayed dialogue between the Saint and his son Adeodatus. Generally, however, the Fathers were of less importance to de Barros' "...positivisme évangelique..." than biblical exegesis. See Révah, "João de Barros," p. 65. de Barros' religiosity, described as "Erasmita," is discussed by A. J. Saraiva, *História da cultura em Portugal* (Lisbon, 1953), II, 566-604, and is best exemplified by *Ropica pnefma* and *Diálogo evangélico sobre os artigos da Fé contra o Talmud dos Judeus*. See the only edition ever published of the latter in the text of I. S. Révah (Lisbon, 1950), p. lxix, lxxxix. For a similar apologetic dialogue involving creeds

using such traditional devices as a syllogism (p. 12), and by interlarding his comments with the examples of traditional authorities. However, classical tradition does not weigh as heavily on João de Barros as it does on Mexía and Pineda, and he shows a spiritual kinship to his fellow linguist Valdés as he wryly observes: "Qualquer cousa por ter preço entre nós, há-de ser dito em grego ou latim..." p. 27). More relevant, therefore, to moral precepts "...que são próprias de todo fiel que confessa a Cristo..." (p. 13) is Scripture, and the author counsels his son "...tomar as leis... não de Platão nem de Túlio, mas da doutrina de Cristo..." (p. 25). He ends his discussion with a florilegium of biblical texts designed to combat "...a viciosa vergonha..."

The author's obviously pedagogic purpose does not negate the possibility of a dialectic, since he shows considerable respect for the son's ratiocinations. When the latter allows that "...é natural que os pais doutrinam of filhos..." with the fallacious explanation that "...com mais amor receberão sua doutrina pois esperam de lhes herdar sua herança... (p. 15), we find none of the peremptory emendations of a Pineda as the father points out that such an argument would be irrelevant should a parent decide to use immoral ends to amass an inheritance for his family (p. 16). The son thus sees his own error and rectifies his statement by distinguishing between the intrinsic worth of sound advice and the incidental encouragement provided by material gain: "Melhor bons costumes... que muita fazenda" (p. 16). Only then does his father admit to having resorted to indirect persuasion: "...o modo dos médicos, que preambulam cousas primeiro que dêem suas mezinhas aos enfermos, para lhe [sic] ser doce e suave o que no seu gosto é azedo e áspero..." (p. 17). [48]

Far more ambitious than João de Barros' simple conversation between himself and his son is Heitor Pinto's monumental *Imagen*

---

rather than individuals, see the refutation of Islam by Gaspar de Leão, *Desengano de perdidos* (Goa, 1573). A modern edition by Eugenio Asensio was published in Coimbra in 1958.

[48] Nonetheless, de Barros does not always rely on reason and personally interpreted authorities in expanding his topic. He dismisses an argument from Seneca on the grounds that "...seria palavra herética..." (p. 12), and depends upon rhetoric as he inveighs against the fruits of "...viciosa vergonha...": "Aqui juramentos falsos, aqui traições, aqui mortes de homens, aqui más sentenças, aqui empréstimos..." (p. 20).

da vida cristã (Part I, Coimbra, 1563; Part II, Lisbon, 1572) which comprises a wealth of philosophical and ascetic teaching regarding the ideal Christian life. The author's explicitly didactic purpose in sculpting an "... estátua e imagen da vida cristã... [49] combined with his respect for the dialogue form, "...à maneira de Platão..." (I, 6), results in eleven colloquies involving interlocutors who are carefully selected as symbols of attitudes necessary for the development of the author's topics. Whether representing a profession, a nationality, or a state in life, the unnamed speakers are chosen as exponents of views proper to, e.g., a jurist, an Italian or a noble. The major exception in each dialogue is the central speaker, for Pinto, like his fellow clerics Pineda and Torquemada, creates a magisterial figure to act as his mouthpiece. Thus, one speaker consistently assumes a didactic relationship with regard to the other interlocutors, nor does the Portuguese friar arbitrarily confer his voice upon any speaker in a given group. The most orthodox passages are invariably given to a Portuguese, a Theologian, a father, or a teacher who engages the others in debates leading to a defense of Catholic precepts. Pinto further reveals himself in his work by allowing the main interlocutors of each dialogue to divulge biographical data which clash with the shadowy presences of the other speakers. Consequently, one finds frequent references to the author's monastic order in form of praise of St. Jerome and of the order's house near Lisbon.[50] Other personal references include glowing allusions to the Portuguese,[51] mention of the author's travels, and a bucolic description of his probable birthplace "...Covilhã... cercada de deleitosos e frutíferos arvoredos..." (IV, 252).[52]

---

[49] Heitor Pinto, *Imagem da vida cristã*, ed. Alves Correia (Lisbon, 1958), I, 1. Future references are incorporated into the text.

[50] See I, 24; II, 31, 63, 82, 136-139, 164; III, 184.

[51] See II, 80.

[52] For the controversy regarding Pinto's birthplace, see Luis Fernando de Carvalho Dias, "Fr. Heitor Pinto, novas achegas para a sua biografia," *Boletim da Biblioteca da Universidade de Coimbra*, XXI (1952), 1. In addition to the foreign setting of some of Pinto's dialogues, the author sometimes mentions the motives of his travels as in II, 155; IV, 263. See Carvalho Dias, pp. 13-30. The most thorough study of *Imagem da Vida Cristã* has been done by Professor Edward Glaser of the University of Michigan. See his introduction to a recent edition of the sixteenth century Spanish translation (anonymous): *Imagen de la vida cristiana* (Barcelona, 1967), pp. 1-167.

An outstanding example of the encyclopedic dialogue, *Imagem da vida cristã* represents the erudition of one who spent "...a mor parte da vida no estudo das letras..." (II, 5). As a result, the dialogic technique is often hidden by a surfeit of authorities both sacred and profane, who are constantly cited in accordance with the author's expressed method: "... que disser será tirado de... autores..." (I, 36). The discussions are usually reducible to a secondary interlocutor's debatable observations which are countered by lengthy clarifications with frequent encouragement and aid from the others. In light of such dogmatism there are few instances of genuine conflict; indeed, the very possibility of disagreement is sometimes precluded: "É tão fundado esse juizo que sem êle será quem lhe contraria" (II, 137).[53] A semblance of dialectic progression can be best found in the mechanics of a syllogism or in the formalism of a scholastic *disputatio* with its ritualistic "demonstração... nego" (I, 200), "...provo-o... concedo..." (II, 205).[54]

Despite his acknowledged admiration for Plato, our Heronymite's pedagogical preoccupation not only slows down the pace of the dialectical exchange, but often undoes even a semblance of the dialogic form. At such times Pinto's discussions assume a homiletic air which may prevail for an entire chapter as is evident from the heading of the last chapter of the "Diálogo da vida solitária": "Da morte eterna e da lembrança da temporal, com uma devota peroração" (II, 148)[55] A somewhat more novelistic example of an interruption of the interlocutory structure is found in "Diálogo da verdadeira amizade" where the speakers pause in their

---

[53] For other expressions implying the futility of altercation, see I, 96, 138; IV, 3, 269. However, there are some instance of spirited debate, e. g., see I, 28 ff, where the opponent, a philosopher, can scarcely wait for the hermit to finish before he "takes the bit between his teeth" ("...soltou as rédeas à boca...")

[54] Pinto furnishes fine examples of "...dispute scholastiche... il metodo dimostrativo per via di argumenti e autorità". See Morigi, p. 127. Other examples of syllogisms are in I, 142, 161, 264; II, 20, 73, 115, 119; IV, 168. For a study of Pinto's eristic technique see Edward Glaser, "Fr. Heitor Pinto's *Imagen da vida cristã*," *Aufsätze zur Portugiesischen Kulturgeschichte*, III (1962), 53-56.

[55] For other examples of homilies, see I, 107, 240; II, 151, 268, 313, 317; IV, 27, 58, 114, 297-98, 301. The author implies that ascetic ends are better served "usando mais de solilóquios que de colóquios..." (II, 54).

conversation to allow one of their number to read some letters on friendship which were found in a notebook bought from an urchin in Madrid.[56] When it is learned that the notebook belongs to the "...teólogo portugues... havia poucos dias que lho furtaram em Madrid..." (III, 195), it becomes apparent that the eighteen-page interval provides an opportunity for another solliloquy by the author.[57]

The failure of Pinto to establish a dialectical interplay among individualized speakers is contrasted by the care with which he constructs the setting for his dialogues. One might even conjecture that Pinto chose the narrative form for his work precisely to allow for detailed descriptions of the backgrounds of his conversations. Thus, the profoundly philosophical tenor of the first dialogue, "Da verdadeira filosofia," unfolds against a background of the willows which line the Mondego river around Coimbra (I, 1).[58] Similar scenes involving leafy glens and purling brooks are situated in such diverse places as Lombardy (I, 194), Piedmont (II, 1), and Lyon (III, 1). The mark of the perceptive tourist is also discernible in Pinto's lengthy description of the harbor at Marseille with the monastery of St. Victor commanding a view of the Mediterranean (II, 155-157), and a dialogue on death is appropriately situated on a manor near Florence amid the ruins of a former civilization (II, 85).[59] Other geographically determined locales are the house of a citizen in a Spanish university

---

[56] That Pinto considers the doctrinal content of dialogue more important than its form is seen in his apology for the interruption: "Não se cortará o fio com ouvirmos carta de amigos" (III, 194).

[57] Variation is also achieved with short stories; e.g., I, 232, 265; II, 61, 153, 165; III, 138-147, 190.

[58] The Mondego and its willows were a poetic commonplace even in Pinto's day. See Ferreira de Vasconcelos, p. 9; Sá de Miranda, "Fábula do Mondego," *Obras* (Lisbon, 1960), I, 79-103; Luis de Camões, *Os Lusíadas*, Canto III, Strophe 135. For a view which sees Pinto's pastoral scenes as influenced by Bernardim Ribeiro's *Menina e moça*, see Eugenio Asensio's review of Dorothy Grokenberger's edition of *Menina e moça* (Lisbon, 1947) in *RFE*, XXXIII (1949), 176-177.

[59] The "peregrino português" in "Diálogo da vida solitária" travelled with "...un cartapácio onde traziam escritos os nomes dos lugares que corriam e as diversidades dos trajes, costumes, leis, e cerimónias que achavam... e outras coisas dignas de memória... (II, 1-2).

town (IV, 1) [60] and an inn in Toledo (II, 67). Less colorful but well chosen for a dialogue on Christian patience in tribulation is a scene in a dungeon where a well-born prisoner is visited by a friend (I, 219). Hence, of the eleven dialogues in *Imagem da vida cristã*, only two are situated in nothing more elaborate than a theologian's house (I, 135) and the chamber of a young lord (IV, 157). [61]

The tradition of the moralistic dialogue in Portugal found a successor to Heitor Pinto in the Carmelite bishop of Portalegre, Amador Arrais. However, what provides the framework of Arrais' *Diálogos* (Coimbra, 1589) is not the panorama of the Christian life, but the more limited prospect of a Christian death. Consequently, the author discards a variety of characters and settings such as are found in *Imagem da vida cristã* in preference for one focal character in a starkly simple setting. As an effective means for maintaining an atmosphere conducive to the theme of "holy dying," the protagonist of *Diálogos* is the bed-ridden invalid Antíoco who never leaves the confines of his sick-room throughout the ten directly presented dialogues. In Antíoco's illness the Carmelite intends an allegorical portrayal of every man's fate as a sinful creature, for "...não há nesta vida verdadeira saúde..." [62] For the Christian, concern regarding where he will live and die is irrelevant, and the self-exiled Antíoco is frequently reminded:

---

[60] Probably Salamanca. See Carvalho Dias, pp. 31-45.

[61] Pinto's dialogues usually end "eclogue fashion" with the setting sun. See Glaser, "Frei Heitor Pinto's *Imagen*...", p. 52. Some are termined abruptly (I, 279; III, 246; IV, 301); and only one, "Diálogo da religião," breaks the pattern as the three pilgrims resume their journey in the cool of late afternoon; see I, 132.

[62] The reference is to the second edition (Coimbra, 1604), p. 219. Future references are incorporated into the text. The significance of Antíoco's illness apparently escapes Fidelino de Figueiredo who regards him as "...um neurastênico disputador..." and sees no value in his illness other than "...excitar-lhe a inteligência e multiplicar os temas da disputa...". The failure to realize the symbolic value of Arrais' central figure leaves Figueiredo at a loss regarding an interpretation of his character: "Não se pode afirmar que esse Antíoco jeremiador seja o modelo pessoal do bom Cristo... porque Arrais está umas vezes com êle e outras contra êle...". See Amador Arrais, *Diálogos*, ed. Fidelino de Figueiredo (Lisbon, 1944), pp. xviii-xix. The name "Antíoco" may well have been chosen for its resemblance to "Antioquia," the city where "Christian" was first coined. See Acts XI, 26.

"Ao bom varão terras alheias seu natural são...no cabo de nossa peregrinação tornaremos àquela pátria que verdadeiramente o é de todos nós..." (p. 248). The ten dialogues comprising Arrais' work thus constitute Antíoco's ascetic peregrination as he gradually learns how to prepare for death (p. 256).

In view of Arrais' moralistic intentions and the allegorical nature of his main interlocutor, one can expect little dialectical conflict in the ten conversations which provide the substance of the work. Indeed, the content of the interchange between the speakers is determined not so much by a dialogic development as by their professional status, which in some instances is implied in their names. For example, the atmosphere is established in the first visit by a doctor called Apolónio who lectures on humors, the symptomatic value of dreams, and engages Antíoco in the hackneyed debate regarding the value of medical science.[63] The second visitor is a preacher named Pauliniano who exhorts the patient to remember "... a adversidade é crisol da virtude..." (p. 30).[64] As Antíoco continues to deteriorate, the sacraments are conferred upon him by another preacher, the wise Sabiniano, who proceeds to instruct the sick man on matters related to Christian doctrine. Of the last three days of Antíoco's life, the first is devoted to a discussion on funerals and inheritances with a canon lawyer who has come to execute the patient's will; the second day is spent with a theologian who discourses on the nature of death; and the final day and the least dialogical of all the conversations is given to prayers, mariology, and extraordinarily graphic sermons as the monk, Olímpio, comforts the dying man in his final hours.[65] The nature of dialogue would lead one to expect the termination of the tenth dialogue to coincide with the death of Antíoco who

---

[63] Obviously a reference to Apollo, the god of healing and father of Asclepius.

[64] The name was probably suggested by St. Paul.

[65] In Chapter LXXX, "Da agonia e morte de Antíoco" there is an indication of the Ignatian "via imaginativa" in such passages as: "Já se destemperou a composição do meu corpo... já o peito se levanta, a voz se enrouquece, já estão frios os pés, e os joelhos, e já meu rosto, os olhos sumidos... "or in" ...olhai para esta imagem de Cristo crucificado... sua cabeça inclinada... o coração... os braços... o corpo..." (pp. 331-344). See Guillermo Diaz-Plaja, *El estilo de S. Ignacio y otras páginas* (Barcelona, 1956), pp. 9-51.

is one of the two interlocutors; however, Olímpio remains to deliver an elegy in Latin (pp. 345-46) and closes with a curiously unascetic eulogy: "...in laudem Coimbrae...onde gastei a flor da minha adolescência..." (p. 346).

Although the primary motivation of Amador Arrais is the spiritual formation of the reader, it apparent throughout the *Diálogos* that the author, like the central figure, is a "...claro engenho ocupado em lição de bons livros... grande estudante devia ser em sua mocedade..." (p. 3). Whether citing Galen on humors (p. 19), Petrarch on poetry (p. 56),[66] or João de Barros on the Portuguese conquests in the Orient (p. 155), he shows himself equally at ease with respect to the various branches of secular learning as he is when delving into the intricacies of religious dogma, and devotes three dialogues to analyzing timely subjects. Thus, in Dialogue III, "Da gente judaica," the patient draws his visitor, the *fidalgo* Aurélio, into a lengthy discussion ranging from a defense of "New Christians" — "Eu [os] tenho por cristãos enquanto se não provar o contrário...," (p. 56) — to a denunciation of the Jews' religious obduracy to which he attributes their woes in Spain and Portugal.[67] Less polemic is Dialogue IV, "Da glória e triunfo dos lusitanos" where a visit from Herculano, just returned from Mauritania (p. 83) is the pretext for a patriotic paean to Portuguese history and maritime exploits.[68] The author's patriotism is also evident in Dialogue IV, "Das condições e partes

---

[66] An example of Arrais' practical familiarity with secular literature is Antioco's Gongoresque greeting to the rising sun on the eve of his death: "Já o sol rompe pelo oriente, e começa de esclarecer no nosso hemisfério com seus raios, e as avezinhas lhe dão as suas alegres alvoradas..." See María Rosa Lida, "El amanecer mitológico en la poesía narrativa española," *NRFH*, VIII (1946), 77-110.

[67] In defending sincere *Cristãos novos* Antíoco mentions as an example "...Apolónio meu médico..." Apparently Arrais' invalid-interlocutor shared none of the fear in which *converso* physicians were generally held by *cristãos velhos* who looked upon them as possible avengers for their people. See Edward Glaser, "Referencias antisemitas en la literatura peninsular de la Edad de Oro," *NRFE*, VIII (1954), 39-62. See especially pp. 44-46. Also see Julio Caro Baroja, *Los judíos en España moderna y contemporánea* (Madrid, 1961), II, 162-211. Caro Baroja mentions Arrais' Apolónio on p. 175, note 55.

[68] Figueiredo underscores the patriotism of much of Portuguese ascetic literature. See Arrais, *Diálogos*, ed. F. de Figueiredo, xvi.

do bom príncipe," as he adduces copious examples from Portugal's royal families in an examination of the ideal Christian king with the appropriately chosen interlocutor, the lawyer Justiniano.

Despite the nationalistic character of these subjects, Arrais maintains the ascetic outline of his work with frequent allusions to Antíoco's illness and imminent death. Moreover, unlike Pinto and the Spanish writers of informative dialogues, the Carmelite is not content to volunteer his information through the performance of a determined speaker; and Antíoco's symbolic function as the universal Christian aproaching judgment is not jeopardized by becoming the equivalent of Pinto's Portuguese priest or Pineda's Philalethes. Rather, each interlocutor displays an admirable competence, and few dialogues can boast speakers who are so completely "...semelhantes pessoas...," (p. 33). [69] But with no one speaker permanently relegated to the status of a questioning pupil, Arrais' seldom-checked tendency to preach results in a non-conversational form not found in his predecessors. For example, in his long discourse on peace-loving kings, the author forgets that Antíoco is conversing with the jurist Justiniano and directly addresses the reader (p. 15). In a similar case, Sabiniano's comments on Colossians I transcends the limits of a conversation with Antíoco and includes a wider audience: "Desejo que tu e quantos me ouvem, se tornem tais qual eu sou..." (p. 199).

It is significant that later Portuguese authors were apparently unaware of the dangers which an excessive reliance on authorities implies for the dialectical progression essential to the dialogic technique. On the contrary, one suspects that the level of a writer's literary aspiration apparently was gauged by the number of allusions which indicated his wide reading. At least such is the case with Diogo do Couto's *O soldado prático* where a revised form indicates that the original draft suffered major modifications with regard to the importance granted to the inclusion of authorities. The first version, which dates from the end of the reign of the ill-fated Dom Sebastião (1557-1578), has a business-like air as the two interlocutors converse in a prosaic style free of re-

---

[69] For the feasibility of compatible speakers in dialogues, see Gilmore, p. 138.

ferences to classical authorities.[70] However, the revised version redacted in 1610 sports a third interlocutor and a repertory of classical allusions in the tradition of Pinto and Arrais. The change is all the more remarkable in that do Couto's intention was not to instruct in the *sapientia perennis* of the scholastic ascetic of his clerical predecessors, but to awaken Portuguese bureaucracy to administrative abuses in the Orient. The fact that the revision was composed to offset counterfeit copies of the original manuscript which had been stolen may explain the author's concern for attempting what he considered a more ambitiously conceived work.[71]

Diogo do Couto followed the example of Pineda and Pinto in making the major figure of *O soldado prático* a spokesman for his own views. Thus, notwithstanding the veteran's description of himself as "...um soldado idiota, que... não sabe falar mais que verdades chãs..." (p. 42), it soon becomes obvious from his perceptive analysis of the ills besetting Portuguese India and his facility with classical and modern history, that the real speaker is the official historian of the Torre do Tombo. The significance of the veteran is underscored by the observation of a second speaker, the despatcher: "Vejo que vos ides mostrando filósofo, humanista, e ainda teólogo..." (p. 99); and becomes even more explicit when he compares the veteran to Antonio de Guevara's Villano del Danubio: "Não cuido que aquele homem do Danúbio falou no senado de Roma mais livre e mais altamente do que vós tendes feito..." (p. 129).[72] However, do Couto's spokesman does not simply lecture to the despatcher and the third speaker, the nobleman. Indeed, it would have been hazardous to do so, since, contrary to a Philalethes who has the weight of moral philosophy behind him, do Couto's spokesman is a satirical commentator on the political establishment of his time.[73] The result is a realistic

---

[70] See Diogo de Couto, *O soldado prático*, ed. M. Rodrigues Lapa (Lisbon, 1954), pp. xxv-xxviii. References to this edition of the revised version are incorporated into the text.

[71] See do Couto, p. xxviii.

[72] See Antonio de Guevara, *Reloj de principes o libro áureo de Marco Aurelio* (Valladolid, 1529), III, 209.

[73] For the use of dialogue and fictional names as a means to criticizing with impunity, see Gilmore, pp. 136-137. This strategem little availed do

conversation as the veteran criticizes while the despatcher and, especially, the noble attempt to exculpate themselves. Given the contradictory positions of the two apologists and the author's indignation, the three dramatic dialogues often reach degrees of heated exchange not commonly found in the genre.[74]

The trenchant social criticism of *O soldado prático* serves to distinguish the dialectical structure of do Couto's dialogues from those of Pinto and Arrais where opposition is usually mild and academic or, at most, censorious and moralistic. Rather than dismiss the historian's use of the dialogic technique as exceptional, though, it may be more to the point to question those theories which claim to trace a progressive deterioration of the dialogue form insofar as they apply to the genre's trajectory in Portuguese letters.[75] Indeed, neither the weighty moralism of the religious writers nor the fiery political diatribes of do Couto constitute a twilight of the dialogue in Portugal, as can be seen from an examination of the subsequently written *Corte na aldeia* by Rodrigues Lobo, perhaps the finest example of the genre in Portugal and our major concern.

Couto who was hounded by the targets of his satire. See do Couto, pp. xxix-xxx.

[74] An indication of do Couto's intentions for writing a dramatic dialogue is the author's division of the three dialogues into scenes.
The veteran's shrill complaints at times threaten the balanced atmosphere basic to the conversational spirit of the dialogue form; whence the author's attempts at creating a feeling of cordiality at the beginning and end of each dialogue with effusive welcomes and adieus.

[75] Such a theory is Hirzel's who stresses that the dogmatism of the dialogue in the Iberian Peninsula was a reason for its ultimate disappearance. However, he never considers the genre as anything more than an Italian import. See Hirzel, II, 389-390. His position is certainly an extreme one in view of the more than one thousand dialogues written in Spain alone between 1525 and 1600. See L. A. Murillo's article "Diálogo y dialéctica en el Siglo XVI español," *RUBA*, IV (1959), 55-57.

Chapter IV

THE FICTIONAL AND DIALECTICAL ELEMENTS OF
CORTE NA ALDEIA E NOITES DE INVERNO

Throughout the sixteen dialogues of *Corte na aldeia e noites de inverno* Francisco Rodrigues Lobo carefully combines didactic content within an imaginative framework in a manner not often equalled by his predecessors in the Iberian Peninsula. We have already seen that such authors as Amador Arrais and Gaspar Luis de Hidalgo used the dialogic technique as a means for ascetic instruction or for light entertainment. It has also been pointed out that the interlocutors of such dialogues were intended either to amuse or to furnish information. It will now be shown that the eight speakers who appear in the course of Lobo's invented conversations are more ambitiously conceived than were earlier interlocutors in an effort to realize both aspects of the dialogue and thus provide the reader with the profitable pastime which is the ideal of the Renaissance writer. Indeed, the very title of Lobo's work indicates the didacticism of a manual of courtly values ("corte na aldeia") as well as a diversion suitable for the long hours of winter nights ("noites de inverno").

With regard to Lobo's pedagogical intention, there is a paradoxical air about "corte na aldeia" in that the sophistication of a court is not commonly portrayed against the simple background of a rustic setting.[1] An explanation for the paradox,

---

[1] In her *Castiglione y Boscan...*, Morreale describes the Renaissance conception of a court as "...la antítesis con la sencillez idealizada de la vida campesina..." (p. 114). The same critic describes the court as "...ciudad

however, can be found in the Portugal of Rodrigues Lobo where the loss of national autonomy in 1580 and the subsequent dissolution of the royal court at Lisbon had forced many former courtiers to retire to their rural estates. [2] As Lobo explains: "Depois que faltou a Portugal a corte dos sereníssimos reis...retirados os títulos pelas vilas e lugares do reino e os fidalgos cortesãos por suas quintãs e casais, vieram a fazer corte nas aldeias, renovando as saudades das passadas com lembranças devidas àquela dourada idade dos portugueses..." (p. 1). [3] With the historical dispersal of a central court throughout the provinces as his point of departure, Lobo may have been influenced in choosing a name for his dialogues by the titles of earlier peninsular works which also mention palace and hamlet. Possible literary examples included such treatises as Antonio de Guevara's *Menosprecio de corte y alabanza de aldea* (Valladolid, 1539) and Luis de Palmireno's

---

por antonomasia..." in her article, "El Mundo del cortesano," *RFE*, XLII (1958-59), 233. The juxtaposition of the two was normally effected for moralistic purposes with a representative of the court chastened by a villager who lectured on the superiority of the simple life of the *Beatus ille*. As examples of the widely spread use of this longlived device one can cite the fifteenth-century dialogue by an anonymous Spanish writer, *Diálogo entre el rey y un rústico* (see Murillo's dissertation, pp. 36-38) and the seventeenth-century dialogue by the Englishman Nicolas Breton, *The Court and the Country or A Brief Discourse between the Courtier and the Country-Man* (n. p., 1618). See William G. Crane, *Wit and Rhetoric in the Renaissance* (N. Y., 1932), p. 124. Lobo was no doubt aware of the paradoxical nature of his title, since, in his discussion of courtesy, he identifies the term by ultimately distinguishing it from the behavior proper to a villager: "...é ...o bom modo dos que vivem nela [i.e., a cidade] em diferença dos aldeões..." (p. 234).

[2] The economic plight of some noble families under Phillipine domination made their rural retirement a modest one. See Oliveira Martins, I, 112-119; M. Pinheiro Chagas, *História de Portugal* (Lisbon, n.d.), VII, 188-191, 353-355; Fortunato de Almeida, *História de Portugal* (Coimbra, 1926), IV, 172-175, 124-129; Damião Peres, *História de Portugal* (Barcelos, 1933), V. 269-272.

[3] The elegiac tone of *Corte na aldeia* with reference to the loss of the royal court at Lisbon is limited to a few incidental allusions. Thus, Solino refers to the time "...em que éramos troianos... [e Leonardo]... viu luzir o que agora está cheio de ferrugem..." (p. 272). Leonardo laments "...falta a Portugal há tantos anos esta criação da corte..." (p. 285). However, D. Júlio's curiosity with regard to "...os nossos príncipes passados"... (p. 44) is no less great than his desire to learn more about the new dignities conferred from Madrid, as he explains "...agora com diferentes homens se acrescentaram [estes cargos] no serviço real de Espanha..." (p. 229).

complementary texts *El estudioso de aldea* (Valencia, 1568) and *El estudioso cortesano* (Valencia, 1573). However, aside from an interest in court and village as is shown in his title, Guevara's attack on the courtier's existence coupled with his defense of the rustic life has nothing in common with Lobo's dialogues. [4] Similarly, Palmireno's instruction for youths about to move from province to palace reflect an historical situation far removed from Lobo's Portugal. [5]

In the second part of his title Lobo expresses his more artistic aspirations towards contributing to a literature of diversion in the guise of "...uma conversação de amigos [e] umas noites de inverno melhor gastadas que as que se passam em outros exercícios prejudiciais à vida e à consciência..." (p. 2). The common situation prompted by the tedium of a wintry eve had occasioned several works which may well have suggested to Lobo the second part of his title. An outstanding example is Aulus Gellius' *Noctium atticarum liberi viginti*, a collection of anecdotes extremely popular

---

[4] Guevara's popularity is indicated in Lobo's explicit references to *Reloj de príncipes o Libro áureo de Marco Aurelio* (Valladolid, 1529) and to *Aviso de privados y doctrina de cortesanos* (Valladolid, 1539). See pp. 18 and 282. For a study of Guevara's popularity in Portugal see P. Felix Lopes, "Traduções manuscritas portuguesas de F. Antonio de Guevara, "Estudios acerca de Fray Antonio de Guevara in *Archivo Ibero-Americano*, XXIII (1946), 605-606. For the pre-Renaissance perspective of Guevara's works in general, see María Rosa Lida, "Fray Antonio de Guevara, Edad Media y Siglo de Oro español", *RFH*, VII (1945), 346-388. For a study of *Menosprecio...*, see E. Correa Calderón, "Guevara y su invectiva contra el mundo," *Escorial*, XII (1943), 41-68. On p. 55 Correa Calderón points out that much of the influence of *Menosprecio...* on later writers derived from the title itself: "La antinomía, corte y aldea... pasa a ser fácil eco, nueva versión de conceptos."

[5] Palmireno's earlier work pretends to "...instruir los mozos de tal modo que antes que lleguen a esta ciudad, pierden las rústicas costumbres" (p. 4). In the second treatise, the author follows his pupil to the city which he identifies with a courtly milieu: "...mi aldeano es venido a la ciudad, y por haber mudado de asiento le llamo cortesano." The aim is now to develop further the pupil's "...facilidad de tratar con la gente..." (p. 3). As in Guevara, Palmireno's reader has the option of living in two distinct places, a court or a village. However, Palmireno's intention is contrary to Guevara's and to that of most Renaissance writers. In his *El estudioso de la aldea*, the author exclaims: "Beati qui habitant urbes..." and considers village life bearable only for the old: "...que tanto aprovecha la aldea al cortesano viejo... otro tanto daña al niño que se encona en aquellas toscas y groseras costumbres... ya queria sacarlo del [sic] aldea..." (p. 20).

during the Renaissance.⁶ Expressly designed as an entertainment ("ludere"), the informal articles were the fruit of a long winter which the author spent in the country ("...per hiem in agro..."). Also widely read in the Iberian Renaissance were Pero Mexía's *Diálogos* which the author composed "...en las noches largas del invierno pasado..." in an effort to pass the idle hours, (V. "Carta nuncupatoria"). Closer in time and spirit to *Corte na aldeia e noites de inverno* was Antonio de Eslava's *Noches de invierno* written to "...entretenerte [i.e., el lector] y aliviarte de la gran pesadumbre de las noches de invierno... ."⁷

The dialogue's dual purpose as a genre ideally suited for instructive diversion is indicated not only in Lobo's title but is also clearly expressed in the first colloquy where an interlocutor offers an analysis neatly summarizing our author's *ars dialogica*:

> ...o melhor modo de escrever são os diálogos escritos em prosa, com figuras introduzidas que disputem e tratem matérias proveitosas, políticas, engraçadas e cheias de galantaria, sendo a primeira figura da obra o autor dela; e esse que vá guiando e introduzindo as mais, que sejam apropriadas àquelas matérias de que hão de tratar entre si. E, além de ser este estilo mais alto, mais vulgar, mais excelente, inclui em si a lição de todos os outros modos de escrever... (pp. 21-22). ⁸

---

⁶ Written sometime in the second century A. D., the work's "...neat, short, chapters... made it specially suitable for use in florilegia and collections of anecdotes..." See Aulus Gellius, *Noctium Atticarum liberi viginti*, ed. Hazel Marie Hornsby (London, 1936), p. xii. References to Aulus Gellius are found in the indices of Mexía's *Silva...*, Pinto's *Imagem...*, and Pineda's *Agricultura...*

⁷ Eslava acknowledges the influence of Aulus Gellius in the prefatory sonnet, "Del hermano del autor" in the second tercet:

> Y en trágicas historias y muy regidas
> con lengua aristotélica y platónica
> imita a un otro Gelio en sus católogos.

⁸ Although *Corte na aldeia* is the only example of Lobo's use of the dialogic technique, there is a marked tendency in his other writings towards conveying didactic content through conversation. It has been observed that his eclogues "...não passam de diálogos...". See Costa e Silva, 10. See also Pontes, 280. That Lobo himself would not consider his eclogues dialogues follows from his stipulation that dialogues be written in prose. Regarding his pastoral novels, it has been said that they contain "...gentle rustics... who propose to each other questions of a somewhat metaphysical nature..."

The Horatian dictum "delectare et prodesse" clearly determines the inclusion in *Corte na aldeia e noites de inverno* of "...matérias proveitosas, políticas... [como também] engraçadas e cheias de galantaria... ." Lobo again paraphrases the principle at the close of his dialogues through another interlocutor who describes the contents of ideal conversations as "...matérias e sujeitos ...escolhidos...proveitosos e agradáveis aos ouvintes..." (pp. 327-328). For Lobo, therefore, neither humorous anecdotes nor academic exercises suffice of themselves as the substance for a proper dialogue. However, while stressing the need for both profit and pleasure, Lobo seems to give the palm to the latter, since the combination of "...todos os ...modos de escrever..." is aimed at creating a variety which "...mais costuma entreter a deleitar os ânimos dos homens..." (p. 21).

In his analysis of the dialogic technique Lobo implicitly mentions the "continuable" character of conversation which permits both the inclusion of many subjects and moods as well as the temporary terminations which further ensure "deleite" by avoiding monotony. For this reason, our author can divide the work internally into separate dialogues as well as offer a sequel to the work itself: "Até nos gostos... a muita continuação causa fastio, pelo que os autores discretos por não cansarem...os juízos dos curiosos, dividem seus volumes em partes..." and terminates "...servindo esta e as passadas [noites] de uma primeira parte que se continuará..." (pp. 327-328). [9] For Lobo "deleitar" is the

---

See M. E. M., "Leaves from the Portuguese Olive-No. VI: Rodrigues Lobo, "*Dublin University Magazine,* LVI (1856), 69. This observation seems to imply that Lobo is alone in creating philosophical shepherds, which, of course, is obviously not the case. The most famous pastoral novel of the Peninsular is replete with "...questions of a somewhat metaphysical nature...". See Jorge de Montemayor, *Los siete libros de Diana,* ed. E. Moreno Baez (Madrid, 1955), pp. xi-xxiv.

[9] Lobo ends with "Se este estilo... for bem aceito, sairá brevemente à luz outro volume de diálogos..." In the "Al lector" to the Spanish translation of *Corte na aldeia* Morales expresses the hope that Lobo would not lose much time before writing a sequel. With regard to internal divisions each dialogue in *Corte na aldeia* is roughly uniform and, in contrast to so many dialogues of the period, credibly brief enough for an evening's chat. Each ends with an allusion to the late hour except the last when Livio announces a projected absence of a few days. Since his part in the dialogues is paramount it is decided that the conversations cannot go on. See p. 327.

result of a variety of topics and moods which, in turn, are united most conveniently through conversation.

In examining *Corte na aldeia* as Lobo's practical application of his theory regarding the dialogue, one is at first puzzled by the author's stipulation that "...a primeira figura da obra [seja] o autor dela..." (p. 21), since Lobo himself does not appear in his dialogues, as does Luis Milán, nor does he cast any one speaker as an obvious exponent of his own views. With the role of "...a primeira figura..." defined as "...guiando e introduzindo as mais..." it would seem that the "first" speaker is a narrator who constructs the world in which the interlocutors act.[10] In support of this view is the fact that *Corte na aldeia e noites de inverno* is a narrative dialogue in the tradition of *Il Cortegiano*, and consequently opens with an extensively described setting:[11]

> Perto da Cidade principal da Lusitânia está uma graciosa Aldeia que com igual distância fica situada à vista do mar Oceano, fresca no Verão, com muitos favores da natureza, e rica no Estio e Inverno com os frutos e comodidades que ajudam a passar a vida saborosamente; porque, com a vizinhança dos portos do mar por uma parte e da outra com a comunicação da ribeira que enche os seus vales e outeiros de arvoredos e verdura, tem em todos os tempos do ano o que em diferentes lugares costuma buscar a necessidade dos homens..." (p. 5).[12]

---

[10] For the narrator as representing an attitude especially designed for his work, see Wolfgang Kayser, *Interpretación y análisis de la obra literaria* (Madrid, 1961), pp. 262-283.

[11] The marked similarities and dissimilarities of *Corte na aldeia* to *Il Cortegiano* will be pointed out throughout the following analysis. For the moment it is sufficient to emphasize the major difference between the structure of Lobo's work and Castiglione's: the latter's historically illustrious men and women gathered in a Renaissance palace for four nights represent a world far removed from Lobo's fictional representation of several rather ordinary bachelors who meet for sixteen wintry nights to discuss sundry topics. See Jorge, pp. 309-312. However, Jorge's "Não dei fé em ponto algum de transcrições..." seems to have overlooked at least one: i. e., Castiglione's "...dulce y amada compañía..." (p. 34) become Lobo's "...doce e amada companhia..." in *Corte na aldeia* (p. 202). However, while Castiglione used the phrase to describe the major speakers in setting the opening scene, Lobo uses it to refer to the characters of an interpolated story.

[12] The setting for *Corte na aldeia* is an example of Lobo's sensitivity to bucolic scenery. For a detailed study of Lobo's poetic landscapes in his pastoral novels, see Jorge, pp. 236-248; Pontes, pp. 79-96. However, the

While there is no mention of the name of the village, the wealth of details indicates that Lobo may have chosen Sintra as the "aldeia" of his title. Within the work the author provides additional clues as in a speaker's reference to "...a nossa serra para a parte do mar..." (p. 100), or by alluding to "...a Cidade [Lisbon]..." as the destination of an easy day's journey.[13] The narrator completes the physical details of his literary world by keeping an early winter setting as the background: "...uma noite de novembro em a qual já o frio não dava lugar a que a frescura do tempo convidasse ao sereno..." (p. 6).[14]

Taking shelter from the winter chill for sixteen consecutive nights are the interlocutors, a group of close friends of diversified backgrounds who gather for "...aprazível conversação ou quieto e moderado jogo..." (p. 6). The author avails himself of his self-appointed role as narrator to provide a cast of characters prior

---

ideal landscape described in the opening paragraph of *Corte na aldeia* ("...tem em todos os tempos do ano o que em diferentes lugares costuma buscar a necessidade dos homens...") seems to jar with the winter weather which is the background for the dialogues.

[13] Well known to the English reader through George Byron's "Childe Harold's Pilgrimage," XVIII-XXIII, Sintra's charms had already been sung in Portugal's literature before Lobo. The *serra* appears as a woman in Gil Vicente's *Triunfo do inverno* where Verão sings of "...Sintra... la sierra más hermosa... refrigerio en los calores..." See Gil Vicente, *Obras completas*, ed. Marques Braga (Lisbon, 1952), IV, 315-316. For a description of the thickly wooded slopes to which Lobo refers see D. João de Castro's letters from Penha Verde, his estate in Sintra, in Elaine Sanceau, D. *João de Castro, Knight of the Renaissance* (London, n. d.), pp. 36-39. Later in the century Sintra was immortalized in *Os Lusiadas*, V, III:

Ficava o caro Tejo e a fresca serra
De Sintra, e nela os olhos se alongavam...

In his article on unedited materials dealing with Lobo's life and works, C. A. Ferreira reproduces a letter by our author wherein he describes a visit to "O mosteiro dos capuchos da serra de Sintra." See Ferreira, pp. 280-283. In his letter Lobo describes "...a serra em cujos primeiros vales e subidas há tanto que louvar em sua graciosa verdura, alegres soutos, debuxados penedos, cristalinas fontes, e sombrios arvoredos..." His description of his trek on p. 280 ("...entrando mais pela espessura da montanha para a parte do mar...") is remarkably similar to his speaker's in *Corte na aldeia*.

[14] The winter setting occasionally rises to the foreground in references to the drizzle ("...chuva miúda...," p. 50), the roaring fireplace (p. 76), and Solino's heavy cloak (p. 244). In describing a forest glade Lobe is careful to point out that the vines "...ainda não estavam despidos de suas folhas..." (p. 101).

to beginning the dialogues themselves. Unlike the *dramatis personae* of Pineda and Castiglione, Lobo's interlocutors are neither cyphers for doctrinal ends nor historical figures. Rather, as in the Platonic dialogues, each is a literary creation designed with an eye to a competent development of the subjects to be discussed. Also, since the topics are treated successively as informal conversations, certain speakers required for later discussions are only summarily mentioned in the "program." Thus, the author hints: "Fora estes havia outros de quem em seus lugares se fará menção..." (p. 6).

For the first ten dialogues the host is Leonardo, a former resident at the royal palace who has come to spend his final years in the rural calm of the village.[15] Complementing Leonardo's knowledge which he acquired as a university graduate trained in languages and developed throughout a long life (p. 12) is Lívio, a retired lawyer who is given to such scholarly pursuits as investigating the histories of past civilizations.[16] Like the host, Lívio has also come to the village to enjoy an undisturbed old age. A less seasoned perspective is provided by the youths D. Júlio, the only noble in the gathering, and Píndaro, a student. The former is a patriot fond of the hunt[17] while the latter is described as an industrious student with a particular interest in poetry. The fifth member of the group is the onetime palace servant, Solino, a remarkably perceptive old man, practised in barbed though good-natured repartee. While each speaker obviously embodies a definite attitude, the close correlation between character development and dialogic progression makes extremely difficult a facile analysis of *Corte na aldeia* into characters as distinct from plot. Hence, some repetition will be inevitable in discussing first Lobo's character-

---

[15] There is a hint of the weary disillusionment so prevalent in Lobo's eclogues (See Pontes, pp. 41-42) in the author's explanation for Leonardo's retirement to the village "...com a mudança e experiência dos anos, fez eleição dos montes para passar neles os que lhe ficavam da vida, grande acerto de quem colhe este fruto maduro entre desenganos..." (pp. 5-6).

[16] "...Doutor na sua profissão e lido nas histórias da humanidade..." (p. 6).

[17] Lobo says that Júlio is "...muito afeiçoado às cousas da pátria..." (p. 7). Later Lívio remarks: "Bravamente é apaixonado o senhor D. Júlio... pelas cousas da nossa pátria..." (p. 25).

ization of his speakers and, subsequently, the "plot" of the dialogues themselves.

Since Lobo intends to entertain his reader with a variety of perspectives as well as to inform him, he does not create a single magisterial figure such as Mexía's Vásquez, Pineda's Philalethes, Pinto's Portuguese theologian or even do Couto's veteran. Nevertheless, a certain predominance exercised by Leonardo makes of him a kind of moderator of the dialogues, and for most of the winter nights it is his house which provides a comfortable setting for the convivial gatherings.[18] Furthermore, Leonardo is the oldest member of the group, and the narrator accordingly refers to him on occasion as "...o velho..." or alludes to his age as a partial explanation for his point of view on certain issues. For example, he omits love letters from his statement on the art of writing letters with "...deixei-[as] por ser impróprio de minha idade tratar delas" (p. 75). Later he discounts a pessimistic appraisal of the modern epoch with "Já no meu tempo havia os mesmos queixumes de agora..." (p. 272). However, on another occasion he plays the *laudator temporis acti* when he bewails the loss of courtly breeding in Portugal: "...falta a Portugal há tantos anos esta criação..." (p. 285). Even here, though, he tempers his plaint by declaring himself a poor judge of contemporary youth: "...posto que a minha [vontade] era dilatar mais esta matéria nem pela idade nem pela confiança tenho licença..." (p. 286).[19]

More important than his significance as host and his venerability as the senior member of the group is Leonardo's activity in directing the majority of the discussions. On one occasion, when an issue is subject to varying interpretations, he tentatively declares it moot ("...deixando isto por averiguar..." p. 24) and leads the conversation to more fertile fields. Leonardo also frequently assigns topics for discussion and appoints speakers to develop the

---

[18] I. e., "...é uma especie de presidente daquele cenáculo...". See Jorge, p. 326. The names of Lobo's speakers suggest no etymological nor historical connotations, allowing for the possible exceptions of Píndaro and Lívio who are, respectively, the group's poet and historian. "Solino" had already appeared in Spanish dialogues and was usually associated, though not here, with the pastoral tradition. See Murillo's dissertation, p. 135.

[19] For references to Leonrado as "o velho" see pp. 7, 10, 17, 115.

conversations: "Estimarei segui-la [i.e., a escolha] tomando o primeiro voto do licenciado..." (p. 271).

The closest he ever comes to deciding a debate is to evaluate an argument somewhat hesitantly either approving ("não me descontenta essa razão..." p. 136), or expressing a personal reservation ("Não falta...quem queira defender a vossa parte... porém, uma dúvida tenho...," p. 268). The Protean nature of aulic protocol which provides much of the material for the discussions does not require Lobo's host to play the decisive role of Torquemada's or Pinto's. Thus, in analyzing an aspect of courtesy Leonardo explains that he cannot provide a definitive assertion: "...como isto há-de ser em conformidade das matérias, occasiões, e pessoas com que se practica, não posso dar a isso regra ordenada" (p. 188). [20]

Central to Leonardo's role as a permissive moderator is his function as representing only one aspect of Lobo's dialectic which accordingly shows a curious division of the argumentative process among several interlocutors. As a result there is a clear distinction throughout between Leonardo's suggestions for topics and discursive analyses and Lívio's academic definitions of the terms used by his host. Leonardo himself defines his relationship to the historian with: "Pouco pudera eu dizer se não fosse acostado à vossa erudição e autoridade" (p. 188). Thus, when asked to declare "...o que há-de ter uma carta para...ser bem escrita...," Leonardo presents the subject as a *definiendum* to Lívio: "...para eu seguir com autoridade é bem que vós comeceis a principiar a matéria, dizendo que nome é *carta* e o seu princípio..." (p. 30). After Lívio has completed a traditional, normative definition comprising the etymology, genus, and species of the term, he returns the topic to his host: "E pois lhe descubri o nome é necessário... senhor Leonardo que lhe deis agora o ser... ." Leonardo then continues "...passando do nome da carta aos exteriores dela." The two interlocutors, therefore, represent the inductive and the deductive facets of any subject which they discuss with Lívio providing the

---

[20] For Leonardo as moderator, see also pp. 51, 76, 78, 124, 140, 164, 172, 192, 231, 271.

essential definitions and Leonardo the existential exemplifications.[21]

To be sure, Lívio's role is not entirely that of a theoretician, for Lobo attempts to give his learned interlocutor a measure of characterization; eg., just as Leonardo protests having to participate in a romantic interlude with "...pela minha idade pudera já estar aposentado para tal empresa..." (p. 116), the voice of one already disillusioned by age can also be detected in Lívio's comments regarding the same intrigue: "O estilo dos encarecimentos namorados... é pensamento que já me desvelou em outra idade..." (p. 105). The lawyer further shows a similarity to his associate in Lobo's dialectic by sometimes acting as a moderator and suggesting a topic: "Não será fora de propósito divertirmo-nos agora com esta matéria..." (p. 105); or he may allow for an exception with "Em tal caso...piadosamente o consentirei..." (p. 227), or even provide a recapitulation for a preceding discussion (p. 210). However, Lívio most often is the figure of academic authority, and no matter how "...autorizada com razões... costumes ... e ... experiência" another's opinion, he nonetheless insists: "Quero eu acrescentar o que li ..." (p. 244).[22] Occasionally he is quick to take offense when he suspects some of his friends of parodying his procedure: "Parece-me... que de aposta quereis profanar a minha autoridade." On one such occasion Lobo pens a picture of ruffled dignity as his learned speaker closes the evening's

---

[21] The lawyer makes an explicit reference to the argument by definition on p. 313; "[a lógica]... ensina... o verdadeiro modo de definir... descobrindo os géneros, espécies, diferenças, substâncias e acidentes... [e] diversos modos de arguir, provar, e sustentar..." See also pp. 79, 168. For a study of the normative definition as first completely developed by Cicero, see Alain Michele, *Rhétorique et philosophie chez Cicéron* (Paris, 1960), pp. 487-489.

[22] Only once does Lívio dispense with his numerous references in an effort towards attaining brevity, and content himself with a terse outline: "...deixando autoridade, exemplos, preceitos, e cousas infinitas que poderão levar grande tempo..." (p. 170). However, Lívio's pretense at succinctness here merely exemplifies the traditional rhetorical device of brevity. See Ernst Robert Curtius, *European Literature and the Latin Middle Ages*, tr. Willard R. Trask (N. Y. 1953), pp. 387-394. Also see Horst Rudiger, "Pura et illustris brevitas," *Festschrift für Erich Rothacker*, ed. Gerhard Funkes (Bonn, 1958), pp. 345-372.

conversation in his pique: "Não vos quero dar esse gosto à minha custa e não passemos daqui nesta matéria..." (p. 99).[23]

No less important to Lobo's dialogical technique than Lívio's erudition is Solino's humor. As Leonardo embarks upon an analysis of the monarchical system he hints at his relationship to the other two senior members of the sessions with: "Poderei discorrer...se o Doutor...interpuser a autoridade de suas letras...e Solino der [graça] a minhas advertências" (p. 274). Lívio makes even clearer Solino's relevance to the author's general intention of providing profit and pleasure when he remarks on the latter's humorous comments with: "A todas as práticas desta nossa conversação faz parecer agradáveis e saborosas..." (p. 189). Described as "um velho não muito rico..." (p. 6), Solino is the only member of the popular classes in *Corte na aldeia;* and his social origin explains his views, which are always expressed in a homely fashion: "...de mim confesso como povo..." (p. 268).[24] Our author frequently uses his village wit to intersperse the dialogues with amusing intervals, as when Solino irreverently interrupts a lengthy disquisition on table etiquette to caricaturize another speaker's weighty directions: "...me quero eu meter como cebolinha em réstia... para as cousas da mesa tenho feito outro aranzel da cortesia..." (p. 240).[25]

Unlike Hidalgo's Castañeda, however, Solino is not intended merely as comic relief, for Lobo carefully distinguishes between a witty critic and an entertaining *gracioso* and explicitly describes

---

[23] For Lívio as moderator, see also pp. 21, 30, 66, 78, 96, 161, 210, 310-321.

[24] In our discussion of Lobo's theory regarding the proper use of language in Chapter VI we shall have occasion to return to Solino's exemplification of popular speech which, he says, he derives from "...termos das velhas..." (p. 207) and "...libros dos rifões e provérbios das velhas..." (p. 24). Solino may have in mind Iñigo López de Mendoza's *Refranes que dicen las viejas tras el fuego* (Medina del Campo, n. d.), but descriptions of homely speech such as "...termos das velhas..." were common at this time. For example, Pinto attributes his maxims to rustic old men. See Pinto, III, 164. See F. Sánchez Escribano, "Santillana y la colección de *Refranes, Medina del Campo,*" *HR*, X (1942), 354-358.

[25] The burlesque adaptation of the rules of etiquette was a commonplace in the late Renaissance. See Robert H. Williams, "Satirical Rules of Conduct in the Siglo de Oro," *Hispania*, XIII (1930), 293-300.

Solino as "...bem entendido..." (p. 6). [26] Indeed, insofar as the author can be detected in any of his characters, he is no less present in the spirited commoner than he is in the learned Lívio or Leonardo. It is especially significant that it falls to Solino to suggest compiling the series of dialogues which compromise *Corte na aldeia* (p. 27) as well as to support a continuation of the conversations on some future date (p. 327). Furthermore, Solino often acts as an arbiter, appointing speakers ("E para conclusão de tudo, diga Píndaro o que sente neste particular...," p. 105); postponing a topic for another day with "Fiquem essas [histórias] guardadas para amanhã" (p. 189); and even chiding the learned Lívio for an inadequate explanation of quips by observing "Parece-me ... que vos ficou por tratar uma espécie de ditos graciosos..." (p. 228). [27]

Solino's contribution to the structural and thematic development of *Corte na aldeia* will become apparent in the course of our analysis of the work. However, it is important to stress the various aspects of his character, since his sometimes trenchant wit has led critics to minimize the nonhumorous facets of his role or to cast him in the light of a contentious Momus. [28] It is more likely that Solino represents a popular point of view which rarely appears in the Iberian dialogue tradition. Moreover, unlike do Couto's veteran, Lobo's proletarian does not normally rely upon

---

[26] In discussing the place of quips in polite conversation, Leonardo attributes a combination of "...o galante e o sesudo..." to the "...engraçado, que é uma diferença que sempre fiz do engraçado ao gracioso..." (p. 188). Furthermore, Solino's sense of humor, described as "...uma murmuração que ficasse entre o couro e a carne... sem dar ferida penetrante..." (p. 6) coincides with a later description of the wit which is proper to the discreet courtier: "...um picar levemente e com arte..." (p. 170).

[27] For other instances of Solino as a moderator, see pp. 71, 133, 135, 153, 157, 189, 214, 228, 247.

[28] Jorge sees him as "...o tipo mais vivo e característico... pronto e vivo na réplica... franco e leal..." but does not mention his relevance to the didactic content of the dialogues. See Jorge, p. 326. A later critic alludes to Solino's "...coloborando na ponderosa argumentação doutrinária... desenlaçando... aspectos novos e novos problemas..." but does not elaborate beyond stressing his importance in providing "...alívio dessas descargas súbitas e benéficas...". See Carlos Duarte, *A graça portuguesa* (Lisbon, 1923), pp. 86-91. For a view of Solino as *advocatus diaboli* primarily serving an eristic function, see Walter J. Schneer, "Two Courtiers: Castiglione and Rodrigues Lobo," *CL*, XIII (1961), 143.

the argument from authority in his criticisms. Rather, he shows as little concern for the accepted forms of argumentation as he does for the ponderous statements of his friends.[29] When Leonardo's explanation of letters requires a whole evening merely to describe the format of the envelope, Solino, predictably doubts that he will have the patience to endure another meeting. "[Não quero continuar]...se a carta...há-de ser tão comprida como o envelope..." (p. 49). Later, when the conversation takes on a particularly scholarly tone, he complains: "Tendes levantado...o discurso de maneira...e está a matéria dele tão altiva que me parece que eu e Píndaro ficamos esta noite camarço..." (p. 89).[30]

The preceding examples of a commoner's point of view admittedly subserve a humorous function which does not materially alter the points at issue. More significant, however, are Solino's positive disagreements with the hoary commonplaces of genteel conversation. For example, he justifies the perfidy of slaves with the explanation: "... como lhe [sic] temos tomado a cousa mais principal... que é a liberdade, sempre nos têm ódio e nos desejam e procuram mal..." (p. 94). When Lívio counters with famous examples of loyalty among slaves in antiquity,[31] the former palace servant shows himself a disabused realist as he discards traditional authorities for modern facts: "A nós não nos cairam em sorte estes escravos, senão a gente mais bárbara do mundo como é a de toda a Etiópia e alguma escravaria da Ásia...que [a] uns e outros tratam os portugueses com rigoroso cativeiro... e assim se podem estes chamar com razão inimigos mortais dos seus senhores..."

---

[29] Generally Solino's references to authorities and classical sources are vague ones such as "...ouvi dizer a Platão..." (p. 96) or "...ouvi aos poetas..." (p. 267) or are so well known as to be commonplaces, such as "...harpias..." (pp. 8, 133) or "...sereia..." (p. 128). Later, in a dispute with Lívio he sardonically refers to the latter's arguments from authorities as "...os muitos padrinhos da vossa parte..." (p. 326). He also dismisses an appeal to "Platão" and a normative definition with "Não me pesa... para me não dar por vencido de duas razões tão fracas como as vossas..." (p. 307). However, for two instances of Solino as an apprentice scholar, see pp. 146-157, 268.

[30] For more examples of Solino's popular point of view, see pp. 49, 63, 95, 111, 207, 240, 267. His criticisms of the various facets of courtesy will be discussed in the following chapter.

[31] One of the examples adduced by Lívio (the slave who disguises himself as his master to protect the latter from enemies) appears as an illustration in Pinto's discussion on friendship. See Pinto, III, 131.

(p. 96). Aside from cursorily mentioning "...escravos ilustres..." in Portugal also, Lívio leaves Solino's argument unanswered. Later the popular perspective is again evident in Solino's criticism of the aristocratic Júlio's preference for esteem over financial remuneration. As a man of modest means, Solino testily asks: "Como pode ser que obrigue e ganhe mais o que emprega menos? e que vença o cortês com uma barretada o que mereceu um liberal com obra tão custosa como é despender fazenda?..." (p. 268). Here again, Lobo leaves his plebean speaker the victor.

Solino's general disregard for the argument from authority is shared by his social opposite in the gathering, the nobleman Júlio. In resolving the dilemma posed by financial prudence and a liberal generosity, the latter confesses a certain reluctance in having to repair to written proofs: "...repugnando-me um pouco à minha natureza por acudir à doutrina e verdade dos escritores..." (p. 263). Earlier, the young noble had shown a light attitude with regard to the breadth of academic pursuits in a rejoinder to Lívio who had attacked his facetious defense of *alcoviteiras*. In a manner necessarily offensive to the lawyer who is to deliver a lecture on the necessity of a liberal education for the courtier (Dialogue XVI), Dom Júlio ironically praises the procuress as superior in every way to a scholar like Lívio: "Ela ... descreve, enfeita, encarece como um retórico... sabe mais da natureza das pessoas com que [sic] fala que um filósofo... vende o falso por verdadeiro, como lógico... obriga e engana no interesse como legista... não há finalmente arte liberal... de que não saiba e em que não vença a seus professores" (pp. 98-99). [32]

---

[32] Júlio's defense of the procuress can be construed as an example of the rhetorical exercice which has already been mentioned in connection with Mexía's praise of the ass and Palmireno's eulogy in honor of pigs and which is discussed in Pease's article. However, in the present instance it also serves a polemic function in criticizing Lívio's constant reference to academic sources and adds to Júlio's characterization. The literary antecedents for the noble's *alcoviteira* are, of course, Celestina (who is mentioned in Solino's comment of the rhetorical feat: "Ainda me parece... que haveis de chegar a Celestina...", p. 99) and Filtra, the procuress in Ferreira de Vasconcelos' *Eufrosina* which Rodrigues Lobo edited in 1616. For a comparison of Filtra to Celestina, see Asensio's introduction to *Eufrosina*, pp. xiv-xv, lvii-lviii. Also see Lida de Malkiel, *La originalidad artística de la Celestina*, 574-581. Another version of praise for the art of procuring is Don Quijote's defense of the procurer who is sentenced to the galleys: "...por solamente el al-

Less polemically, Júlio's participation in Lobo's dialogic technique takes the form of suggesting topics for discussion and, with regard to scene, playing host for the last five dialogues when a minor indisposition prevents him from leaving his house. He also takes part in an extra-dialogical episode which provides fertile matter for conversations within the dialogues.[33] Generally, however, Júlio's participation follows from his social status as a noble and a patriot. Thus, he shows special interest in the proper form of a letter worthy of a courtier (p. 29) and, on the same subject, requests a description of the royal insignia used to seal envelopes (p. 41). It also follows from his characterization that Dom Júlio champions a hierarchized society based on honor (pp. 263-266) and prizes valor more highly than understanding as a quality for an ideal ambassador (p. 86). Similarly, in defending his views he admits examples only from Portugal's history, since such knowledge, we are told, is incumbent upon member of the aristocracy (p. 25). Again, after asking Leonardo to explain the mottoes on royal escutcheons, the young noble asserts: "Estou contente do fruto que colhi da minha pergunta, por saber curiosidade tão

---

cahuete limpio no merecía él ir a bogar en las galeras, sino a mandarlas y a ser general de ellas..." See Miguel Cervantes Saavedra, *El ingenioso hidalgo D. Quijote*, ed. F. Rodríguez Marín (Madrid, 1947), II, 173-174. In his notes to this episode Rodríguez Marín reproduces an "Elogio de los alcahuetes" by D. Juan Antonio de Vera y Figueroa which was written at the turn of the sixteenth century and which bears some resemblance to Júlio's praise in that procuring is compared to scholarly pursuits:

> La gente más hábil, treznada, e ingeniosa,
> la más sútil y más severa había
> de profesar tan importante cosa.
> ....
> No me engaña afición; usar debiera
> este ejercicio afable dignamente
> la gente en ciencia y calidad primera
> un examen discreto y diligente
> se había de hacer para otorgar el grado,
> y un colegio mayor para tal gente.

However, Lobo prefers that the degree be conferred only upon women: "...posto que o ofício é do género comum a dois, acomoda-se melhor ao feminino" (p. 99).

[33] The episode will be discussed along with other interpolated tales in Chapter VII when Lobo's literary theory will be treated.

notável dos nossos príncipes antigos... que para a minha natural inclinação é a cousa de maior gosto e interesse..." (p. 44). [34]

The remaining member of the initial group is Píndaro whom the narrator describes as "...um estudante de bom engenho..." (p. 6). Píndaro's contributions to the colloquies all bear the mark of the scholar. For example, in an attack on material wealth he draws from an impressive barrage of classical figures and authorities (pp. 141-146). Rodrigues Lobo employs this zealous savant to give an explanation of neo-Platonic love and its expression through Petrarchan poetry, a task incompatible with the temperament of the older speakers and obviously beyond the capacity of the equally young nobleman (pp. 106, 130-132). Later, in Dialogue X, Lobo chooses his student to relate a short story which is to serve as a model for the genre.

Píndaro's tendency to weigh his observations with academic references makes him a likely target for the jibes of the older Solino who clearly cannot as readily bait the authoritative Lívio. [35] Consequently, a current of friendly taunts exchanged between the two runs throughout the dialogues until the final evening when the student's rancor shatters the cordial aura of *Corte na aldeia* in a stinging outburst: "É cousa clara que toda a sua opinião nasceu de uns princípios de gramática que teve, que, depois de ferrugentos naquela idade os alimpou com a cinza do borralho desta aldeia para se levantar contra os que sabem mais... sendo a sua murmuração puras fezes de idiota..." With the moderating influence of Leonardo to quiet the clash, the harmony essential to dialogue is re-established, and Píndaro apologizes for his outburst: "Estava colérico contra o meu amigo, que, ainda que o não pareça no modo com que me encontra, eu o sou na verdade..." Their joint appearance in the first dialogue is mirrored in their departure at the last as Solino agrees to let bygones be bygones: "Nem por este [i. e., pequeno salto] deixaremos de ir juntos para casa..." (pp. 326-327).

---

[34] For a satirical view of the pride of nobles in their coats of arms, see João de Barros, *Ropica Pnefma*, II, 140-142.

[35] Solino and Píndaro are an unlikely duo throughout the dialogues. For references to their friendship as well as to their mutual insults, see pp. 10, 26, 27-28, 29, 33, 89, 111, 146, 164, 189, 219.

Of the three interlocutors who subsequently appear in the course of the sixteen dialogues, one, Feliciano, is a licentiate and a close friend of Píndaro. Arriving in the latter's company on the third evening, Feliciano's role is to complement Píndaro's. Thus, he too defends a Petrarchan view of lyric poetry (p. 50) and launches into a philosophical analysis of love as understood by the Italian neo-Platonists (pp. 128-130). Further similarity between the two students is seen in Dialogue X where Lobo has Feliciano narrate a paradigm short story whose outline is closely reproduced in Píndaro's example. More pertinent to the characterization of both collegians is their resentment when scant attention is paid them one evening after they had carefully prepared their comments. The narrator describes their departure with "[Se levantaram]... assás descontentes com a mágoa dos seus conceitos malogrados que, quando depois de escolhidos não vêm a lume, deixam... a vontade ofendida" (p. 269). Feliciano, the less temperamental of the two, advises the irascible Píndaro against contesting Lívio's projected discourse, "A criação das escolas" (Dialogue XVI), with a strategem culled from experience: "...até em aquilo que eu sei muito melhor que otros quisera antes ouvir aos que sabem, mais que discutirem-me eles... [assim] faço mais certo juízo do meu cabedal para outras ocasiões" (p. 309).

On the sixth evening of *Corte na aldeia e noites de inverno* the group is joined by the prior, "...um clérigo de idade, pessoa, e traje autorizado, que dos mais foi logo conhecido por ser Prior de uma igreja que perto dali ficava..." (p. 115). The author's reason for introducing the new figure at this point is to provide an explanation for the extra-dialogical episode involving D. Júlio's chance encounter with a beautiful pilgrim while hunting in the forest. As a cleric, the newcomer is also admirably suited for presenting a homily on avarice and selfishness with numerous references to Patristic sources (p. 155).

That he is more than merely a village priest is revealed in his absence when Leonardo informs the others of his past: "Antes de tomar aqueles hábitos, parecia muito bem nos de corte e que debaixo dos compridos pode ainda dar lições dela a muitos de capa e espada..." (p. 157). The priest's secular past helps to explain a risqué pun which he later relates to the group (p. 223) [36] and fully authorizes him to analyze the substance of Dialogue XII, "Das cortesias". [37] In the clerical figure of the elderly prior, then, Lobo combines the discernment of Leonardo, the erudition of Lívio, and the spirited humor of Solino, and the host accordingly describes him as "...um discreto e douto cortesão... composto e engraçado no que fala..." (p. 157).

The final speaker to appear in Corte na aldeia is the prior's younger brother, the soldier Alberto, who arrives on the eleventh night. Described somewhat vaguely as "...um homem mancebo, bem figurado..." (p. 211), Alberto is the least developed figure among the eight speakers, since his part in the remaining dialogues derives almost entirely from his profession. Thus, after his brother completes his discourse on courtesy in Dialogue XI, the soldier takes up half of the following visit to narrate an instance of courtesy as exemplified by a gracious Portuguese captain in occupied Flanders who protects a genteel Flemish woman. Alberto's raison d'être is clearly stated in Dialogue XIV where Leonardo mentions the relevance of a military training to a courtier's formation (p. 231). Since no interlocutor present in the earlier dialogues can competently discourse on such a topic, the author is obliged to introduce his final interlocutor mainly to describe the many facets of the life of an ideal soldier, the subject of Dialogue XV. Beyond offering these two vignettes of a soldier's life, one a romanticized episode, the other a generic description, Alberto's role remains minimal.

In light of the preceding paragraphs, it should be obvious that the dialogues comprising Corte na aldeia hardly constitute a

---

[36] As has already been seen with regard to Júlio's defense of the procuress, Lobo is as competent in turning a ribald phrase as he is in describing a pastoral scene. He is the author of three letters, "Carta a Josefa Vaca," "Hospital de Cupido," and "A Maria Tardia" which border on the obscene. See Ferreira, pp. 283-287, 297-298; Jorge, pp. 373-380. Jorge steadfastly refuses to accept this facet of our author's personality preferring to minimize the off-color passages in Corte na aldeia and to consider the letters spurious for no reason except "Mas se Roiz Lobo escreveu isto... o que não era êle capaz de escrever, ó deuses de Píndaro!?" See Jorge, pp. 124-126, 375-380. For a different view of "Carta a Josefa Vaca," see Andrée Crabée Rocha, "As cartas de Francisco Rodrigues Lobo," Colóquio, XXIX (1964), 58-60.

[37] Courtesy and some of the means for attaining it (military life and the university) will be discussed in the following chapter.

tightly knit organic unity. As was shown in analyzing Plato's use of the genre, however, the appearance of spontaneous conversation is often attained only at the price of structural cohesion. This is especially the case with Rodrigues Lobo for whom the dialogue encompasses the elements of all other prose genres. Furthermore, when Solino suggests "...destas noites tão bem gastadas... se faça um ou muitos diálogos que... possam aparecer nas praças [do mundo] à vista dos curiosos..." (p. 27), the author explicitly alludes to the fictional character of the conversations and thus disavows any pretensions to reproducing a concatenation which is naturally developed. Furthermore, the very reference to *Corte na aldeia*'s fictional character as a conversation in literary form provides a pretext for the topics which comprise the opening dialogues. Consequently, the first three evenings are devoted to analyses of such interrelated subjects as the degrees of literary verisimilitude, the natural priority of speech over writing, and the fusion of verbal and written communication in the form of effective letterwriting.

For the fourth dialogue, "Dos recados, embaixadores, e visitas," Lobo depends upon an extraneous, narrated event involving the failure of Solino's servant to deliver a message properly thereby causing his master to arrive late for the soirée.[38] After Píndaro establishes a connection with the preceding discussion by observing that messages are a kind of letter (p. 78), Leonardo and Lívio enlist the others in a session on messages, ambassadors, and diplomatic missions. The author makes no attempt to minimize the distance between the insignificant motive for the discussion and the discussion itself as is clear from Solino's comment: "...não cuidei que [de êste mau jogo que me fez o meu moço] saltásseis a cousas tão diferentes..." (p. 89). However, not all external motivations for the subjects of the dialogues are as contrived as can be seen in Dialogue V where Dom Júlio tells of his encounter with the foreign woman in pilgrim's garb. His enraptured des-

---

[38] Lobo's considerable reliance on extra-dialogical motivation for his discussions is not at all unusual in the dialogues of this period, where "...la presenza di un certo movimento esterno..." enhances the dramatic aspect of the colloquies provided that such external action be "...accessoria..." to the discussions. See Morigi, p. 14.

cription of her beauty directly furnishes the matter for a conversation on poetic hyperbole.

The background episode involving the mysterious pilgrim continues to influence in varying degrees the structure of the remaining dialogues. It has already been shown in analyzing the interlocutors that the prior's appearance in Dialogue VI serves to dispel the mystery surrounding the foreign woman's appearance in the forest. Since her tale involves a conflict between love and avarice, Dialogue VI leads into a detailed comparison between the two forces which extends into Dialogue VII in the form of a debate regarding the relevance of wealth and poverty to ethical behavior. The prior's departure from the scene on the dawn of the eighth day elicits expressions of regret from the remaining speakers who lament the loss of the priest's eloquence and decide to outline the principles of such an effective oratorical style throughout Dialogues VIII and IX. On the tenth day, when Dom Júlio follows the prior and the pilgrim to Lisbon, the speakers seize upon the ardour of their absent companion's infatuation to relate two Italianate novelas and a humorously told short story all exemplifying hardships which are both caused and resolved by love. Later, when the nobleman returns from his trip a bit indisposed and accompanied by the prior and the latter's brother, the group assembles in Dom Júlio's sickroom and continues the discussion on narrative fiction. The accessory plot provides the content for the last five winter nights which are concerned with an analysis of courtesy, its distinction from generosity, and the ways whereby one becomes a courtier whether through service at a royal court, military training, or a university education. When Lívio announces that business in the city will take him from the village for a few days, the dialogues are called to a "temporary" halt.

The varied topics, numerous anecdotes, and contrasting perspectives constituting the "plot" of *Corte na aldeia* are the result of Lobo's theory of the dialogue as a genre comprising "...história verdadeira e fingida... artes liberais e mecânicas... ciências, disciplinas necessárias das profissões particulares... govêrno da vida prática e privada..." (pp. 21-22). Since some of these subjects entail material which is not readily susceptible to an imaginary debate, a union of didactic content and literary diversion is not always the case. [39] As an example of heavy didacticism one might cite Lívio's discourse on the syllabus of the Renaissance university in the final dialogue (pp. 311-321) which could have been uttered as well by a magisterial figure in Pineda's *Agricultura cristiana* or Arrais' *Diálogos*. Nonetheless, even here the pedagogue's allocution is tempered by Solino's not entirely unfounded criticism. [40] Indeed, no matter how well versed the speaker in *Corte na aldeia*, his comments are generally subject to the qualifications of the other interlocutors in keeping with a form of dialectic which is expressly disputatious. In the opening discussion D. Júlio's suggestion "...que poupássemos esta matéria para gastar a noite pondo-a em maneira de disputa..." (p. 12) is repeated in Lívio's description of the ideal interlocutory exchange as one involving "...figuras introduzidas que disputem e tratem matérias..." (p. 21) [41]

Lobo's use of disputation for dialectical development accounts for the numerous examples of scholastic argumentation which are found throughout his dialogues. Similar to Lívio's normative definitions, therefore, the influence of the schoolmen is also detected in many of the subjects which are prepared for discussion in a manner reminiscent of the medieval *disputatio*. The winter chill of Sintra is often forgotten as the speakers verbally parry over "...se é melhor servir-se... de um moço simples e nécio ou de um malicioso ...e esperto..." (p. 92); or, "Com qual de duas cousas se obriga e granjeia mais o ânimo dos homens: se com a liberalidade, se com a cortesia..." (p. 259). It follows that the conversations often progress according to the rules of conventional logic, adducing such figures of thought as cause, effect, antecedent

---

[39] Largely on the basis of *Corte na aldeia*, Lobo received the accolade "...experimentado político, doutrinado... filósofo moral...," see Machado, II, 243.

[40] Lívio's curriculum and Solino's criticism are examined in the next chapter. Further examples of heavy didacticism are found on pp. 109, 161, 234, 244, 275, 293, 306, 313.

[41] For examples of *disputationes* see pp. 92-96, 105, 127, 140, 178, 183, 213, 244, 267, 305, 307, 322. Deductive arguments are most noticeable on pp. 52, 79, 157, 214, 225, 295. cf. Castiglione's similar method as described by Micer Fregoso on p. 47: "...que... pueda cada uno de nosotros contradecir... como hacen los filósofos en las disputas."

and consequent. Especially common throughout *Corte na aldeia* is the argument from analogy which the interlocutors frequently invoke as an appeal to authority whether in citing Plato on the nature of poetry or borrowing from emblem anthologies in comparing love and avarice. [42] However, since Lobo's fundamental aim is the "...satisfação dos ânimos afeiçoados a seus escritos..." (p. 329), he uses the argument from analogy less often as a didactic device than as a means for peppering his conversations with numerous anecdotes which not only support assertions but which also entertain the listeners. [43]

Aside from the author's intention to entertain as well as to instruct, there is a non-dogmatic spirit which pervades *Corte na aldeia* even where the scholastic argumentation is most turgid. [44] For example, when Solino and Píndaro enter the lists, the former charged with a defense of wealth and the latter with its denigration, their numerous appeals to causes, effects, and examples are ultimately discarded by the prior who terminates the bout on an empirical note far removed from the deductive arguments of the two disputants. He decides that both good and evil may be said of wealth if questions regarding intrinsic values are replaced by arguments based entirely upon the uses to which gold is put. [45] A similar shift from the traditionally scholastic dependence on *a priori* value residing in the nature of things to more relativistic *a posteriori* criteria is glimpsed in Solino's criticism of the scholar who exaggerates the importance of theoretical knowledge over pratical experience: "...se o tirardes do bairro de sua profissão, se perde na metade da hora do dia como em beco sem saída,

---

[42] Thus, the lawer's description of love (p. 124) is identical to emblem CV (*Potentia amoris*) in the fourth edition of Andrae Alciati, *Emblematum* (Lugduni Badtavarum, 1593). Also cf. CXL (*Statuam amoris*). For "Cobiça" (*Corte na aldeia*, p. 125), see Emblem LXXXIV (*Avaritia*).

[43] For the various types of arguments from authority, see Chaim Perelman and Olbrechts-Tyteca, *Traité de l'argumentation* (Paris, 1958), I, 308.

[44] For examples see pp. 56, 174, 188, 197, 243, 244, 268, 276, 322.

[45] The prior suggests that they settle the issue "...fazendo a diferença sòmente no uso dêle [i. e., ouro]..." For the shift at this time from *a priori* argumentation based on essences to *a posteriori* arguments based on utility, see José Antonio Maravall, *Los orígenes del empirismo en el pensamiento político español del siglo XVII* (Granada, 1947), pp. 21-28; Eugene F. Rice, *The Renaissance Idea of Wisdom* (Cambridge, Mass., 1958), passim.

para o que eu tenho um estrólabio [sic] que me deu a experiência..." (p. 322). [46]

For the literary historian an even more significant sign of a change of perspective in Lobo's dialogues is found in the ironic finale of the novelistic episode involving the love-struck Lívio and the beautiful pilgrim. Here the author provides a denouement which parodies the spirit of his own pastoral novels: Contrary to the romantic hypotheses of his literary minded friends who diagnose his illness as a case of the *cuitas* of a young blade in love, D. Júlio attributes his indisposition to a case of indigestion, "...que me entreguei ontem mais do que era razão na ceia... de pescado e de marisco, e doces..." (p. 212).

Aside, therefore, from interpolated narrations and such static topics as explanations of etymologies and coats of arms, there is a tendency in *Corte na aldeia* to foment rather than to resolve the reader's doubts. [47] For Solino, the speaker most given to raising objections to traditionally unchallenged views, the content of the colloquies consists of "...dúvidas bem movidas..." (p. 27). Even the pedagogic Lívio avoids sounding peremptory in his preface to "Os movimentos e decoro na prática" (Dialogue VIII), when he says "nomearei alguns vícios... que acreditarão as minhas opiniões, a que eu não posso nem quero dar o nome de preceitos..." (p. 157). Also, similar to Leonardo's reluctance to decide on matters of protocol, the prior in referring to the same subject alludes to the numerous exceptions "...que não cabem em regras tão limitadas..." (p. 244). Further evidence of an inconclusive dilectic involving a vacillation between traditional views and modern experience, between the ideal and defined as opposed to the real and amorphous, in short, between the *a priori* and the

---

[46] In his reference to the astrolabe, Solino's criticism shows evidence of the Portuguese age of discoveries. However, the notion of the wise man as inept in practical circumstances is a common one in the criticism of scholastic philosophy. Cf. Palmireno, *Estudioso cortesano:* "...muchos he visto que decoraban bien, argumentaban mejor, y puestos en cosas del mundo parecían tontos" (p. 5). See Rice, p. 55.

[47] With the passing of the "Ages of Faith" and the advent of widespread scepticism, it is not surprising that in the seventeenth century dialogues "...che lasciano assai dubbioso cui legge a qual parere l'autore inclini..." became more common than earlier. See Pallavicino, p. 263.

empirical will become apparent in an analysis of the three major themes which constantly appear in different contexts throughout Lobo's dialogues; i. e., the meaning of courtesy, the proper use of language, and the varied aspects of literature, Lobo's "outros modos de escrever" which comprise *Corte na aldeia e noites de inverno.*

CHAPTER V

COURTIER AND COURTESY IN *CORTE NA ALDEIA*

A comparison of *Corte na aldeia* with Castiglione's *Il Cortegiano* has revealed that the Portuguese work lacks both the central figure and noble characteristics discussed in the Italian masterpiece.[1] Indeed, Lobo's views regarding courtesy reflect such varying conditions that is impossible to provide a definitive description of his courtier. While he sometimes refers to the benefits of a noble birth, he steadfastly regards all his interlocutors as courtiers although only D. Júlio is a noble.[2] Furthermore, while it is implied that a court is essential to courtesy, D. Júlio considers a chat with his friends in the village as more conducive to courtliness than life in a palace: "Aonde [sic] vós estais é a corte, e a falta desta me podia na corte fazer aldeão" (pp. 211-212). It would appear, therefore, that Lobo's dialogues provide flexible interpretations of "courtier" and "courtesy" which distinguish

---

[1] See Schneer: "...the courtier is always taken for granted in *Corte na aldeia*, but at no time is an ideal courtier presented as a recognizable central figure..." (p. 142). Schneer ventures that perhaps the vaguely defined "cortesão" is equivalent to "homem" (p. 146). By coincidence this is the interpretation given to the term by the Spanish translator Morales who points out in the "Al lector": Estos [diálogos] son útiles y necesarios a todo género de gentes y una escuela universal donde puede aprender uno a ser hombre y merecer el nombre." Certainly "hombre" is here equivalent to one whose faculties are fully developed. See William Harrison Woodward, *Studies in Education during the Age of the Renaissance* (Cambridge, 1924): "The courtier was the ideal personality as the Renaissance conceived it" (p. 232).

[2] While Lobo predicates courtesy of "...os bem nascidos..." (p. 259), he refers to his interlocutors as "...cortesãos tão discretos..." (p. 174).

these related terms from the unequivocal definitions found in *Il Cortegiano*.[1] In the following pages I shall analyze these two concepts according to the formulation which they receive throughout *Corte na aldeia*.

The major discussion regarding courtesy and the courtier is found in Dialogue XII which takes place against the background of Dom Júlio's chivalric adventure with the foreign pilgrim. With the return of the noble to the village, Lívio ventures that a discussion on courtesy would be especially opportune: "...não sei eu melhor ocasião que falar em cortesias... que é matéria que beta muito bem com as das noites passadas" (p. 233). In presenting a group of interlocutors who embark upon an analysis of courtesy, the twelfth night of *Corte na aldeia* strongly resembles the point of departure for *Il Cortegiano*. The similarity, however, soon ends as Lobo proceeds to comment on the practical steps which one must take in order to become a courtier. Our author's pedagogic approach contrasts sharply with Castiglione's paradigma of an ideal, well-born courtier untouched by real circumstances.[4] Thus, when Alberto elects his brother, the prior, to lead the discusison, he explains the latter's competence for teaching courtesy by alluding to his early years in the royal palace "...temos presente o senhor prior, a quem está melhor que a todos o cargo de nos fazer cortesãos por doutrina, assim como o pode ensinar a todos com o exemplo" (p. 233). While not discounting the value of a noble birth, Lobo therefore implies that anyone can become a courtier through instruction and practise. Since, then, courtesy presupposes a learning process, it is more convenient for our

---

[3] For the univocal use of the notion "courtier" in both Castiglione and Boscán, see Morreale, *Castiglione y Boscán...*, pp. 116-117. Also see her article, "El mundo del cortesano," *RFE*, XLII (1958), 229-260.

[4] See Castiglione: "Mi obligación es ahora solamente de declararos cuál ha de ser un perfecto cortesano... mas no mostraros como lo habéis de hacer puntualmente para serlo" (pp. 70-71). The same *apriori* approach presuming a type of Platonic courtier is found in Lobo's contemporary Gerónimo de Salas Barbadillo, *El Caballero Perfecto* (Madrid, 1620). See the edition of Pauline Marshall, *University of Colorado Studies in Language and Literature*, II (1949), pp. ix-xxiv; Bernardo Blanco-González, *Del cortesano al discreto, Examen de una Decadencia*, I (Madrid, 1962).

author to provide a lecture on the rules of courtliness than to postulate an ideal like Castiglione's Platonic noble.[5]

The prior begins his lecture by defining courtesy in a manner which underlines the close relationship between "court" and "city": "...[cortesia] é... um vocábulo particular que tem entre nós a significação mui larga, porque no seu verdadeiro sentido ainda é mais estreito que o latino, que é *urbanidade,* derivado de *urbs,* que quer dizer cidade, e, assim, é o comedimento e bom modo dos que vivem nela, em diferença dos aldeãos, e cortesia é dos que seguem a corte em diferença de uns e outros" (p. 234). Essential, then, to courtesy is a sense of measure or decorum ("comedimento") which regulates the way one acts ("modo") when observing the rules of conduct peculiar to life in a city.[6] Since his definition would preclude the possibility of one's being a courtier anywhere but in a court or city,[7] the prior broadens

---

[5] Schneer's attempts to find a "central figure" in *Corte na aldeia* stem from his failure to recognize the implications of Lobo's prescriptive, as opposed to Castiglione's paradigmatic, point of departure. See José G. Herculano de Carvalho, "Um tipo literário e humano do Barroco, o 'cortesão discreto'," *Boletim da Biblioteca da Universidade de Coimbra,* XXVI (1963), p. 12: "Em nenhum dos diálogos ou qualquer dos seus passos se pretende [Lobo] traçar um retrato e nem mesmo propor uma definição do cortesão discreto, isto é, do perfeito cortesão." Other examples of prescriptive manuals of courtesy which involve no central figure are Giovanni della Casa's *Il Galateo* (Venice, 1558) and Stefano Guazzo's *La civile conversatione* (Venice, 1579). Future references to the former work are from the edition of Giovanni Tinivella (Milan, 1954). In the preface to the English translation by R. S. Pine-Coffin (London, 1958), the translator points out the prescriptive approach presumes no particular social level, whence the absence of a convenient, describable model. See pp. 16-17. Exactly the same opinion is expressed by Margherita Morreale in a study of the free Spanish translation by Lucas Gracián Dantisco (Zaragoza, 1593). See her article "Una obra de cortesía en tono menor: *El Galateo Español* de Lucas Gracián Dantisco," *BRAE,* XVII (1962), 47-89. See especially p. 66: "En el *Galateo* falta un sujeto susceptible de descripción, bien sea como individuo o como miembro de una clase social." A comparison of both *Il Galateo* and *La Civile conversatione* which contrasts their *a posteriori* method with the *a priori Il Cortegiano* is found in John Leon Lievsay, *Stefano Guazzo and the English Renaissance* (Chapel Hill, 1961). See pp. 39-46.

[6] See Herculano de Carvalho: "Tudo se resume afinal no amor da ordem...de ser moderado..." (p. 19). By the same token, a lack of measure ("descomedimento") is equivalent to "descortesia." See Arrais, p. 136.

[7] Similarly, Guazzo points out that civil conversation does not imply that only city dwellers can be civil: "...il vivir civilmente no dipende dalla città..." (p. 16).

the term to include measured behavior in three contexts: the ceremonies of religious ritual, the protocol of aulic settings, and the etiquette of ordinary social relationships. While only aulic protocol is, properly speaking, courtly behavior, the prior considers etiquette ("...bom ensino...") as an extension of courtesy into a less august milieu and declares that he will limit himself to outlining courtesy as it is observed among social equals.

Lobo's lecturer reminds his listeners that a threefold division of courtesy it not only logically convenient but also historically sound. Thus, he traces all polite behavior to the vanity of kings who usurped the ceremonies of religious functions in order to exalt themselves in the eyes of their subjects (p. 235). In time such ceremonies were adopted for regulating the general behavior of genteel society. [8] The kneeling worshiper became the subject obliged to address an arrogant monarch by kneeling on one knee and, finally, the ordinary well-bred man who properly greets his friends by bending the left knee. Similarly, titles like "Majesty" and "Highness" were originally addressed only to the deity. With their adaptation to regal pomp, salutations previously used for speaking to royalty such as "Your Grace" fell to the level of polite conversation in turn relegating the pronoun "you" to affectionate or ill-mannered usage. Since the transition from religious veneration to civil behavior was effected through a courtly setting, the prior suggests that his remarks, while concerned with proper conduct in ordinary polite society, will nonetheless reflect their historical source in the civilizing influence of a royal court: "Bom ensino é tratamento de homens bem doutrinados ou por

---

[8] The same theory regarding the origin of courtesy is found in *Il Galateo*. Cf. the Spanish translation: "...hase usurpado este nombre [Dios] después acá...llamándose los hombres títulos extraordinarios...y alguno viendo esta costumbre tan nueva la llamó ceremonia." The reference is to the edition of Barcelona,1796 (pp. 189-191). See also Pineda who chides nobles for making their pages address them while kneeling: "...os igualáis con todo lo que se puede dar a Dios, y aun excedéis en lo que de santo pasa, pues a Dios sirven en pie o con una rodilla los que os sirven a vos con dos" (p. 325). Less censorious is Guazzo's comparison of etiquette to: "...le sacre ceremonie [che] hanno forza nel conspetto di Dio" (p. 17). Guazzo also refers to the Spanish king who is "...quasi como idolo adorato" (p. 70).

experiência da corte e da cidade, ou por ensino de outros que nela viveram... (p. 235). [9]

Lobo's clerical courtier defines the decorum ("...comedimento...") which is the touchstone of courtesy as a measured comportment in both actions ("inclinação") and words ("palavras", pp. 235-236). He also alludes to the ecclesiastical origins of courtesy by not sharply distinguishing the courtier's willful obedience to an impersonal code from the virtue of religious humility: "Esta cortesia no exterior difere mui pouco da virtude da humildade, e tem o mesmo fruto entre os homens da terra que o Evangelh promete no céu aos humildes, que é serem levantados..." (p. 236). In comparing courtesy to a virtue Lobo implies that a courtier is one who has attained the habit of moderating every aspect of his social behavior. [10] As a habit, therefore, courtesy may be considered an acquired nature which enables a commoner to appear as well-bred as the traditional, nobly born blueblood. [11] Moreover, since there are degrees of habituation, the most well-born courtier will be the one who has longest observed the precepts of courtesy. Thus, while granting that anyone may aspire to being a courtier, Lobo also acknowledges the added, though not essential, advantages provided by a noble birth, since the latter entails that one's formative years be spent in a milieu marked by polished manners. For this reason alone a life at court is the surest way to secure the habit of courtesy:

---

[9] Lobo's frequent references to a royal court need not contradict the popular character of his village court as is implied by Schneer (p. 150). For the late Renaissance "...the court stood for the central impulse and acknowledged standard of every higher activity of the community." See Woodward, p. 253.

[10] Identification of habit and virtue was the official position of scholastic ethics; i.e., virtue and vice constitute the two kinds of habit. See Aristotle, *Categories*, VIII, 9A. della Casa also classified courtesy as "...o virtù o cosa molto a virtù somigliante" (p. 150), as did Lobo's contemporary D. Francisco de Portugal (1585-1632) in his posthumously published *Arte de Galantería* (Lisbon, 1670): "...[cortesía]...es una virtud...debida a la razón, un hábito del bien..." (p. 34).

[11] The same reference cited above from Aristotle also postulates a close relationship between habit and character with the former considered as a kind of "second nature," a theory commonly held by Lobo's predecessors. For example, see de Barros' *Viciosa vergonha:* "A criação e disciplina fazem costume...e hábito é segunda natureza..." (p. 11).

"...e têm mais destas partes [da cortesia] os que por criação da meninice tomaram este leite como são os filhos dos que no mesmo serviço [no palácio] gastaram a vida" (p. 284).

In considering the courtier's noble birth a mere advantage as opposed to the traditional view which had stipulated illustrious forebears as a necessary condition of courtesy, Rodrigues Lobo leaves it doubtful whether any intrinsic difference exists between appearing to be a courtier and actually being one. Certainly, until the neophyte courtier succeeds in fully acquiring a behavior attuned to polite norms, his mannerisms can only be described as a studiously practised role. Both the prior and his brother accordingly describe the dialogues of *Corte na aldeia* as a rehearsal ("ensaiar") for anyone who should like to appear well-bred in a real court (p. 231). Since *Corte na aldeia* makes no mention of a spiritual modesty which would parallel decorous actions and words, one wonders whether Lobo's courtier is ever anything more than a manikin of manners. When Feliciano advises the headstrong Píndaro to be less assertive in advancing his views, the reason given is that a modest mien provides a convenient feint for evaluating more effectively the weaknesses of one's peers. [12] Similarly, in offering a model for gallant courtesy, Alberto describes a soldier whose real motives turn out to be nothing more than a craving for public recognition. For him the battlefield

---

[12] cf. Palmireno's *Estudioso Cortesano* where the author advises his student to feign dullness as a tactic: "...para acomodar [se] a la materia..." (p. 64). For the more common view of the courtier as one dedicated to spiritual rectitude through self-knowledge, see Castiglione's insistence that external modesty mirror an interior humility: "...lo de fuera muchas veces da señal de lo de dentro... Esto que se ve de fuera da...noticias de lo de dentro..." (pp. 181-183). See also p. 191: "...Aquello que se ve de fuera es lo menos...". For other examples of the desirability of moral probity for the courtier, see Tinivella's introduction to *Il Galateo* (pp. 46-47; 78-82), Guevara, *Menosprecio...*, pp. 29,52; *Libro aureo...*, fol. 86; Guazzo, pp. 16, 37; Palmireno, *Estudioso Cortesano*, p. 217: Pinto, I, 70, 260, II, 119, 138, III, 106, IV, 123, 131, 172, 258; Arrais, pp. 148-150, 167; Eslava, p. 66; Salas Barbadillo, pp. 37 ff. For self-knowledge as the source of the traditional notions of humility and modesty, see Uurich von Wilamowitz-Moellendorf, "Erkenne dich Selbst," *Reden und Vortrage* (Berlin, 1929), II, 171-184. See Eliza Gregory Wilkins, *The Delphic Maxim in Literature* (Chicago, 1929), pp. 85-115. Miss Wilkins points out that the very injunction to "know thyself" was for the humanist a call to modesty and moderation (*modestiae mediocritatisque*). See p. 85.

is an opportunity for eliciting the admiration of others ("...ocasião de se mostrar gentil-homem...", p. 251). [13]

A wholly external view of courtesy is rendered more obvious by the prior's discussion of the four major occasions for polite social intercourse: casual encounters, visits, formal dinners, and walks with one's friends. In each instance courtesy is reducible to a simulated humility as a means to ensuring an equally diffident reception from an acquaintance. In this way both parties maintain their dignity. As the courtiers compete in their efforts to appear humble, their social mannerisms assume the air of a contest in self-effacement: "...os dois termos em que se sustenta [a cortesia] são humilhar-se uma das partes, e a outra querer se melhorar na humildade, porque, quanto um mais se aproveita dela, mais obriga ao outro se querer mostrar bem ensinado" (p. 236). Having established a show of humility as the premise of polite activity, the prior proceeds to give more specific precepts pertinent to concrete situations. [14]

---

[13] For a study of the trend of the courtier away from questions concerning substance and spiritual sincerity towards a concern for appearance and (social) popularity, see Vladimir Jankélévitch, "Apparence et manière," *Homenaje a Gracián* (Zaragoza, 1958), pp. 119-129. Thus, as in the case of the Spanish Jesuit, Lobo's courtesy is also a matter of external performance for the sake of acquiring the favorable opinion of others. The goal is no longer ascetic (γνωθι σεαυτον) but social (προς αλλους). There is no doubt that our author was highly esteemed by the Jesuit who praises Lobo in his *El Criticón*. See *Obras completas*, ed. Arturo de Hoyo (Madrid, 1960), p. 1005; "Éste sí que será eterno... Miradle y leedle, que es la *Corte na aldeia* del portugués Lobo!" Of course, the cultivation of appearance to ensure success is itself an ancient strategem. See Cicero, *De Oratore*, II, 41: "Si vero assequetur, ut talis videatur, qualis se viderai velit." Almost as ancient is the warning that failure to known oneself results in an excessive preoccupation with external performance at the cost of spiritual development. See Jean Daniélou, *Platonisme et théologie mystique. Essai sur la doctrine spirituelle de Saint Grégoire de Nysse* (Paris, 1944). Note pp. 45-46 where the author contrasts the notion προς αλλους ("...s'étant laissé séduire par la variété des choses exterieures...") with that of γνωθι σεαυτον ("...un retour à soi par l'élimination des choses étrangères..."). That dissimulation at the cost of internal rectitude had become a concern to the Renaissance moralist is clear from Alciati's Emblem CLXXXIV (p. 662) where the motto γνωθι σεαυτον is explained as "...mentem non formam plus polere... forma nihil si sola forma est."

[14] Whether the example is a soldier or two friends, Lobo consistently uses the expression "mostrar-se" to describe courteous behavior, thus reinforcing his earlier assertion that humility is the appearance ("... no

With regard to casual encounters, the initiative for showing oneself well-bred falls to the man who enjoys certain temporary advantages such as meeting a friend who is standing still, greeting from horseback an acquaintance who is walking, or, in cases when both are walking, coming upon a friend from a higher elevation or from the right (pp. 236-237). In each situation the party so favored should be the first to salute the other with a slight bow ("mesura") or by doffing his cap. More complicated are the rules for welcoming a guest who pays a social call. Rather than multiplying his advertences, Lobo's perceptor omits visits which require extraordinary tact such as calling upon sick or bereaved friends and prefers to define the role of the gracious host. The latter greets his caller by going outside his house and shows further deference by insisting that his guest precede him upon re-entering. Maintaining a position of inferiority, he ushers his guest to his own chair and proceeds to seat himself to the left. At the end of the visit, our gentle host leads his departing guest by the left hand to the place where he had greeted him outside his house (p. 238).

More elaborate precautions are necessary in giving a dinner party when care must be taken to seat the guests in an order of declining importance beginning with the end of the table to the right of those seated ("cabeceira").[15] To facilitate serving, one

---

exterior...") of humility. I find no basis whatsoever for the assertion by Herculano de Carvalho that "...este culto da ordem, do equilíbrio, e da modéstia exterior [é] nada mais do que uma homenagem ... da verdadeira virtude... a humildade sincera... aquela interior modificação das paixões..." (p. 23). Such a view is applicable to an earlier age. See José Antonio Maravall, "La Cortesía como saber en la Edad Media," *Cuadernos Hispano-Americanos,* LDXXXVI (1965), 528-538. Marvall's distinction between the formalism of *adab* among the Arabs and the Christian regard for knowledge as a reflection of a "fondo ético" suggests a precedent for the exteriorization of manners in *Corte na aldeia*. Certainly one can predicate Maravall's description of *adab* ("modo idóneo de expresión de una sociedad fatigada y decadente, pero todavía civilizada") of seventeenth-century Portugal.

[15] The importance given to a proper dinner represents a charge of attitude from the previous century when banquets were viewed as the questionably moral offspring of Roman bacchanalia. Thus, in his *Diálogos,* Mexía allows for "convites..." only when marked by sobriety ("...orden y templanza...") and the guests number no more than nine representing the Graces and the Muses. See p. 67 ff. For a similarly grudging permission, see Guevara's *Aviso de privados,* p. 41.

side of the table should be left free and not a moment wasted in providing water for all to wash their hands (p. 239). As a mark of special regard, Lobo's host selects the choicest morsels for his friends' plates and, at the end of the meal, is sure to thank the diners for accepting his hospitality before they can express their gratitude for the invitation (p. 240). More detailed instructions regarding proper eating habits are but lightly touched upon in *Corte na aldeia*. The prior simply points out that moderation must be the rule in eating and drinking and that one should not talk excessively while others eat nor eat while others converse.[16] Of capital importance is a discreet choice of words lest repugnant associations dull the appetites of the others.[17]

The prestige associated with a position to the right of any group, already mentioned in deciding questions of precedence in visits and dinners, also dictates the proper order for a stroll with one's acquaintances.[18] So that all may share in this honor, courtesy demands that positions be reversed at some point in the walk. The ritualistic formalism of the prior's precepts becomes especially obvious as he suggests that newcomers be offered a place to the right of the group and they should humbly decline the offer in preference for a place to the left. In no case should the participants turn their backs on one another, a social offence which the speaker attributes to the influence of foreigners. Should space not permit the party to walk abreast, smaller groups should be formed.

The priest's social casuistry falters in resolving an unforeseen disruption in the order of the strollers such as when one of them stops to pick up something which he has dropped. Only slightly daunted, however, he hazards that courtesy would seem to oblige one's neighbor to the right to do the honor. Injecting a light

---

[16] Lobo's sparse comments on table manners constitute a bare outline of such lengthy expositions as Guevara's "La templanza al comer a la mesa de los señores." See Chapter XII of *Aviso...* . Also cf. Palmireno's seventeen pages on dining manners in *Estudioso Cortesano*, pp. 63-80; and Don Quijote's advice to Sancho in *Don Quijote*, VI, 246-252.

[17] cf. della Casa, pp. 178-180: "Di quali materie dobbiamo astenerci de favellare per no recare noia...".

[18] cf. D. Francisco de Portugal, p. 57: "...[desde la izquierda] ha de servir la parte del corazón."

note into this heavy formalism which converts a friendly promenade into an intricate ballet, Solino notes that a definite ruling would be most helpful in avoiding a clash of heads if two or more walkers should stop simultaneously to pick up a fallen object (p. 242). The priest is more certain in the case of a disruption caused by one of the party who halts to greet a passerby. Here the "offending" member of the group should be readmitted only after begging pardon and resuming the stroll by going to the left. Once again the earthy Solino steps in to raise the problem of certain unavoidable interruptions which may occur when a promenade is on horseback. But the prior reminds him that, as a habit akin to virtue, courtesy can apply only to the conduct of rational creatures (p. 244). Consequently, no apology is necessary when a promenade is interrupted by a participant's horse. [19]

Solino's queries serve both to introduce a humorous note into the prior's long-winded disquisition as well as to point out that no amount of legislating can foresee all the situations where a show of courtesy is required. Consequently, while not minimizing the importance of rules, the prior adds that he has provided only the barest outline for the would-be courtier to follow and cautions: "...há cem mil galantarias e extremos que não cabem em regras tão limitadas..." (p. 244). [20] Obviously the habit of courtesy presupposes a sense of timing whereby the courtier adapts his activity to any situation which may arise. But Lobo nowhere explains precisely how such a sense is acquired beyond implying that it is the mark of the discreet man ("discreto") to know when he should display his humility to gain the greatest social benefit: "...saber escolher as ocasiões ... é o mais verdadeiro

---

[19] Solino's example is not as frivolous as may appear. See D. Francisco de Portugal, p. 124: "No parece razón que tengan parte en las finezas de un alma las acciones de un caballo."

[20] It is significant that both della Casa and Guazzo agree that the Spanish were to blame for needlessly multiplying the minutiae of proper behavior. See della Casa, p. 201; Guazzo, p. 69. Jankélévitch attributes the growing body of protocol to the increasing importance of a proper appearance in all possible circumstances: "...les manières prolifèrent à l'infini, selon les éclairages et les modes d'être" (p. 124).

toque do entendimento..." (p. 205).[21] Even more thorny is the problem of a judicious choice of courteous phrases where the very abundance of possibilities makes it impossible to attempt a classification. The former courtier therefore terminates his lecture with the observation: "As cortesias que consistem em palavras... se não pode pôr limite" (p. 244).

Although Lobo does not expressly summarize the phrases most frequently uttered by the courtier in specific situations, he would no doubt consider polite clichés, insofar as they are an aspect of social ritual, as a merely convenient façade of scant intrinsic worth. Indeed, Dialogue XII begins and ends with the saw: "Cortesia e falar bem, custa pouco e vale muito" (pp. 235, 248).[22] Feliciano goes even further in revealing the hypocrisy implicit in humble expressions which serve only to conceal a reluctance to inconvenience oneself in reality: "...palavras de cortesia não obrigam a pessoa... à falta de verdade e obras se introduziram no mundo os comprimentos que são um engano de toda jurisdição..." (p. 240).[23] Only Solino defends the use of courteous catchwords ("...são a melhor coisa do mundo...", p. 248), but it is apparent that his motives stem from selfish convenience. For example, he uses the phrase "Beijo as mãos de Vossa Mercê" with the explanation: "Essa [expressão] me custa a m'm bem pouco; porque não gasto nela mais que palavras e

---

[21] cf. Gracián, *El político D. Fernando el Católico:* "...astucia [es] ...valerse siempre de la occasión..." (p. 40). Also cf. *Oráculo manual:* "...conocer las cosas en su punto, en su sazón, y saberlas lograr..." (p. 203).

[22] A light attitude regarding the easy convenience of courteous phrases is common at this time. For example, see Gracián, *Oráculo...*, p. 183: "[La cortesía]...cuesta poco y vale mucho...". See A. H. Williams, pp. 293-295.

[23] For a similar view of polite expressions, see della Casa, p. 190: "...sono parole vane e ne' superflui titoli...senza significato ma non pertanto a noi non è lecito de mutar... . In his *Coloquios satíricos* Antonio de Torquemada rails against similar "...palavras vanas y mentirosas, sin rima ni razón." See Bataillon, *Erasme et Espagne,* p. 695. Feliciano's rueful comparison of large words and small deeds was anticipated by Guevara, *Libro aureo,* fol. 106: "...cuán fácil cosa es bien hablar y cuán difícil es bien obrar...". For a dialogic portrayal of opposing views regarding polite phrases, see Juan Baptista de Vossa, *Sossia Perseguida* (Madrid, 1621), pp. 10-12. One interlocutor charges that courteous clichés are "...complimientos escusados..." while his friend defends them as "...cierta especie de virtud, por medio de la cual los hombres se aman y disponen en buena voluntad unos para otros...".

essas, com as abreviaturas de agora, são já muito menos" (p. 246). [24] In a parody of the prior's comments, Solino goes on to demonstrate that one can readily accept the demands of etiquette with a show of humble words and actions while in reality ensuring one's own comfort, "E quanto a todas as... entradas e saídas como são o lavar das mãos, mesuras, e prolfaças, [sou] liberal como nas eiras." (p. 241) Indeed, Lobo's witty commentator synthesizes the remarks of the others regarding the divergence between sincere humility and the courtier's merely apparent meekness by attributing all forms of polite behavior to a type of mental reservation: "...o verdadeiro cumprimento em que se declaram os demais e que serve de lei mental a todos é... todo sou vosso, tirando fazenda e corpo" (p. 244).

In Dialogue XIII a discussion unfolds which dramatically shows the tension between Lobo's view of courtesy as a kind of social façade and the traditional notion that courtesy is necessarily entailed by a hierarchy of values. The controversy is couched in terms of a debate concerning which create a greater sense of obligation, courteous acts or generous favors. As the exponent of the traditional view, Dom Júlio begins with the premise that honor is the highest value. Since courteous acts rendered to one in public add to his honor, it follows that one will be more grateful to a courtier than to a wealthy benefactor who merely alleviates a financial burden. The young nobleman obviously presumes that the arbiters of values are the members of the privileged classes: "Mas o honrado, o nobre, o cavaleiro, o cortesão, o brioso, o discreto, e o rico antes quer [sic] que o honreis que não que o enriqueçais" (pp. 264-265). Conversely, liberality serves to oblige only those who are motivated not by honor but by material interests and whose values are as inferior as their social rank: "... a gente que se obriga do interesse é de muito menos condição... o pobre, o humilde, o perseguido, o homiziado, o vagabundo, o taful..." (p. 264). Thus, a courteous act which obliges a

---

[24] Gracián Dantisco would limit the phrase to letters (p. 65), while Guevara resoundly condemns it as completely absurd ("...mucha torpedad..."). See his *Epístolas familiares*, ed. J. M. de Cossío (Madrid, 1952), I, 190.

king is clearly far more worthy than a largess which indebts a begger. [25]

Opposed to Dom Júlio is Solino who views the question primarily from the perspective of the dispenser of an act of courtesy or generosity and only secondarily from the position of the recipient. The problem becomes a matter of deciding which act requires the greater sacrifice, adding to another's honor with words and ceremonies or alleviating material distress. Solino argues that the benefactor who parts with his goods earns far more merit than the courtier who pretends to be humble in deference to another while actually losing nothing: "...como pode ser que obrigue e ganhe mais o que emprega menos... e que vença o cortês com uma barretada o que mereceu um liberal com obra tão custosa como é despender fazenda..." (pp. 267-268). [26] Solino proceeds to minimize the importance of courtesy by assuming a critical view with regard to honor, so that was for the noble Júlio a valid recognition of one's worth appears to Lobo's commoner as a pretentious desire for self-aggrandizement. [27] Thus, he repeats the

---

[25] The archaic character of D. Júlio's argument is made clearer by comparing it to a fifteenth-century treatise on the art of giving in a hierarchized society. See D. Pedro, *O Livro da virtuosa benefeitoria*, ed. Joaquim Costa (Porto, 1940). The medieval author finds the value of a largess entirely in the intention of the giver and not at all in its material worth: "...na voluntariosa tenção tem o benefício sua perseverança ... não no acto que logo trespassa...não em riqueza e dons, nem no proveito.... Os benefícios não podem ser tangidos com as mãos, mais [sic] trazidos em o coração" (pp. 49-50). Thus, financial generosity is inferior to conferring honor, since it involves tokens "...que podem ser tiradas e perdidas... cousas vãs em que jaz fundada a nossa cobiça..." (p. 51). For a completely utilitarian view of courtesy as a means to obliging others, see Gracián, *Oráculo...*, p. 222: "La cortesía no da sino que empeña, y es la galantería la mayor obligación."

[26] The first part of Solino's argument betrays the attitude which gradually made wealth an increasingly important adjunct of virtue. See his defense of wealth on pp. 146-153. A similar view of the need for material signs of charitable solicitude is found in Pinto, I, 186-190. See Hans Baron, "Franciscan Poverty and Civic Wealth in Humanistic Thought," *Speculum*, XIII (1938), 1-38. See especially pp. 20-36.

[27] For examples of agreement with Solino's jaundiced view of courtly honor, see Pinto's comments regarding those who frequent courts: "...cegos com os fumos da soberba..." (II, 42). See also Pineda on those who would seek honor at court: "...no se acuerdan ni aun de quien [sic] son, cuanto más de Dios" (p. 370).

charge of the previous night that courtesy springs from pompous vanity and defends liberality insofar as it is concerned with practical issues: "...a cortesia não satisfaz mais que a vaidade, e a largueza acode ao principal da vida..." (p. 268). Even so, D. Júlio maintains that generosity creates restrictive bonds by obligating the receiver: "...o generoso [faz] mercês, que... são grilhões da liberdade dos homens" (p. 269).

Although the completely formal character of courtesy in *Corte na aldeia* relegates to a secondary position such traditional prerequisites as moral integrity and ancestral honor, it is not enough for Lobo's courtier to master the sundry rites and phrases of polite society in order to gain social acceptance. Genteel gatherings would be dull affairs indeed if the participants needed only to know the mechanics of proper gestures and polite clichés. Indispensable, therefore, to Lobo's courtier is an ability to engage in any discussion which may arise while visiting, dining, strolling, or meeting with his friends. The fact that Lobo's interlocutors themselves possess this ability doubtlessly explains why our author frequently refers to them as courtiers, for, unlike the more traditional courtier who had to exhibit certain physical skills proper to his rank, Leonardo and his friends perform in a milieu where conversation is the only real exercise.[28] Hence, the subject discussed in *Corte na aldeia* must command an impressive repertory of topics which are acquired either at first hand through experience or vicariously through acquaintances and reading: "...não é justo que faltem ao discreto palavras com que mostre que tem conhecimento de todas [as cousas]..." (p. 188).[29]

---

[28] See Jorge: "O Lobo esse não cura de exercícios físicos nem da iniciação nas belas artes; alheio a deportes e a estética ...concentra-se todo na lição didáctica do saber, da expressão e da maneira" (p. 311). Also see Schneer, p. 149.

[29] For the same reason Guazzo would make it essential that his reader be able to "...ragionar mezzanamente... de diverse cose" (p. 79). Cf. Gracián, *Oraculo manual:* "Es munición de discretos la cortesana... erudición, un prático saber de todo lo corriente; más a lo noticioso, menos a lo vulgar..." (p. 157). See William Harrison Woodward, *Vittorino da Feltre and other Humanist Educators* (Cambridge, 1912), pp. 189-190: "Distinction in social life was marked by power of conversation...". Cf. Wm. G. Crane, p. 78: "...wit was shown by the ability to discourse on any topic".

To aid his reader in collecting the topics suitable to polite conversation, Lobo has Leonardo outline a spectrum of subjects ranging from fine arts to warfare (p. 188). [30] However, it is significant that even in conversation, gentility is regarded as an appearance which may or may not correspond to more substantial qualities. Lobo's host implies a kind of knowledge which is more appropriate for name-dropping than for weighty discussions: "Fica... que advertir ao discreto a mecânica genal dos termos e nomes dos principais instrumentos com que se exercitam as artes... as peças e nomes... com que se arma um cavaleiro... os nomes de um edifício bem fabricado... saber a cor e o nome a todas as pedras de valia... e outras coisas semelhantes a estas... que andam sempre na praça ordinária da conversação..." (p. 188). The ability to converse on a number of matters at a moment's notice completes Lobo's theoretical analysis of courtesy. It now remains to determine the areas where his courtier may most readily attain and perfect the social poise which results both from a display of propriety in actions and words as well as from a convincing performance as a knowledgeable conversationalist.

The last three nights of *Corte na aldeia* are devoted to discussions of the three occupations which provide the most ample opportunities for acquiring and perfecting the habits proper to a courtier: "...a corte, ...a milícia, e ...a universidade... são os três exercícios nobres em que os homens se ocupam, apuram, e engrandecem..." (p. 217). As the standard for all polite behavior, the first to be analyzed is the court with Leonardo elected the principal speaker. The former palace resident prefaces his remarks by pointing out that the years have dulled his memories of Portugal's extinct court and warns that his comments will be incomplete: "...há tanto que dizer dela [i. e., a corte] que de necessidade hão-de passar muitas pela malha a quem vive há tantos anos neste desvio..." (p. 272). [31] However, he singles out four

---

[30] Similarly, Palmireno enjoins his student to enrich his vocabulary and provides an example with a list of nautical topics: "...y al mismo modo puedes hacer en cosas de agricultura o de arte militar...". See *El Estudioso en aldea*, pp. 157-163.

[31] Leonardo's diffidence resembles the author's when apologizing for his "...corte na aldeia, composta dos riscos e sombras que ficaram dos cortesãos antigos e tradições suas..." (p. 1).

aspects of every court which teach one how to become courteous ("cortês"): the example of the king and his ministers, the diligence of those who solicit royal favors, the elaborate decorum required to serve noble ladies, and the contact with foreign visitors to the palace (pp. 272-273).

Daily contact with a prince provides the fledgling courtier with a thorough training in the protocol observed in a throne room, e.g., the ceremonies and regulations regarding bowing, salutations, and the costumes appropriate for specific functions (pp. 272-273). Even more relevant to the sense of moderation which shapes courtly conduct is the king's example of voluntary obedience to law: "...[a pessoa real] deve obedecer a lei e fica sendo lei para todos os inferiores para a imitação dos costumes e virtudes que no príncipe estão mais certos que em outra pessoa particular..." (p. 274). In time the courtier may even dispense with an exteriorly imposed discipline if he can emulate the sovereign's temperance in freely subjecting himself to the demands of reason: "os reis se sujeitam mais à lei e à razão que [são] obrigados de forçoso poder..." (p. 275).[32] It follows that best suited to the office of a king as an example of self-discipline is the eminently rational man. "Porém, entre os que são governados por razão... era devido o nome de rei...ao que no entendimento fizesse vantagem aos outros homens..." (p. 276). For both king and courtier, therefore, the rule of reason results in a predisposition for observing the many precepts demanded by courtesy: "...são mais observantes das leis... [e são mais] sóbrios, temperados, recolhidos, e honestos" (p. 278).

When he turns to the example provided by the king's ministers, Lobo's speaker becomes somewhat ambiguous. On the one hand he alludes to a minister's role as a royal adviser and the need for such virtues as justice and goodness. As such the minister provides

---

[32] Leonardo describes here the classical notion of the eminently rational king such as can be found in Xenophon's *Cyropaedia*. See the translation of the latter work by S. J. Watson and H. Dall (London, 1855), pp. 3-9. For a discussion of the traditional view of the king as the eminently rational man in the Golden Age of the Peninsula, see Maria Angeles Galino Carillo, *Los tratados sobre educación de príncipes (siglos XVI y XVII)* (Madrid, 1948). Especially see pp. 118-135.

a noble model for a courtier.[33] Leonardo also implies, however, that a successful minister may have become so thanks to devious means necessary to offset social disadvantages which sometime hinder an ambitious young climber in his bid for social respectability. From such a minister the courtier can learn the value of diligence as a substitute for insufficient talent when vying for royal favors: "...posto que o eleger privado está na vontade do senhor, a diligência faz nesta parte muitas vezes o ofício da natureza..." (p. 280).[34] Such diligence may entail a careful study of the prince's character with a view to discovering those traits which should be disembled if one hopes to win his favor: "...estuda...a sua natureza, inclinação, e costume, para se...fingir aquele que lhe convém ser para o contentar..." (pp. 280-281). Leonardo proceeds to mention examples of outstanding courtiers who gained their masters' friendship by aping a physical defect such as a limp, laughing at their jokes, or purposely losing in card games (p. 281). Once patronage is attained such men continue to provide a lesson in courtesy by combining a performance of humility ("...o mais alto lugar...se sustenta com os maiores extremos de humildade...") with a parallel show of power to discourage rival courtiers. Lobo's lecture on social graces points with apparent

---

[33] Here Lobo echoes Castiglione in regarding the courtier as the king's moral adviser. Indeed, without the courtier's high aim, Castiglione, like Solino, would consider courtesy as so many "...leviandades y vanidades puras..." (p. 413). In this specific context Lobo compares an evil courtier to a poisonous current flowing into a fountain from which a nation drinks (p. 280). Our author attributes the image to "...o nosso bom português Francisco Sá de Miranda..." who had used it in his "Carta a el-Rei João III". See Miranda, *Obras*, II, 33. It is also to be found in Castiglione, pp. 420-423, Guevara, *Libro aureo...*, p. 32, and Pinto, I, 211.

[34] In encouraging his courtier to be diligent in his quest for gaining a favorable impression in society, Lobo is merely following out the implications of a courtesy which allows for no perogatives due to natural benefits. Della Casa also alludes to those who have won favor by their efforts rather than by their moral character or social origins: "...e potré ...nominare di molti... i quali essendo più altro da poca stima, sono stati e tuttavia sono apprezzati assai... sono pervenuti ad altisimi gradi, lasciandosi... che erano dotatti di quelle più nobile e più chiare virtù..." (p. 150). Cf. Gracián, *El político...*, p. 57: "Más alcanza... una mediana habilidad con aplicación que no un raro talento sin ella." Classical precedent was available in Cicero's observation: "...ipsum ingenium diligentia etiam ex tarditate incitat". See *De Oratore*, II, 25.

approval to courtiers who further secured their privileged posts by ruthlessly maneuvering in order to discredit their rivals in court.[35]

Our author's cavalier acceptance of hypocrisy as a basic ingredient in the courtier's formation is even more obvious when Leonardo analyzes the forms of courtesy which should be observed when soliciting a favor. As always the courtier submits his will to a standard of behavior. But unlike the monarch's standard which is reason and the minister's criterion which is reducible to whatever is calculated to please his lord, the petitioner must be deferent to anyone who may aid him in realizing his aim. While his external behavior is therefore similar to that of the palace resident, his sobriety is the result not of long habit but rather of a continuous effort to ingratiate himself at every turn of his quest: "...acomodar a vontade com a [de quem o favorece] em um voluntário cativeiro, fazendo-se com todos os ventos para o contentar..." (p. 291).[36] Our author outlines an etiquette of obsequious groveling whereby his petitioner surpasses all his acquaintances in humble greetings, surrendering his seat to every caller, and exuding modesty in his dress, dining habits, and conversation. In promoting a type of behavior which may be considered reprehensible, Rodrigues Lobo once again shows that courtesy implies considerable superficial humility, which is taken

---

[35] In teaching his young courtier the subtleties of social climbing ("...maneras de subir...") Palmireno also counsels attaining the protection of the powerful while awing and discrediting one's rivals. See *Estudioso Cortesano*, pp. 185-186. This tactic had been deplored by the more moralistic de Barros in his *Viciosa vergonha*: "...fazendo-se honrado... desonra os outros..." (p. 9).

[36] Cf. Correa Colderón: "El cortesano ha de ...perder su personalidad hasta el punto de hacer suyos odios y amistades de quienes les conduzcan" (p. 47). Thus, Palmireno advises his *Estudioso Cortesano*: "pregunta que es lo que más les contenta, y acomódate..." (p. 25). The ability of the retainer to present a pleasing exterior to everyone was commonly symbolized by the cameleon. See Alciati, Emblem LIII. The analogy is that the courtier also "...se transforma en el color del lugar que le ponen." See Gracián Dantisco, p. 60. In criticizing social duplicity, de Barros puts into the mouth of Entendimento in *Ropica Pnefma*: "Se me não falecer língua, não me falecerá ventura, porque me tenho feito um camaleão..." (p. 58). Within *Corte na aldeia* Solino contemptuously refers to those who would pride themselves on the right phrase at the right time as "...camaleões da cortesia..." (p. 268).

for granted in a society with little regard for real worth. Thus, he describes the demeaning courtesy of the petitioner as a practical means for coping with the inescapable duplicity of the times.[37] "E como neste tempo os homens estão já desenganados de quão pouco valem merecimentos...lhes tem mostrado a experiência a verdade daquele rifão que cada um dança segundo o amigo que tem na sala..." (p. 285).

A less grim means for acquiring courtly manners is the intricate ritual which must be observed if one is to serve the ladies of the court.[38] There is an echo of the theory which had detected the roots of courtesy in religion in the ceremonious behavior which Lobo considers essential to courtly love: "Os cortesãos... se lhes descobrem e ajoelham como a deusas, lhe [sic] fazem festas... como a deidades...estão pendurados de seus favores... como de oráculos, as acompanham como as cousas sagradas...tudo é veneração e humildade com que as engrandece" (p. 285). By tempering his every act to please the object of his devotion, the palace swain cultivates the attributes proper to the most punctilious courtier, striving for elegance in dress, verbal dash in expressing his conceits, grace in dancing, and valor in defending his lady's honor. He is also capable of abnegation when he humbly resigns himself to the vagaries of feminine caprice: "Quê esquivança não sofre? quê riquezas estima?...vela de noite, não descansa de dia, não se entristece com a pena, não faz conta de agravos, nem estima desprezos..." (p. 285). But such selfless service stems from motives which are hardly altruistic. On the contrary, for the lucky suiter the favor of a noble lady may prove to be a step towards achieving

---

[37] The times were often invoked to rationalize the hollowness of social courtesy. See della Casa: "...non è peccato nostro, ma del secolo..." (p. 191). Guazzo admits "...hoggidi... non nega... siamo statti introdotti costumi perversi..." (p. 35). D. Francisco de Portugal agrees that substance has suffered, but he refers to the coresponding perfection of form: "...no se puede negar que las edades presentes están estragando las costumbres pero están mejorando las buenas artes..." (p. 87).

[38] Cf. Castiglione: "Sin damas no hay corte" (p. 291). Later D. Francisco de Portugal referred to the presence of women in court as constituting "...una escuela de todas las buenas maneras" (p. 23). Cf. Maurice Magendie, *La politesse mondaine et les théories de l'honneteté en France au XVIIe siècle, de 1600 à 1660* (Paris, n. d.): "Rien ne peut mieux polir les mœurs des hommes qu'un commerce suivi avec les dames..." (p. 88).

public acclaim: "...de seu voto toma a fama informações para os fazer grandes na opinião de todos" (p. 273).

In his comments on the example of king and ministers, the hardships of petitioners, and the service of gentlewomen, Leonardo has stressed the relevance of court life to polished manners and temperate behavior. When he explains why it is advisable to cultivate foreign acquaintances, the speaker prefers to emphasize the importance of an impressive collection of data which the courtier can interject into his conversations. Like Torquemada's interlocutors, Lobo's courtier has an avid curiosity regarding exotic lands: "...a vária notícia de costumes e condições de gente e dos ritos e leis de províncias..." (p. 286). Whatever he sees, hears, or learns from the foreign traveler at court can be profitably used to color his remarks with a cosmopolitan hue: "...para a conversação civil e perfeição do homem bem nascido..." (p. 287). Elaborating upon his list of general topics necessary for anyone who hopes to appear cultivated, Leonardo enumerates for the benefit of the arm-chair traveler the characteristics of various countries: "...as excelências particulares e os defeitos das províncias...como a gentileza da França, a fúria de Inglaterra, a fortaleza da Alemanha..." and hints darkly at "...a crueldade de Hungria, a infidelidade de Turquia...a luxúria de Catalunha, a gulodice de Berberia..." (p. 288).[39] Less imaginative but equally desirable for social ease in any conversation are the facts of economic life which can be learned from contact with mercants and traders. The speaker ends his remarks with a catalogue of merchandise ranging from Syrian scents to Indian ivory (p. 288).

Also insisting on the courtier's need of a wide range of knowledge for taking the lead in any conversation is Alberto, the prior's soldier-brother. Nonetheless, he prefers the army to the court as an ideal way to acquire courtesy, arguing that it is far better actually to see the exotic lands and customs about which one is expected to converse than to rely on the hearsay of court gossip: "Pois a vista, que é só a que de todo satisfaz o ânimo e enriquece

---

[39] Cf. Guazzo, p. 19: "...a ciascuna natione, a ciascun paese, e a ciascuna terra sono date e infuse per la natura del luogo, per lo clima del cielo, e per l'infuso delle stelle certe virtù e certe vitii che sono loro propri, innati, e perpetui" (p. 19).

o entendimento ninguém a tem mais vária que o soldado..." (p. 304).[40] Moreover, a soldier's first-hand contact with alien peoples is gotten not only from travel but also from the camaraderie with the men of many nationalities who constitute the cosmopolitan armies of the time: "...um exército se compõe de gente de muitas nações que por soldo, irmandade, socorro...se ajudam uns aos outros..." (p. 303). Any courtier, therefore, is more likely to enhance his social prestige while chatting with cultivated friends if he refers to personal experiences encountered on a foreign campaign than if he repeats the curiosities overheard in the comfort of a palace drawing room. Equally important in an imperialistic age is the ability to discourse upon the technical aspects of military strategy, and Lobo's veteran warns against the glib charlatan who strews his remarks with jargon culled from military manuals: "...só os experimentados nas armas podem falar pròpriamente." However, since the author himself provides his reader with convenient lists of military terms through Alberto's detailed enumerations (p. 305), it would seem that Lobo is less insistent than his speaker regarding the need for actual military experience as a preparation for knowledgeably discoursing on the technical aspects of warfare.

More pertinent to Alberto's defense of a soldier's life is his contention that honor is a necessary condition for courtesy. Like Júlio, the soldier would consider social distinction as indispensable for polite behavior, but unlike the young noble, Alberto repudiates an inherited prestige in favor of the honor which fame bestows upon an outstanding display of valor: "...a honra...de um soldado não consiste no apelido de sua família...senão na opinião em que está tido entre os amigos e contrários segundo seu valor e mereci-

---

[40] The theory that sight is the superior sense dates at least from the *Timaeus,* 47A. Adding to this notion the ideal of Homer's much-traveled hero Odysseus, the Renaissance polymath was, like Alberto, one who acquired wide experience in his voyages. See Pinto, II, 83: "Como ver muitas cousas acaçala o engenho, e desta vossa peregrinação vos resulta muita experiência... e conhecimento de grandes e várias cousas, dai-a por bem empregada." Cf. Cervatnes, *El Licenciado Vidriera* in *Novelas Ejemplares,* ed. R. Schevill and A. Bonilla, (Madrid, 1927), II, 17: "...pues las luengas peregrinaciones hacen a los hombres discretos...". A change is seen in Guazzo, p. 11: "...meglio s'apprende la dottrina per l'orrechie che per gli occhi...".

mentos" (p. 297). [41] For our man risen from the ranks the warrior is more worthy of honor than the scion of a noble house, since he has achieved recognition entirely on his own merits: "...só o soldado é filho de suas obras e se pode chamar honrado por si mesmo..." (p. 299). To be sure, Alberto does not scorn an impressive pedigree, but he observes that for the well-born combatant the past should serve as a stimulus for adding to the glory of his ancestors and not as a surrogate for personal exploits. To confirm his argument he appeals to numerous examples of noble families whose social status is entirely the result of the courage of a plebean warrior-ancestor (p. 299).

Alberto also argues that the soldier, more so than the palace attendant, is obliged by severe sanctions to observe the minutiae of protocol: "...os soldados se desvelam para andarem apontados até em miudezas de que na corte se descuidam os mais advertidos..." (p. 298). Unlike Leonardo's courtier who alters his behavior according to the whims of the grandee from whom he solicits a favor, the soldier subjects his every action to an iron code: "...o falar...o responder...o perguntar...cada coisa tem na guerra suas leis estabelecidas..." (p. 298). In fact, the penalty for violating a tenet of proper conduct may be more severe than an accident suffered in battle, since even an inadvertent slight of another's honor often provokes a fatal duel.

At this juncture in his discourse, the speaker betrays a blatant inconsistency: On the one hand he defends the army as an institution which best fosters an observance of courtesy largely because it allows for the threat of a duel as a punishment for incivility: "...como...está sujeito a dar satisfação por um caminho tão breve [i.e., o duelo], qualquer soldado prático está mais advertido que o melhor cortesão no bom ensino..." (p. 299). Simultaneously, however, Alberto decries dueling as a barbaric disregard for established legal procedures and an irksome reminder of restrictive trivia: "Duelo ...é um combate de homens...que com muito rigor os castigam; procedendo todos sobre miudezas e pontos...impertinentes...introduzidos pela bizarria e fonfarria [sic] soldadesca..."

---

[41] The theme of the soldier as the self-made man owing to his deeds was common in Lobo's day. For examples, see Mexía, *Silva*, XXXVI; Guevara, *Libro aureo*..., p. 25; do Couto, p. 70; Cervantes, *Don Quijote*, I, 157.

(p. 300). As in the debate regarding the fatuous nature of courteous actions and phrases, Alberto also is clearly inconsistent as he acknowledges the demands of military protocol and the sanctions of dueling while conceding a theoretical condemnation of both. [42]

Less controversial as a means for acquiring the courtier's temperate habits is the army's Spartan regime. Similar to the coutier's suffering devotion to his lady and his pains in soliciting political favors, Alberto's soldier finds ample opportunities for exercising a willful submission to trial as a step towards mastering a courtier's sense of discipline and moderation. The ascetic note is even more pronounced in Alberto's description of the hardships of military life: "...dormiram as noites sem despirem a malha e couraça...a necessidade é cozinheira, o escudo...a mesa, o morrião o púcaro, e a fome a iguaria... (pp. 300-302). [43] The monastic character of military life is emphasized by the need for an unquestioning obedience which does not allow for an occasional infraction even when crowned with success: "...vieram os reis e generais a castigar bons successos, quando fora da obediência e ordem militar se conseguiram..." (p. 302). An extension of military obedience which is also generally useful in a more social setting is the ability to maintain a discreet silence when the situation warrants: "...o segredo...vence ao maior que se deve aos negócios civis e cortesãos..." (p. 303). [44] The pior's brother ends his discourse with a list of qualities which attest to the soldier's habit of orderly behavior: "E todas estas leis, costumes, e sujeições fazem a um homem tão apurado, polido, discreto, amável, secreto, brando, e animoso..." (p. 303).

---

[42] Cf. *Corte na aldeia*, p. 775 where Leonardo refuses to discuss how to compose a letter challenging one to a duel: "...por não me embaraçar com o duelo, que está reprovado...". The traditional courtier was supposed to be a skillful swordsman precisely to be able to defend his honor. See Giuseppe Toffanin, *Il Cortegiano nella trattatistica del Rinacimento* (Naples, n. d.), p. 57.

[43] For a comparison of the asceticism of the soldier to that of the monk, see do Couto, p. 215. Cf. Cervantes, *Don Quijote*, III, 154-158.

[44] For the importance of keeping secrets, see Mexía, *Silva de Varia Lección* [Anvers, 1544], I, fol. 4; Guevara, *Aviso...*, fol. I; *Menosprecio...*, pp. 7, 111. Cf. Alciati, Emblem XXII: "Non vulganda consilia". See pp. 81-82: "Quod non minus occulta esse debeant consilia ducum et principum, quam fuerit olim domicilium Minotauri labyrinthus." For the secret as a means to dissembling a courteous exterior, see Jankélévitch, p. 125.

Although the relation between army life and courtesy is exemplified in the speaker's case, Solino singles out two flaws in Alberto's reasoning. First, while it cannot be denied that honor has historically often been earned by acts of personal valor in battle, the character of modern warfare renders anachronistic the concept of individual combats where one may prove his mettle. Solino refers, instead, to the wanton loss of life ("...homicídio comum...," p. 305) which typifies a modern military onslaught.[45] Even more fundamental is his second point: honor no longer enters as the primary motivation for joining an army. On the contrary, as was hinted in Alberto's reference to the international composition of an army and the importance of financial remuneration ("soldo"), the modern army is described by Solino as a band of brigands whose dubious loyalty is bought with gold and a license for libertinage: "...os soldados não são outra coisa que soldados pagos e armados em dano da república, roubadores de honras, ladrões de fazenda, blasfemos, jogadores, insolentes, espadachins, matadores, rufiões, adúlteros, sacrílegos, incestuosos, e perjuros..." (p. 305).[46]

Lívio attempts to counter Solino's charges by recalling the traditional worth of the soldier and reaffirming the *apriori* ideal of honor as the stimulus for choosing a military career and, consequently, of warfare as a means for attaining individual heroism: "...a quem a honra obriga a que se queira avantajar do vulgo..." (p. 309). However, he cannot discredit the factual worth of Solino's argument which is based on personal experience: "...[as pessoas] com quem eu tratei correndo tantos lares e

---

[45] Vindicating Solino is do Couto who laments that honor is no longer paid the valorous soldier. See pp. 171-173. Regarding the conflict between individual valor and modern warfare, see Cervantes, *Don Quijote*, III, 158.

[46] Solino's arguments against warfare's indiscriminate killing and pillaging bear a resemblance to Erasmus' *Querella Pacis*. See the translation of Élise C. Bagdat (Paris, 1924), pp. 167-168, 198-199. The Dutch humanist also criticizes the brigandage of mercenaries and specifically mentions sacrilege, adultery, and incest (p. 168). He also discounts honor as a motive for becoming a soldier (p. 198). For the place of Erasmus in Portugal, see Marcel Bataillon, *Études sur le Portugal au temps de l'humanisme* (Coimbra, 1952), pp. 9-100. For another view of the immorality of the professional soldier, see Pineda, I, 92-94, 137. Also III, 326-327, where Pineda expresses his concern for the moral rectitude of those who would choose either the court or the army as a way of life.

estalagens como João-de-espera-em-Deus." [47] Even Lívio concedes that there are many men who enter a military career for ignoble reasons and who therefore cannot be considered as candidates for honorable fame (p. 307).

Lívio is less hesitant in his defense of a university education as a means ideally suited for attaining the rank of courtier. Of the three occupations discussed in detail in *Corte na aldeia* an academic preparation allows for the greatest popular representation, since as many students come from the families of wealthy commoners and religious communities as from the nobility.[48] Indeed, even well-born students are predominantly second and third sons deprived by promogeniture of an inheritance and consequently obliged to earn their own living: "...são filhos segundos ou terceiros...que ficaram sem herança e procuraram alcançar a sua pelas letras..." (p. 320). Not only does the university teach the precepts of courtesy to a wider segment of the population than do attendance at court and military life, but it also incorporates a theoretical knowledge of all other pursuits: "...nas escolas... todas [as criações] se aprendem em diferença de outras profissões, em que só por experiência e comunicação chegam algumas sombras das vivas cores da sabedoria..." (p. 311). While the court attendant depends upon favors and the soldier upon military distinctions to merit general acclaim, Lívio's courtier excels by giving evidence of an awareness of all areas of knowledge: "...se

---

[47] For Solino's observations as representing the wide-spread abuses of the time, see Pinheiro Chagas, VII, 188: "Não se pagava ao exército... não tinham remédio senão deixá-los [os soldados] viver na plena indisciplina." For a discussion of Solino's reference to "João-de-espera-em-Deus" as a Portuguese version of the wandering Jew, see Carolina Michaelis de Vasconcelos, "O judeu errante em Portugal, "*Revista Lusitana,* I (1888), 34-44. See the postscript to this article in *RL,* II (1890), pp. 74-76. For a dissenting opinion which seen João-de-espera-em-Deus as an Iberian legend regarding John the "Beloved Apostle" who is a symbol of the traveler-sage, see Marcel Bataillon, "Pérégrinations espagnoles du juif errant", *BH,* XLIII (1941), 81-122. See especially pp. 111-121.

[48] In the later Renaissance arms and letters tended to vie with each other rather than to cooperate as a means to social prestige. Some would give the palm to learning: See Mexía, *Silva,* fol. 190; Guazzo, p. 64: "...la nobilità è figluola della scienza e la scienza nobilita il suo possessore...". See Woodward, *Vittorino da Feltre...,* p. 186.

faz homem com saber, merecimentos, e suficiência para se aventajar [sic] do vulgo" (p. 312).[49]

Lobo's scholar describes his program for acquiring courtesy as a ladder whose rungs constitute the traditional academic disciplines. Accordingly, the future courtier first masters the medieval trivium of grammar ("...o primeiro degrau das letras..."),[50] logic, and rhetoric (pp. 313-314). Lívio proceeds to assign the fourth rung to poetry which an earlier age would have included as an aspect of grammar.[51] A crucial step ("...tão necessária ao cortesão") is geometry which inculcates the sense of proportion and measure required for the subsidiary disciplines of music and architecture (pp. 314-315).[52] Only then can the student go on to astronomy, the various branches of philosophy, and natural theology. Similar to the discipline of Leonardo's courtier and Alberto's soldier, is the student's measured actions and words which stem from a stoic ethic: "[a terra] é a chave que abre os segredos da natureza, que ensina a viver com disciplina... une as diferenças, restitui o governo com ordem, rege as cidades com

---

[49] Leonardo had also described his rational courtier as one who stood out from the crowd: "...fizesse vantagem aos outros homens" (p. 270). Lívio's reference here to the student's superiority over the crowd ("vulgo") repeats his description of the soldier. However, Lobo nowhere tells us in *Corte na aldeia* what he thinks of the mass. For a study of changing views regarding the crowd in the late Iberian Renaissance, see A. Porqueras Mayo and F. Sánchez Escribano, "Función del 'Vulgo' en la preceptiva dramática de la Edad de Oro," *RFE*, L (1967), 123-143.

[50] For the image of grammar as the first step to learning, see Woodward, *Vittorino da Feltre...*, pp. 210-211. Cervantes used the same metaphor in *Don Quijote*, V, 32: "...el primer escalón de las ciencias... es el de las lenguas...".

[51] For the classification of poetry as a separate discipline in the Renaissance curriculum, see P. O. Kristeller, "The Modern System of the Arts: A Study in the History of Aesthetics," *Journal of the History of Ideas*, XII (1951), 510.

[52] In Portugal the pedagogic value of music and arithmetic as a means to decorum had been extensively studied by Jerónimo Osório, *De Regis Institutionis et Disciplina* (Coimbra, 1589). See the translation of A. J. da Cruz Figueiredo, *Da Instituição real e sua disciplina* (n. p., n. d.), pp. 335-345. For a study of the evolution of the notion ἁρμονία καὶ ἀριθμός see Leo Spitzer, *Classical and Christian Ideas of World Harmony, Prolegomena to an Interpretation of One Word, 'Stimmung'* (Baltimore, 1963). See especially p. 125.

justiça..." (p. 316). [53] Lívio completes his program with a detailed disquisition concerning the divisions of philosophy and theology. In this way Lobo provides his readers with a catalogue of courses ranging from physics and ethics to apologetics and biblical exegesis (pp. 316-319).

Like the speakers of the two preceding nights, the scholarly lecturer insists upon a rigorous regimen if his student is to cultivate the courtier's decorous comportment. Corresponding to exigent noblewomen and military martinets are the stern schoolmaster and competing schoolmates: "...qualquer pequeno descuido se rebate... obrigando a todos a compostura do rosto, a quietação do corpo, a modéstia no traje, a pontualidade na cortesia, ao cuidado no falar, e a não se querer algum fazer singular entre os outros" (p. 320). Once again, however, there is a hint that, similar to his predecessors, the scholarly courtier is more intent upon impressing his peers than in actually plumbing the subjects described in the ladder to courtesy. Certainly he cannot be considered philosophically indifferent to the opinion of others: "...a universidade [é] uma corte especulativa... aonde [sic] à vista dos doutores... na lição dos mestres...na comunicação dos nobres, na convenção modesta dos religiosos...está o nobre em uma contínua lição de polícia, tendo por palmatória de seus erros a vergonha de os cometer à vista de tantos censores, guardando a advertência de lhes fugir à curiosidade com que se espreitam..." (pp. 319-320). Reminiscent of Leonardo's lists of remote places and their products and Alberto's catalogues of military terms is Lívio's onomastic cornucopia of the schoolman's stock in trade which he explicitly offers as a means to giving an authoritative ring to one's comments: "...nomes e termos naturais...que na prática comum

---

[53] For the importance of the Stoic teaching regarding nature as an ethical standard in the Renaissance as well as a discussion of the cosmic harmony mentioned in Lívio's discourse, see Leontine Zanta, *La Renaissance du Stoicisme au XVIe Siècle* (Paris, 1914). See especially pp. 76-85. Although it would be rash to impute the secular character of Lobo's courtesy to a stoic ethic, it is undeniable that the stoicism of the late Renaissance paved the way for a naturalistic morality. See Zanta, pp. 333-339. Also see Jorge de Sena, *Uma Canção de Camões*, pp. 453-455.

parecerão peregrinos, e de que é bem que o homem cortesão se não ache alheio" (p. 315). [54]

True to his role as the scrutinizing gadfly of *Corte na aldeia,* Solino subjects Lívio's analysis of a courtier's formation to a spirited criticism by seizing upon the highly theoretical character of the traditional curriculum: He underlines the scholar's incompetence when faced with issues which are not confined within the narrow limits of his own interests "...se o tirardes do bairro de sua profissão... se perde na metade da hora do dia..." (p. 322). Furthermore, the specialist's tendency towards using a professional jargon renders his conversation unintelligible to the layman and consequently improper for the normal social events which call for courteous behavior: "...vos deixam o entendimento em jejum, sem darem um bordão à comum e civil conversação..." (p. 323). [55] Less pertinent, perhaps, is our critic's observation that the discipline of the classroom often results in a student's knowing less about a science than is the case of a courtier who is motivated by a sincere desire to learn (p. 325). A more telling refutation of Lívio's equating the attitude of the student with the attitude of the courtier is Solino's appeal to facts which indicate that there is no necessary connection between academic training and courtly discipline. While some scholars are in fact courtiers, the academic community is generally no more characterized by courtesy than the army or the palace retinue. The truth baldly put is simply that "...muitos letrados não fazem um homem cortesão..." (p. 325). [56]

---

[54] Here Lívio's student shows himself as quite typical. See Woodward, *Vittorino da Feltre...*, p. 223: "Philosophy included just enough information to understand the allusions to astronomy, geography, or natural history...". As has been shown with regard to the learning of the palace resident and the soldier, "Science... was regarded mainly as an aid to vocabulary or as helpful in understanding classical allusions" (pp. 238-239).

[55] In calling attention to the scholar's impracticality and penchant for jargon, Solino shows himself an heir of Erasmus' *Praise of Folly.* See the edition published in Ann Arbor, 1960, pp. 89-91. See also Guazzo, p. 72: "...gli litterati... discorrono con quei termini... [che] offendono l'orecchio...".

[56] That learning and social comportment are far from identical is also the view of Lope de Vega's character Laurencio in *La Dorotea:* "...esto del magisterio es para las escuelas, no para las conversaciones". See the edition of E. B. Morby (Valencia, 1958), p. 170.

The amorphous character of Lobo's courtier which was noted in the opening paragraphs of this chapter can now be attributed primarily to a lack of a single ideal method for acquiring the habit of courtesy. To be sure, each of the three "schools for courtesy" which are discussed on the final nights of *Corte na aldeia* provides necessary aspects of a courteous formation such as the palace attendant's ceremonious behavior, the soldier's valor, and the student's brilliance in conversation, and each contributes in some degree to the discipline, poise, and the conversational fluency which will be for him most helpful: "...deixando a eleição do voto a quem o tiver desapaixonado..." (p. 329). However, none is wholly satisfactory. The purpose of the author, of course, is to provide his reader with a combination of all three as an aid to attaining the well-informed opinion necessary for his own social needs.

The absence of a completely uniform courtier in *Corte na aldeia* results from Lobo's stress upon behavior and appearance at the expense of substance and motive. The absolute standards of an earlier age have given way to the mercurial dictates of social expediency in a more fluid society.[57] Hence, the courtesy of *Corte na aldeia* is merely a means to a means, insofar as its goal, social acceptance, is itself to be used in accordance with personal motives which lie beyond Lobo's prescription. Our author merely contents himself by implying that a noble nature cannot be inferred form gracious behavior. For example, the courtly discretion of the foreign ambassador is really a ruse for concealing his motives ("...encubrindo, desculpando...") while shrewdly evaluating which situations can be best turned to his advantage (p. 87). Similarly, his apparent generosity is in reality an attempt to buy the confidence of others with bribes in order to educe their own hidden motives: "...[para] saber o aviso, o secreto, o intento, a cautela...

---

[57] To be sure, the *Caballero Perfecto* of Salas Barbadillo, published a year after *Corte na aldeia,* maintains the traditional prerequisites of the Iberian gentleman's "profound religiosity and exaggerated sense of honor". See editor's preface, p. 1. However, for an analysis which reveals a growing difficulty at this time "in preserving whole, absolute ideals in a relative world" see Monroe Z. Hafter, *Gracián and Perfection. Spanish Moralists of the Seventeenth Century* (Cambridge, Mass., 1966). See especially pp. 89-146.

que convém...e para mover os ministros e validos, em cuja mão ou conselho está o seu negócio ..." (p.82). [58] Whatever his social origins, Lobo's courtier acts in conformity with traditional ideals for reasons which no longer need imply a moral commitment to those ideals.

---

[58] Cf. p. 246 where Lobo gives as a motive for certain courtesies: "... para granjearem ânimos e vontades alheias...". See Gracián, *Oráculo...*, p. 177: "Cifrar la voluntad"; p. 158: "El arte de mover voluntades". Our frequent references to Gracián indicate that Lobo's courtier might be better imagined as looking forward to the *Discreto* than back to the *Cortegiano* as some of his critics have attempted, thereby missing his originality in their zeal to trace his indebtedness to previous writers.

CHAPTER VI

THE SOCIAL USES OF LANGUAGE IN *CORTE NA ALDEIA*

In his dedicatory preface to *Corte na aldeia* Rodrigues Lobo addresses his noble patron D. Duarte as the protector of the Portuguese language.[1] While our author intended the honorary title as an expression of gratitude for the Duke's literary patronage, the encomium is nonetheless a significant indication of Lobo's own regard for the proper use of the vernacular.[2] We have already seen in the preceding chapter that Lobo considers courtesy largely a matter of social grace in conversation; i.e. his courtier is distinguished by his ability to speak well whether simply commenting on the topic of the day or arguing the policy of his monarch in a foreign court. When Lobo's interlocutors attempt to pinpoint the prior's most courtly characteristic they accordingly single out his eloquence: "...o falar bem leva tudo após si..."

---

[1] Lobo addresses his Maecenas of the House of Bragança as "protector da língua e nação portuguesa..." (pp. 1-2). For the importance of the Dukes of Bragança as literary patrons at this time, see Luis de Matos, *A corte literária dos Duques de Bragança no renascimento* (Lisbon, 1956), pp. 13-26.

[2] In Lobo's pastoral novel *Primavera*, the hero Lereno appeals to his devotion to Portuguese as the reason for composing romances in that language: "...eu como mais afeiçoado à nossa língua portuguesa fui o primeiro que nela cantei romances." See *Primavera*, II, v (p. 191). Despite his claim to being the first to compose romances in Portuguese, Lobo followed Gil Vicente and others. See José Ares Montes, *Góngora y la poesía portuguesa del Siglo XVII* (Madrid, 1956), p. 185. Lobo's professed devotion to his language did not prevent him from composing most of his *Romances* in Spanish which he subsequently used again in his panegyric to Philip III, *La jornada...*

(p. 157). [3] The following discussion of Lobo's views regarding language as found in *Corte na aldeia* will therefore involve both his defense of Portuguese as the language spoken by his courtier as well as his analysis of the rhetorical principles which the courtier will observe if he hopes to make a winning impression in society.

In the first dialogue Lobo explicitly states that the peculiar virtue of his chosen form, the dialogue, derives from its affinity to colloquial speech: "...a melhor escritura é a que retrata com mais semelhança a fala e conversação dentre os amigos" (p. 22). A subject which naturally suggests itself is the intrinsic worth of the language spoken by the interlocutors. The topic assumes added relevance in the case of *Corte na aldeia*, since the literary suitability of the vernacular at this time was occasionally criticized. Although Leonardo refers somewhat ruefully to unnamed compatriots who would demean the mother tongue as clumsy and unresourceful, [4] our bucolic courtiers, however, make it quite clear that for themselves the problem is entirely academic, since they do not subscribe to such misgivings. In fact, their normally gracious host can scarcely conceal his impatience whenever the subject is broached ("...ouço de má vontade..."), and D. Júlio contemptuously dismisses the partisans of such a view as fools who

---

[3] For other writers who expressly assign eloquence to the first place of the courtier's qualities, see Valdés, p. 5; Mexía, *Diálogos*, p. 244; Guevara, *Reloj...*, fol. 25; *Aviso...*, fol. 13, 114; Castiglione, p. 78. Milan, p. 79. The works of these and other writers of the period are marked by "...la buena cantidad de páginas dedicadas a las normas del buen hablar, lo que prueba como era la conversación el atractivo principal del hombre bien criado." See Celina L. Cortazar, "El Galateo español y su retrato en el *Arancel de necedades*," *HR*, XXX (1962), 319-320. See also Magendie, p. 250.

[4] No less a figure than Gil Vicente had insinuated that Spanish was more malleable than his own language. See his introduction to *Triunfo de inverno* where he explains his reason for using Spanish in the play: "...quem quiser fingir / na castelhana linguagem / achará quanto pedir." See *Obras*, IV, 265. Cf. Camões' eclogue "Que grande variedade vão fazendo" where an interlocutor exclaims: "Nota e vê, Umbrano, quão bem soa o verso castelhano." See *Obras* (Lisbon, 1955), II, 18. See Albin Eduard Beau, "Sobre el bilanguismo en Gil Vicente," *Homenaje a Dámaso Alonso* (Madrid, 1960), I, 217-225. For a list of Portuguese writers who occasionally preferred Spanish to their own language, see Eugenio Asensio, "España en la época filipina," *RFE*, XXIII (1949), 75-80. See also Ares Montes, pp. 119-120; M. Rodriguez Lapa, *Lições de literatura portuguesa, época medieval* (Coimbra, 1964), p. 405.

speak ill of the language because their own ineptitude prevents them from using it well: "...não basta que a falem mal, senão que se querem mostrar discretos dizendo mal dela, e o que me vinga da sua ignorância é que eles acreditam a sua opinião..." (p. 25).[5] The nightly sessions thus begin with a topic which is obviously popular: an apology of Portuguese.[6] To be sure, their remarks are more dithyrambic than critical and provide little of the dialectical exchange which we have seen in some of the topics already discussed.[7]

---

[5] Júlio's view had been expressed earlier by António Pinheiro in his *Panegírico de Plínio* (Lisbon, 1541). Pinheiro's opinion, in turn, was quoted in the prologue to Ferreira de Vasconcelos' *Eufrosina*: "Desgraçados portugueses... que por desculparem sua negligência culpam a pobreza da língua...". See Asensio's edition, p. 8. The sentiment is also found in the prologue to Francisco de Morais' *Palmeirim de Inglaterra* (Évora, 1567). See the edition of Lisbon, 1786, I, iv.

[6] The defense of the vernacular as a theme especially popular in Renaissance dialogues has been noted by Herzl, II, 389-390: "Wie aber der lebendige Dialog schliesslich fast mit Notwendigkeit aut den Gebrauch der Muttersprache führt, so konnte es auch für ihn kaum ein geeingneteres Theme geben als die Erorterung der sie betreffenden Fragen — der Fragen, welche Rechte sie selber gegenüber die lateinischen Weltsprache habe...". As examples Hirzel mentions Bembo and Castiglione in Italy, Valdés in Spain and Lobo in Portugal. For a general study of the theme and the different issues involved from one country to another, see Vernon Hull, *Renaissance Literary Criticism, A Study of its Social Content* (Gloucester, 1959), pp. 16-36, 82-100; 153-173. Also see Thérèse Labande-Jeanroy, *La question de la langue en Italie* (Strasbourg, 1925). See pp. 8-10, 17-27; M. Romero-Navarro, "La defensa de la lengua española en el Siglo xv," *BH*, XXXI (1929), 204-255; Erasmo Buceta, "La tendencia a identificar el español con el latín," *Homenaje a Menéndez Pidal* (Madrid, 1925), I, 85-108; Rafael Lapesa, *Historia de la lengua española* (Madrid, 1962), pp. 195-218. In Portugal the problem arose owing to the purists' demand for a classical standard in Latin and, with increasing momentum, to the popularity of Spanish as a literary medium. See F. Rebelo Gonçalves, "História da filologia portuguesa. Os filólogos portugueses do Século XVI", *BF*, IV (1936), 1-13; Albin Eduardo Beau, *Die Entwicklung des Portugiesischen Nationalbewusstseins* (Hamburg, 1945), pp. 36-40, 80-85; A. E. Beau, "A valorização do idioma nacional no pensamento do humanismo português," *Estudos* I (Coimbra, 1959), 349-370; Luciana Stegnano Picchio, "La questione della lingua in Portogallo," in her edition of J. de Baros' *Diálogo em louvor da nossa linguagem* (Modena, 1959), pp. 5-64; Edward Glaser, "On Portuguese 'Sprachbetrachtung' of the Seventeenth Century," *Homenaje a Dámaso Alonso* (Madrid, 1961), II, 115-126. Also see Ares Montes, pp. 117-136.

[7] Lobo's speaker follows the tradition of the abstract praise which was the rule rather than the exception until the more seriously linguistic approach

Of the five interlocutors of the first dialogue, the learned Lívio appropriately assumes the responsibility for defending Portuguese. He begins his eulogy with an enumeration of purported vocal qualities: "...É branda para deleitar...doce para pronunciar...para falar é engraçada com um todo senhoril, para cantar é suave...a pronúncia não obriga a ferir o céu da boca com aspereza nem a arrancar as palavras em veemência do gargalo..." (pp. 25-26). The notion that his language displays a perfect balance between the extremes of harsh palatalization ("...o céu da boca...") and guttural velars ("...o gargalo...") is emphasized in a later context when Lívio contrasts the rounded euphony of Portuguese with the marked preference of other languages for one point of articulation at the expense of another: "Todas as nações orientais...oprimem a voz na garganta quando falam...e todos os mediterrâneos referem as palavras aos paladares da língua...e todos os ocidentais...mastigam a palavra entre os dentes e as pronunciam na ponta da língua... mas os que estão mais isentos dela [i.e., tal pronúncia] são os portugueses..." (p. 161). [8]

As he proceeds to point out the reputed flexibility of Portuguese, Lívio's words assume a cadent grandeur appropriate to the subject: "[É] grave para engrandecer, eficaz para mover... breve para resolver e acomodada às matérias da prática e escritura ... para pregar é sustanciosa com uma gravidez que autoriza as razões e as sentenças [9] ... nem tem infinita cópia que dane, nem

---

formulated by Duarte Nunes Leão, *Origem da língua portuguesa* (Lisbon, 1606). See Stegnano Picchio, pp. 36-40.

[8] Lívio's pride in the euphony of his language is a commonplace. See Stegnano Picchio, p. 21: "...l'eccellenza del portoghese sulle altre lingue in virtù di una maggiore appertura de boca... sarà argomento topico dei grammatici cinquenteschi... argomento tanto più curioso quanto più inconsistente e lontano dal vero." Signora Stegnano Picchio attributes the argument less to scientific reasons than to an attempt to equate Portuguese with the ideal of perfect balance as described by Horace in the *Ars poetica:* "...graecis dedit ore rotundo / Musa loqui, praeter laudem nullius avaris..." (322-323). Cf. de Barros, *Diálogo em louvor...*, pp. 78-79. Unless otherwise stated, future references to de Barros are to this work.

[9] In calling attention to its adaptability for eulogies, writing and conversing, the speaker is probably intent upon proving that his language can be used for the traditional three styles of classical antiquity. See Cicero, *Orator,* 17. However, Lobo nowhere mentions the three styles aside from a reference to "...*bom* ou *mau, humilde* ou *altivo estilo* de escrever..." (p. 31; author's italics). For an explicit relation of Portuguese to the three

breviade estéril que a limite [10] ...nem é tão florida que se derrame, nem tão seca que busque o favor das alheias [11] ... escreve-se da maneira que se lê, e assim se fala" [12] (pp. 25-26). The Doctor links this remarkable combination of oratorical virtues, lexical wealth, and othographic regularity to the salient features of other languages. [13] With regard to her Romance sisters, for example, Portuguese has the warmth ("familiaridade...") of Spanish, the smooth charm ("...brandura...") of French, and the elegance of Italian. Lívio's patriotism and his interest in philology lead him to claim for his language the prestige of classical antiquity. [14] Consequently, he ascribes Greek origins and Latin pronunciation to

---

styles, see Manuel Severim de Faria, *Discursos políticos* (Lisbon, 1624). See the edition of 1791, pp. 58-59.

[10] In pointing out the lexical adequacy of Portuguese, Lobo is careful to show that his language, while rich, does not violate the dictum "Indecorum est nimuium." See Quintilian, *Institutio oratoria*, XI, I, 91. Our author attributes an excess of words to Italian, since he considers verbosity a trait proper to Italians: "Como a língua italiana é mais copiosa... aos que na nossa falam muito... chamaram *homens de parola*, como se lhes chamara *italianos*" (p. 181). Cf. Arrais, p. 56: "...e tenho por melhor linguagem a nossa portuguesa que a italiana porque em menos palavras contém maiores conceitos...".

[11] For other writers who stress the adequate vocabulary ("cópia") of Portuguese see de Barros, p. 81; Ferreira de Vasconcelos, pp. 7-8; Morais, I, iv; Fernão Álvares do Oriente, *Lusitania transformada* (Lisbon, 1606). I quote from a later edition (Lisbon, 1781), p. 222. Also see Severim de Faria, p. 49.

[12] Here Lobo subscribes to the theory that orthography should reflect the pronunciation of words and not their etymology. For a discussion of the two approaches to spelling in Renaissance Portugal, the phonetic and the etymological, see Rebelo Gonçalves, pp. 8-9. Despite Lívio's optimism, Portuguese orthography in the Renaissance (and until recent years) was notoriously inconsistent, whether the standard was phonetic or etymological. See José Joaquim Nunes, *Compêndio de gramática histórica portuguesa* (Lisbon, 1956), pp. 190-195.

[13] For a similar view which actually traces to foreign sources the lexical and phonetic variety of Portuguese, see Álvares do Oriente, p. 219: "...encorporou em si a graça da pronúncia e dos melhores vocábulos das outras [línguas], fazendo-se entre todas um ramalhete composto de diversas flores."

[14] "Tem... a pronunciação da latina, a origem da grega..." (p. 26). Lobo gives no reason for attributing a Greek origin to Portuguese. However, the notion of a Greek substratum of the Peninsular's languages had been developed in Valdés' *Diálogo de la lengua*. See pp. 21-25. Our author may also have in mind the legend which attributed the founding of Lisbon to Ulysses and his Greeks. The legend found epic expression in Gabriel Pereira

Portuguese and even imputes a modest reserve to his countrymen's speech as a reason for raising the language to the august rank of Hebrew, the Holy Tongue: "E se a língua hebreia, pela honestidade das palavras, chamaram santa, certo que não sei eu outra que tanto fuja de palavras claras em matérias descompostas quanto a nossa" (p. 26). [15]

Despite his lavish praise, Lobo's speaker is concerned with a large number of foreign loan words which, he says, threaten to convert the language into a linguistic patchwork: "Só um mal tem [a língua] e é que pelo pouco que lhe querem seus naturais, a trazem mais remendada que capa de pedinte" (p. 26). To safeguard the integrity of a specifically Portuguese vocabulary, Rodrigues Lobo advances a conservative view throughout the dialogues whereby he would forbid borrowing any foreign word unfamiliar to the general speaker, including Latin words, their etymological similarity notwithstanding. [16] It follows that Lobo, contrary to many of his Renaissance compatriots, does not adhere to the view that the vernacular is merely a corrupt form of its classical ancestor, and one would seek in vain in *Corte na aldeia*

---

de Castro, *Ulisseia* (Lisbon, 1636) and António de Sousa de Macedo, *Ulissipo* (Lisbon, 1640). For a study of the former, see Edward Glaser, "The Odyssean Adventures in Gabriel Pereira de Castro's *Ulysseia*," *Bulletin des études portugaises*, XXIV (1963), 25-75. See especially notes 36-37 for the place of the legend in seventeenth-century Portuguese historiography. Lobo's claim to a Latin pronunciation was a common argument in favor of its superiority in relation to the other Romance vernaculars. See de Barros, p. 77; Severim de Faria, p. 64. However, see below, no. 16.

[15] That Portuguese was intrinsically modest had been expressed by de Barros in contrasting the language with Spanish: "Verdade é ser em si tão honesta e casta que parece não consentir em si uma tal obra como *Celestina*. E Gil Vicente cómico, que a mais tratou em compostura que alguma pessoa destes reinos, nunca se atreveu a introduzir um Centúrio português; porque como o não consente a nação, assim o não sofre a linguagem" (pp. 79-80). Of course, not even Lobo can seriously accept this theory, since, as was indicated in Chapter IV, note 36, he himself is the author of two extremely risqué letters.

[16] Like other compatriots, our author is apparently not at all disturbed by the contradiction implied in his championing Portuguese over other Romance vernaculars in virtue of its similarity to Latin while simultaneously defending his language as superior to Latin itself in every way. See Beau, *Die Entwicklung...*, p. 38.

for the theory that greater lexical purity results from emphasizing the relationship of Portuguese to Latin. [17]

Lobo's disagreement with the purists is clearly shown in an exchange between Píndaro acting as a proponent of the classical standard and Leonardo. The student suggests a gradual Latinization of the vernacular by progressively increasing the number of Latin derivatives: "Não tenho por grande erro quando a conversação é entre doutos, usar algumas palavras tiradas do latim, quando forem melhores que as com que nos podíamos declarar em português" (p. 178). His reason is that, in time, Portuguese will become as "pure" (i.e., as similar to Latin) as Tuscan: "...se isto se fora introduzindo, viera a nossa língua pouco a pouco a se aparentar com ela [i.e., a língua latina] e ficar tão polida como a toscana," p. 178). Leonardo objects strongly, questioning the wisdom of following the example of Tuscan, which, for all its similarity to its forebear, has been contemptuously labeled the lees of Latin ("borra da língua latina..." p. 178). [18] In opposing a classical standard which would imply relegating the vernacular to the status of a corrupt tonge, Leonardo proposes an autonomous view. Rather than prescribe a non-Portuguese criterion for propriety, therefore, the speaker identifies the structure of his language with its actual use: "...que a linguagem mais pende do uso que da razão..." (p. 178). [19] Solino echoes the host's call for independence from a Latin standard by pointing

---

[17] Identifying the vernacular with the language of the Roman empire was one of the manifestations of the Renaissance fever for emulating classical antiquity in imperialist Portugal. The notion is found in *Os Lusíadas*, I, XXXIII where Venus is said to compare the Portuguese to the Romans in virtue of "...os fortes corações..., a grande estrela / ... / e ... a língua, na qual quando imagina / com pouca corrupção crê que é latina." Cf. de Barros, pp. 85-86; Arrais, p. 56. See Rebelo Gonçalves, p. 10; Lapesa, p. 203. For a study of Romance vernacular as a corrupt form of Latin, see Remigio Sabbadini, *Storia del Ciceronianismo* (Torino, 1886), pp. 128-130.

[18] For the pejorative notion of Tuscan as a remnant of Latin, see Labande-Jeanroy, p. 27.

[19] Cf. Cicero, *De oratore*, II, 20: "Ita loquamur... quae nos usus docuit...". This was the general notion during the High Renaissance. See Margherita Morreale, "Una obra de cortesanía en tono menor: "El 'Galateo español' de Lucián Gracián Dantisco," pp. 78-79. However, the classical notion took on added importance in Renaissance Portugal, since general use was the most effective means for countering the threat of Spanish. See Beau. *Die Entwicklung...*, p. 83.

to the viability of his language as an adequate means of expression: "...tenho raiva sabendo que a língua portuguesa não é manca nem aleijada, ver que a façam andar em muletas latinas os que a haviam de tratar melhor" (p. 179). [20]

Besides Latin a less likely source for new words in Renaissance Portugal were Oriental languages and their terms which refer to an abundance of products and institutions previously unknown in the West. Lobo, however, appears singularly unimpressed with the linguistic fruits of imperialistic expansion and cautions repatriated travelers not to adulterate the language with verbal borrowings. [21] Speaking through Leonardo, he mentions with disapproval those explorers who, bent upon publicizing their far-flung voyages, constantly refer to exotic places in terms of an equally exotic jargon to the great confusion of their less venturesome compatriots. Whenever the topic turns to the commercial traffic to India, such men proudly display the words which they learned in the various ports of call: "...em colhendo na prática Ormuz, Malaca, ou

---

[20] In contrast to such writers as Severim de Faria, Lobo's praise of Portuguese is little concerned with other languages, whether pointing out their shortcomings or, in the case of Latin, developing parallels. Indeed, our author's rather cool acknowledgement of Latin as the parent language has little precedent among his predecessors in the sixteenth century among whom only Fernão de Oliveira in his *Gramática da linguagem portuguesa* (Lisbon, 1536) chose not to accentuate the Latin character of the tongue. See Beau, "A valorização do idioma...," (p. 359). Lobo's intransigence regarding neologisms from Latin is certainly at variance with de Barros' advice: "Assim que podemos usar dalguns termos latinos que a orelha bem receba..." (p. 81). Cf. Castiglione who encouraged borrowing words from Latin, French, and Spanish, pp. 87-90. Lobo's stand is less harsh in practice, since he allows his speakers to coin "...paroleiro... posto que a frase seja italiana..." (p. 181). Our author's cautious use of Latin may be considered as an aspect of his resistance to the cultism which characterized the Gongorism of his day. See Ares Montes, pp. 124-136.

[21] Again Lobo stands at opposite poles from de Barros and others who exulted in both spreading Portuguese among the Orientals as well as borrowing from their languages. For de Barros as "...imperialista da língua portuguesa..." see Hernâni Cidade, "João de Barros, o que pensa da língua portuguesa, como a escreve," *BF*, XI (1950), 281-303. See also Eugenio Asensio, "La lengua compañera del imperio," *RFE*, XLIII (1960), 399-413. For a study of the spread of Portuguese as a sign of imperialistic power as well as a tool for evangelization, see Beau, *Die Entwicklung...*, pp. 38-39.

Sofala, não sabem dar um passo sem palanquins, bajuns, catanas, bois, larins, e bazurrocos..." (p. 184). [22]

To counter the dual threat of Latin and foreign influences, both of which serve only to undermine a national vocabulary, our author urges the Portuguese to consider the vernacular as quite literally a mother tongue, comprising only the vocabulary which is used by women. [23] His reason is not only that women are less likely to study Latin, but also that they are generally restricted to the domestic scene and thus have minimal contact with foreign languages: "Por isso se chama língua materna porque nas mulheres que menos saem da pátria, se corrompe menos o uso da fala comum..." (p. 175). [24] But simply knowing which words properly belong to a language will not lead automatically to its effective use. Drawing heavily from the traditional precepts of polite speech. Lobo accordingly devotes a considerable part of *Corte na aldeia* to discussing the use of language in polite conversation.

Our author divides his analysis of eloquence into two parts: the choice and use of the words uttered and the physical aspects conducive to an effective delivery. Lobo is impressed by the need for presenting a pleasing appearance and emphasizes that it is no less imperative for polite conversation than what is actually said: "... e não consiste este bem [i. e., o falar bem] só nas razões discretas e palavras escolhidas, senão no bom modo e graça de as dizer..." (p. 157). In Dialogue VIII one finds Lívio's comments on the speaker's gestures and social decorum while Dialogue IX comprises Leonardo's views of the rhetorical structure of polite speech. Both speakers stress that remarks are intended for the gentleman in normal conversations and not for the student of oratory. Neither pretends to a technical exposition. Thus, Leo-

---

[22] Despite our author's disapproval, all these words have made their way into the language and are discussed at length in Sebastião Rudolfo Delgado, *Glossário Luso-Asiático* (Coimbra, 1919), I, 81, 109, 133, 231, 513; II, 142.

[23] See Cicero, *De Oratore*, III, 2: "...facilius enim mulieres incorruptam (linguam) antiquitatem conservant, quod nullorum sermonis experte, ea tenent sempre quae primae dedicerunt." Cf. Castiglione, p. 99; Guazzo, p. 45; Cervantes, *Don Quijote*, VI, 30. Cf. Amado Alonso, p. 175; "Lengua propia es ni más ni menos que la lengua natural... la lengua materna...".

[24] Elsewhere Lobo includes women among "...pessoas que não sabem ou que não têm obrigação de o [i.e., latim] entender..." (p. 184).

nardo avers that the sparse character of his advice falls far short of the traditional manual of rhetoric with its detailed precepts and lists of figures (p. 174), while Lívio describes his remarks as mere opinions: "...a que eu não posso nem quero dar o nome de preceitos..." (p. 162).

His claims to an unpretentious simplicity to the contrary, Lobo nonetheless betrays a heavy reliance in both dialogues on formal rhetorical treatises. The very point of departure of both discussions is the traditional dictum that regulations cannot substitute for talent and practical experience: "...a graça não se aprende, é mero dom da natureza..." (p. 158). With no absolute rules available, Leonardo reminds his listeners that no pedagogic method can guarantee the rhetorician predictable results: "...não posso fazer escola de falar bem..." (p. 174). True to his tandem role, Lívio makes the equally hoary qualification that art improves upon nature: "...todas as coisas dela [i. e., a natureza] se aperfeiçoam e melhoram com a arte..." (p. 158).[25] Further similarities to classical theory will become apparent in the following analysis, combined, to be sure, with important modifications in view of Lobo's more modest aims. We shall proceed by reversing the order in which the two interlocutors appear and first consider Leonardo's more specifically rhetorical comments on the content of conversation as they are found in Dialogue IX.[26]

Described by Solino as a new rhetoric for the Portuguese language (p. 174), Leonardo's discussion develops five directives for

---

[25] See Cicero, *De oratore*, I, 25: "Sentio naturam primam, atque ingenium ad dicendum vim afferre maximam"; II, 35: "Non possum... non ingenio prima concedere, sed tamen ipsum diligentia etiam ex tarditate incitat." Cf. Quintilian, II, XVII, 19-21; XI, III, 11. Leonardo admits that the opinions comprising his "new rhetoric" "...à força se hão-de misturar com os da latina..." (p. 174).

[26] The order which Lobo observes in presenting his rhetoric and the importance which he gives to externals shows the change of emphasis from the classical preoccupation with composing a convincing argument to the courtier's concern for presenting a pleasing appearance in social gatherings. Cicero and Quintilian, of course, also stress the physical aspect of delivery, e.g., "Est enim actio corporis quaedam eloquentia..." (*Orator*, 55). Cf. Quintilian, XI, III, 14-176. However, the Romans give prior consideration and a more detailed treatment to the orator-lawyer's arguments.

correcting the most common errors ("...vícios...") which are found in polite conversation: [27]

> Falar vulgarmente com propriedade.
> Fugir da prolixidade.
> Não confundir as razões com brevidade.
> Não enfeitar com brevidade as palavras.
> Não descuidar com a confiança.

In his insistence that the courtier speak the vernacular ("...falar vulgarmente...") Leonardo affirms the Renaissance regard for natural dignity in speech. The colloquial ideal, therefore, unites discriminating selection and general comprehension: "...qual os melhores falem e todos entendam..." (p. 178). [28] The alternatives to this ideal may range from an unnatural affectation to its opposite of lowly crudity. Lobo's polite speaker observes a proper mean by rejecting regionalisms, foreign accretions, and capricious inventions which render ordinary communication unnecessarily difficult: "...sem vocábulos estrangeiros, nem esquisitos, nem inovados..." (p. 175). Furthermore, as the natural expression of a modern society the vernacular reflects changing institutions and new phenomena by allowing for new words and discarding archaisms: "...vocábulos... nem antigos e desusados, senão comuns e correntes..." (p. 175). Lobo's host draws a parallel between lexicon and fashion whereby he would no more utter a dated word than he would wear an outmoded costume. Here Solino interrupts to illustrate with a caricature of the speaker addicted to obsolete words: "...homen de barba larga, penteada sobre os peitos, com

---

[27] In his reference to the speaker's faults or errors as "vices" Lobo uses the Ciceronian term *vitii*. See *De oratore*, III, 11.

[28] See Castiglione's aversion to affected (i.e., unnatural) speech, p. 88. Cf. della Casa, pp. 218-255; Pinto, I, 80; II, 76; III, 23; IV, 284; Gracián Dantisco, pp. 12-13; Cervantes *Don Quijote*, V, 95-96. For the Renaissance notion of natural perfection in language see Ramón Menéndez Pidal, "La lengua en tiempo de los reyes latinos (del retoricismo al humanismo)," *Cuadernos hispano-americanos*, III (1950), 9-24; Rita Hamilton, "Villalón et Castiglione," *BH*, LIV (1952), 200-202; Lapesa, pp. 188-233. For a study which contrasts this ideal of discriminating selection to the later ideal of learned invention, see Jole Scudieri Ruggieri, "Premessa allo studio linguistico del *Agricultura cristiana* de Fr. Juan de Pineda."

carapuça redonda e pelote de abas pregadas, que vos conte histórias de El-Rei D. Manuel..." (p. 180). [29]

To attain the unaffected simplicity which he describes, Leonardo advises his listeners to give every word its primary meaning by carefully avoiding stylistic arabesques: "...o falar próprio é com palavras naturais e menos figuras de retórica para ornamento delas, e não usar dos tropos, de alegorias, metáforas, translações, antonomasias, antífrases, ironias, enigmas e outras muitas..." (p. 176). Aside from extraordinary situations which he does not specify, Lobo would apparently limit the rhetorical repertory of polite conversation to three figures: Metaphor ("...translação..."), synecdoche ("...antonomasia..."), and irony. But even these are subject to carefully defined restrictions, e. g., while admitting that metaphor is customarily used in circumlocutions, abbreviations, embellishment, and catachresis ("...acudir à pobreza da língua..."), Leonardo would allow only the first two types. Thus, one may occasionally employ circumlocutions to avoid scabrous expressions: "...para evitar palavras desonestas..." (p. 176). [31] For example, rather than refer to someone as a drunkard, one may speak of him as "fond of the vine" or "lost to Bacchus" to "heedless of himself". The second permissible use of metaphor involves highly idiomatic expressions which succinctly condense a total situation such as is suggested by the phrase "He was left high and dry" ("...ficou em seco...," p. 177). [32]

---

[29] A similar theory is found in Castiglione, pp. 79-94. For a comparison of obsolete words and the clothing of a by-gone era, see Gracián Dantisco, pp. 136-137. For a clear statement of the need to keep abreast of the language "...en que cada dia se inventan de nuevo palavras..." see Torquemada's *Jardín...*, p. 255.

[30] Lobo's grudging permission for the use of some rhetorical figures is quite different from the attitude of Cicero and Castiglione who stress the orator's need to give his speech color and melodic qualities through figurative expression. See *De oratore*, III, 38; Castiglione, p. 93. Cf. Michel, p. 342.

[31] See *Rhetorical ad Herennium*, IV, 34: "Translatio... sumitur obscenitatis vitandae causa..." Cf. della Casa's advice for avoiding "...parole deshoneste..." (p. 222). For the use of circumlocution to avoid improprieties, see Sanford Shepard, *El Pinciano y las teorías literarias del Siglo de Oro* (Madrid, 1962), p. 71.

[32] The metaphors which Lobo permits are later described as "...tão usadas e próprias que parecem nascidas com a mesma língua..." (p. 52). For a study of such idiomatic constructions which were originally metaphors,

The remaining types of metaphors are normally unnecessary, since catachresis implies lexical poverty while embellishment too often offends against unaffected speech (p. 177). [33]

A less elaborate form of periphrasis is *antonomasia*, a subspecies of synecdoche whereby the speaker refers to a well-known entity in terms of a common noun which is epitomized by the subject designated. [34] Since the subject must we well known if the allusion is to be readily understood, the figure is limited to conversations between speakers of common cultural milieus: "Só nas pessoas ou partes do mesmo reino será mais aceita" (p. 177). For the Portuguese of Lobo's day, then, "the Poet" meant Camões while "the Historian" referred to João de Barros. Similarly, "the City" was Lisbon and "the game preserve" referred to the popular summer spa for Portuguese nobility at Almeirim (p. 177). In each case the reference is to an entity which has become a symbol of the class to which it belongs: "...a grandeza deu superioridade das outras do mesmo nome."

As the third permissible exception to the general rule of proper designation, irony is normally used to enliven conversation with a wry humor. Since the figure entails a discordance between what the speaker says and what he intends his listener to understand, he should clearly show that his words are not to be given their normal meaning: "A ironia consiste mais na graça, riso, ou dissimulação do que fala, que nas palavras... (p. 177). Leonardo divides irony into two kinds depending upon the degree of semantic modification. The first kind involves an expression which may imply the exact opposite of what it describes such as when a weakling is contemptuously called a Hercules or when a woman of easy virtue ("...pouco casta...") is singled out as a veritable Helen (p. 177). [35] Less radical a change is envolved in the second

---

see Perelman and Tyteca's discussion of *métaphore endormie* in *Traité de l'argumentation*, II, 546.

[33] Lobo is apparently unaware of the problem which he has created with regard to replenishing the language; i.e., he insists that all words bear the stamp of the mother tongue, that they be discared when obsolete, and that they be employed in a minimum of figures.

[34] For a discussion of the traditional use of antonomasia, see Perelman, *Traité...*, I, 235.

[35] Lobo's definition of irony is found in Cicero, *De oratore*, II, 269; III, 203. In making Helen a model of chastity, Lobo apparently is extending

type of irony which substitutes the reverse namecalling of the first ("...escárnio...") with a subtle statement. Leonardo's examples include describing a coward in battle with phrases which at first sight seem to apply to a hero; i.e. of the timorous soldier who never even seized his lance in battle, one may say that the lance never fell from his hand. Concerning his comrade in arms who fled the field one may say that the enemy could not even come near to him. Similarly, the apparent recommendation "He never asked for anything" may, in circumstances known to both speaker and listener, refer to one who always stole what he wanted. [36]

Despite the lengthy exposition of his first premise for a new rhetoric, Leonardo is more concerned with the second common error of speech which is verbosity: "...tenho por pior de todos [os atoleiros] o da prolixidade" (p. 181). He warns that one may be careful in using simple language and in generally calling things by their proper names and yet be guilty of never allowing an interlocutor to enter into the conversation: "Há muitos homens tão palavrosos que nos não deixam tomar carta na conversação... é vício de que se há-de fugir como da peste..." (p. 181). The garrulous speaker not only defeats the end of conversation which is a reciprocal exchange of views, but he necessarily frustrates his own intention to impart information, since his listeners are hard put to cope with his bombast: "...a prática comprida não a comprende [sic] a memória..." (p. 181). [37]

One must, however, avoid prolixity by incurring the third error of proper speech which is extreme brevity. If the former makes retention difficult by taxing the hearer's memory, the latter eludes comprehension entirely with its enigmatic concision. In short, both

---

her role as a symbol of feminine beauty to include feminine virtue as well. Perhaps he has in mind Cicero's *De inventione*, II, I where the painter Zeuxis could not find a proper model for a painting of Helen from among the five most beautiful virgins of Croton.

[36] This example seems to be suggested by *De oratore*, II, 248 where a description of a thieving servant ("...in furace servo...") is said to be equally applicable to an honest one: "'Solum esse cui domi nihil sit nec obsignatum nec reclusum': idem in bono servo dici solet."

[37] Leonardo's insistence on brevity to avoid the danger which verbosity entails for memory is probably suggested by Horace. *Ars poetica*, 335-337: "...esto breve ut cito dicta / percipiant dociles teneantque fideles... / omne supervacuum pleno de pectore manat." Cf. Cicero, *Orator*, 221; *Rhetorica ad Herennium*, I, 15.

prolixity and extreme brevity are detrimental to the clarity which is essential to language (p. 181). Leonardo explains that the third fault ultimately derives from an immoderate desire to express oneself succinctly: "...posto que a brevidade seja louvada..." (p. 182). Citing the example of the "Latin poet" who attained brevity only at the price of clarity, Leonardo urges his friends to strive for explicitness no less than for concision: "...o cortesano nem há-de dizer as cousas em três palavras nem em trezentas" (p. 182). [38]

Quite different is the brevity which Leonardo mentions in the fourth error: "Não enfeitar com brevidade as palavras". Lívio interrupts his colleague to explain that such brevity is culpable even in intention, for it proceeds from a vain virtuosity and involves a forced attenuation of expression. The speaker no longer proposes to communicate succinctly but rather to gain admiration for his concision even while he may leave his listeners in the dark: "Serve de névoa para as cousas que se tratam" (p. 182). [39] The Doctor shows contempt for anyone who bedecks his speech with a show of elliptical artifice: "...muito se me parece esse erro de abreviar com o de enfeitar as palavras... é um trabalho não sòmente escusado mas odioso..." (p. 182). For Lobo, then, sparseness can be just as conducive to artificiality and obscurity as verbal excess.

---

[38] "Quando queria ser breve ficava escuro..." (p. 181). Here Lobo's debt to Horace is explicit. See *Ars poetica*, 26-27: "...Brevis esse laboro / obscurus fio..." For brevity as the correction of garrulity, see Horst Rudiger, "Pura et illustris brevitas," pp. 353-359.

[39] For artificially elliptical speech as a fault see Plato's *Phaedrus*, 267 B: "There is nothing left but a heap of 'ologies' and other technical terms invented by ...Georgias and others who have rules for everything and teach how to be long or short at pleasure." See also Quintilian on diminution ($\mu\varepsilon\iota\omega\sigma\iota\varsigma$), VIII, III, 50. The rhetorical brevity so deplored by Lívio had been forecast in the previous century by such writers as Milán whose Valencian-speaking interlocutor in *El Cortesano* exclaims: "E tan cortesano el corto parlar que voria sensa parlar eser inteso..." (p. 310). Cf. Castiglione, p. 82. Subsequent to Lobo, of course, brevity became the touchstone of artful expression and clever conceits (for brevity in Lobo, see below, Note 68). Gracián fully accepted the inevitable result of such extreme concision in speech: "Las verdades que más nos interesan vienen siempre a medio decir... La arcanidad tiene visos de divinidad... tal vez conviene la oscuridad para no ser vulgar..." See *Oráculo manual*, pp. 158, 194, 208.

Leonardo's final precept concerns the need for cautiously choosing the topics of conversation in order to avoid offending one's listeners. Our speaker counsels extraordinary care at social events such as weddings and christenings which abound with tempting occasions for relating risqué puns to the embarrassment of female guests: "...é mais necessário ao discreto levar as rédeas na mão, por que ele não perca os estribos e a elas se não mude a cor" (p. 183). [40] Lobo's taboos seem somewhat extreme, since they include mentioning the word "leg" when women are present: "...porque nas mulheres é parte oculta e nos homens [é] manifesta..." (p. 183). However, since his demand for clarity lends him to banish such strained periphrases as "sustainers" (...sustinentes...") and "ambulators" ("...andadeiras...") he has no recourse but to forbid such topics completely when the company comprises speakers of both sexes. [41]

The tactless speaker commits an even more serious *faux pas* when he gossips about an absent figure in the presence of a friend or relation of his victim. This example of an imprudent choice of topic often takes the form of a negative criticism of customs, professions, or opinions which number adherents among the listeners. A casual conversation, therefore, must never serve as the occasion for expressing a controversial opinion: "...é perigoso... ainda que seja em matéria leve..." (p. 184).

Complementing Leonardo's theoretical analysis of the subjects and words proper to conversation is Lívio's graphic comments on the physical aspects of the speaker's delivery. The Doctor warns that his advice is intended only for the man with normal faculties. Thus, in outlining the qualities essential to an ideal voice the speaker omits handicaps such as stammering and lisping and the harsh tones of rustic speech: "...a voz do gago... do cicioso... [e] do rústico grosseiro..." (p. 159). For the normal speaker the desideratum is a phonic application of the golden mean: "O meio em todas as cousas é a perfeição delas..." (p. 160). Consequently, one should avoid such extremes as mumbling and artificial

---

[40] Castiglione also refers to blushing ladies in the presence of indiscreet speakers. See p. 243.
[41] For a different opinion which encourages periphrasis in such cases see Gracián Dantisco, p. 112.

articulation or a booming bass and shrill soprano. Tempering his speech to fit the circumstances, the popular conversationalist has a voice which is like the ideal language; i. e., "...clara, branda, cheia, e compassada..." (p. 159). [42]

No less important for a pleasing performance in conversation are facial expressions and bodily gestures. Here Lívio alludes to Cicero and Quintilian, although he admits that the precepts of classical oratory are more applicable to the pulpit than to the drawing room. [43] Nonetheless, even the ordinary speaker will learn to accompany his comments with measured motions which are neither spiritless and wooden nor disconcertingly animated: "nem há-de parecer estátua... nem bonifrate..." (p. 159). Continuing to rely on the golden mean, [44] Lívio suggests that the eyes should add sparkle to one's words with a clear gaze and not evoke ambiguous feelings such as pity or scorn by staring forlornly or squinting myopically. Even one's eyebrows can defeat an attempt to be cordial by coming together in a scowl or arching in surprise. Similarly, the head and limbs should accompany the tenor of the conversation with discreet movement, "...mostrando-se grave, composto, ou inclinado segundo as matérias sobre que fala..." (p. 161). However, the greatest possibilities for giving a pleasing performance in conversation depend upon a judicious use of manual gestures: "...não falando com ambas elas [i. e., as mãos] nem chegando com alguma [sic] perto da vista dos ouvintes..." (p. 162). [45]

---

[42] Cicero refers to the same vocal qualities in *De oratore*, III, 41-42, 227; cf. *De Officiis*, I, 37 where the orator is told to develop a voice "...ut clara sit, ut suavis..." cf. Castiglione, p. 89; della Casa, p. 227.

[43] See p. 158: "Esta doutrina [de Cícero e Quintiliano] parece que convinha então aos oradores como aos pregadores...".

[44] Lívio's frequent use of the golden mean shows the adaptability of the ideal for manifold uses, whether ethical, as in the case of courtly behavior, or linguistic or esthetic. See Whitney J. Oates, "Horace and the Doctrine of the Mean," *Classical Studies presented to Edward Capps* (Princeton, 1936), pp. 260-267.

[45] Allowing for the differences which follow from changing the speaker's role from that of barrister to gentleman, Lívio's advertences follow closely Cicero's as found in *De oratore*, III, 216-227. For the importance of eyes and gestures in speaking, see Castiglione, pp. 89-90. Cf. Woodward, *Studies in Education...*, p. 247.

Lívio follows his exposition with an enumeration of seven habits which often characterize the boor in conversation. Termed "vices" as was the case with Leonardo's directives, three of the defects stem from excessive complacence while the remainder are the result of the speaker's ignorance of the rules of courtesy: [46]

> O primeiro é escutar-se um homem a si próprio quando fala, por se contentar no que diz.
> O segundo, repetir outra vez o que tem dito, com os olhos nos ouvintes, para que lho gabem.
> O terceiro, deter-se tanto nas palavras como que as vai pesando, e compondo para as dizer.
> O quarto, ir-se arrimando a bordões para que lhe acudam entanto as palavras.
> O quinto, ir à mão ao que quer responder, por querer falar tudo.
> O sexto, bracejar muito, e dar grandes risadas a seus próprios ditos.
> O sétimo, borrifar as palavras com a humidade da boca, por falar com veemência.

The first three are closely related ("encadeados"), for the speaker who is struck by his own importance is less interested in imparting ideas than he is with hearing himself speak.[47] As a result, he repeats what he is all too willing to consider an effective phrase while eagerly evaluating the reactions of his listeners. Solino illustrates the second trait with a few of the catch phrases dear to the conceited speaker: "...e metem de quando em quando um 'entendeis-me?' 'estais comigo?' 'digo bem?' 'que vos parece?' 'não sei se me declaro?' (p. 164).[48] An even more

---

[46] "os três primeiros nascem do amor próprio que cada um tem a suas coisas que os gregos chamaram *Filaucia*, os quatro seguintes, ou da ignorância ou do descostume e falta da doutrina cortesã" (p. 163). In Alciati's *Emblematum*, *Filaucia*, the *morbus maximus* of Narcissus, is followed by *Garrulitas* which entails a lack of decorum in speaking. See emblems LXIX and LXX.

[47] Cf. Gracián's *Oráculo manual*, aphorism 141: "No escucharse... Querer hablar y oirse no sale bien..." (p. 189).

[48] Cf. Gracián Dantisco who advises that a gentleman should converse "...hablando sin repetir muchas veces una misma palabra..." (p. 113). The fault had been exploited for comic purposes by Gil Vicente in his *Auto dos físicos* where each of the three doctors is characterized by a favorite profes-

intolerable sign of oratorical vanity, however, is the third shortcoming which leads the pompous speaker carefully to weigh every word, savoring each syllable before deigning to utter it: "...soltando-as [i. e., as palavras] por compasso... é vício que fará ser aborrecível a todo o mundo que o tem..." (pp. 164-165).

Less closely linked are the habits which comprise the second group of unpleasant traits in conversation. Perhaps the most common involves the inexperienced speaker who is unable to find the proper word at the precise moment and attempts to conceal his confusion with certain actions and clichés. Lívio realistically describes some of the more common actions such as toying with an interlocutor's vest button, brushing lint from his lapel, or tapping him on the chest. When words fail completely, the boor may have recourse to even more noisome habits: "...com as mãos esgravatando os dentes ou bulindo nos narizes... tirando cabelos da barba e mordendo as unhas, e outros vícios semelhantes que servem como uns espaços e recramos [sic] a que lhe acodem as palabras" (p. 165). Less trying to the bystander are the clumsy speaker's verbal crutches ("...bordões...") which take the form of tiresome phrases: "...metem um 'diz', 'assim que digo', 'tal e qual', 'sim senhor',... 'então'" (p. 165). [49]

The fifth example of the rude speaker involves an instance of garrulity as well, since it refers to the man who precipitates answers to his own questions in his eagerness to say everything. Thus, he dominates the scene with a torrent of words: "Esses tais... falam a duas mãos por que querem que vá tudo por êles..." (p. 166). [50] Still, even at his worst he is less annoying than the speaker who flails wildly with his arms guffawing no less at his

---

sional question: "Entendeis-me?" "Ouvi-lo?" and (for the Spaniard Mestre Anrique) "Habéis mirado?" See *Obras*, VI, 109-118.

[49] Cf. Valdés who uses the same term ("bordones"): "...[llamo bordones] a essas palabrillas y otras tales que algunos toman a que arrimarse quando, estando hablando, no les viene a la memoria el vocablo tan presto como sería menester..." See p. 149.

[50] Lívio does not mention the opposite fault (silence) aside from citing two proverbs showing that silence is golden and not subject to rules of correct speech. For the equating of silence and discretion which is Lívio's position, see Alciati's Emblem XIX: "Prudens magis quam loquax"; cf. Milán, p. 79; Guazzo, p. 39. However, della Casa disapproves of silent members of social gatherings (pp. 238-240).

own heavy witticisms than at those of his friends. At this point Lívio observes that one should greet the puns of others with a moderate laughter while concealing any sign that one is amused by one's own jokes.[51] However, far more grave a transgression of propriety than any of the preceding is the final fault: "...borrifar com umidade o que dizem e as vezes a quem os escuta..." (p. 169).[52]

Leonardo's views regarding irony and Livio's comments on the laughter which is proper for a gentleman are clear indications that Lobo considers humor an essential element of conversation. Indeed, the Doctor alludes to laughter as a defining property of human nature: "Pois é definição e diferença do homem ser animal racional e a sua própria paixão é ser risível..." (p. 168).[53] It follows that a completely humorless conversation fails to appeal to the whole man as *animal risibile* and is, to a degree, a failure. Lívio compares the relation between comic spirit and a social gathering to the importance of salt to a meal: "...o sal é uma graça e composição da prática... e esta [graça]... se declara no que obriga a riso e alegria... sem sal todas as iguarias são sem sabores e desgostosas, assim a prática onde a sua graça falta é puro fastio..." (p. 186).[54] By the same token, an excess of humorous quips has the same effect on conversation that too much salt has in one's food (p. 188). Hence, the imprudent speaker who is profligate with his puns necessarily upsets the measured wit proper to the clever gentleman and descends to the level of a jester. As an appendix to his comments Leonardo therefore warns "...que não

---

[51] "...não há-de rir... com a boca aberta... nem com um riso mole e afeminado..." (p. 168). For the traditional regard for a "mild type of laughter" see Mary A. Grant, "The Ancient Rhetorical Theories of the Laughable," *University of Wisconsin Studies in Language and Literature*, XXI (1924), 146-148.

[52] Cf. della Casa, p. 258: "E alcuni altri spuntano addosso e nel viso a coloro con quali raggionano..." Cf. Gracián Dantisco, p. 7.

[53] The same scholastic definition appears in Castiglione, p. 212.

[54] The identity of salt and interest in conversation is facilitated by the etymology of *sensaboria* (boredom) which is "sem sabor" or "without taste." Thus Lobo can define: "Sal quer dizer graça, que é o contrário da frieza e sensaboria..." (p. 186). For salt as a synonym of humor in conversation see Cicero, *De oratore*, II, 62-68; *Orator*, 87; Quintilian, VI, III, 119; Castiglione, pp. 69-70. For a discussion relating salt, witticisms, and *graça* in conversation, see Morreale, *Castiglione y Boscán...*, pp. 160-163, 212-216.

seja a prática toda de graças, nem toda sem elas, se não uma certa liga com que se componha o galante e o sesudo, que é uma diferença que sempre fiz do engraçado ao gracioso..." (p. 188). [55]

An analysis of a major source of wit in conversation is found in Dialogue VIII when Lívio comments on barbed criticism ("murmuração"). The Doctor concedes that many would consider no other kind of humor quite as effective: "...posto que alguns digam que sem esse sal a mais discreta [prática] é fria e pouco saborosa." [56] But he warns that the negative character of a humorous lampoon comprises a threat to social sensibilities thereby requiring extraordinary tact. The clever speaker is enjoined to moderate his remarks by scrupulously evaluating them in light of the immediate circumstances: "...o que fala, com quem, e diante de quem..." (p. 176). [57] As examples of acceptable squibs the speaker points to Solino's frequent sallies which neither embarrass those who are present nor attack absent members of the speaker's social circle: "...que a todos agradam... aos ouvintes não fazem fastio, tão pouco aos ofendidos causam queixumes" (p. 171). To be effectively humorous, then, the satirist's rapier should have a fine point and be deftly wielded: "...o discreto... há-de... picar levemente e com arte e graça da conversação..." (p. 170).

The speaker is less likely to incur resentment if he develops a facility in relating the comical anecdotes and repartees which add immensely to enlivening conversation. Lobo devotes all of Dialogue XI to analyzing and exemplifying the humorous short story ("...contos graciosos...") and the clever remark ("...ditos agu-

---

[55] Lobo's *gracioso* who constantly jokes corresponds to Cicero's equally reprehensible *scurra* (buffoon). See *De Oratore*, II, 245. For the same distinction see Castiglione, p. 272, della Casa, p. 213; Gracián's *Héroe*, p. 199. For a discussion of the humor proper to the "free man" (the ancestor of Lobo's courtier) as opposed to the Latin buffoon, see Grant, pp. 83-90.

[56] Cf. Júlio's opinion: "...na murmuração se acha mais certa [a graça]..." (p. 185). Castiglione admits to reservations similar to Lívio's on the subject of satirical humor. See pp. 213-219.

[57] Lívio's "...três coisas..." are probably suggested by Cicero's "...tria videnda sunt oratori: Quid dicat et quo loco et quo modo...". See *Orator*, 43. For the same advice, see Quintilian, VI, III, 94; Castiglione, p. 219; Guazzo, p. 45.

dos...") as the traditional constituents of a droll conversation.[58] Of the two the more readily adaptable to an informal chat is the latter: "...não pode haver graça melhor aceita que a dos ditos agudos e galantes..." (p. 222). Once again acting as the spokesman for our author, Lívio defines *dito* as a word or pithy phrase which expresses either a profound thought or a humorous conceit: "...muito do entendimento [ou] de graça..." (p. 222).[59] The Doctor abandons the former after classifying it as a type of aphorism ("sentença...") and promises to consider it on another occasion: "...a sentença... terá em outro dia o seu lugar..." (p. 222).[60]

---

[58] Lobo's analysis of the two sources of humor closely follows the traditional distinction between the funny narrative and the witty saying. See Cicero, *De oratore*, II, 59: "Duo sunt enim genera facetiarum... quorum alterum re tractatur; alterum dicto. Re, si quando quid tamquam aliquid fabella narratur... sals tota narratio... in dicto autem ridiculum est id quod verbi aut sententiae quodam acumine movetur." Cf. Castiglione's distinction between "...el hablar largo y no interrumpido..." as opposed to "...dichos prestos y agudos..." (p. 207). See Grant, pp. 95-108; August Haury, *L'ironie et l'humour chez Cicéron* (Leiden, 1955), p. 55. As a narrative involving plot, character, and setting, the *conto* is properly a literary genre and will accordingly be treated in our discussion of Lobo's literary theories in the following chapter.

[59] Here again Lobo closely follows Cicero in dividing the pithy expression into thought-provoking aphorism and the pun. See *supra* Cicero's "...ridiculum est id quod verbi aut sententiae..." cf. Castiglione, p. 214: "...donde se funden los motes para hacer reír, se pueden fundar las sentencias graves para loar y reprehender." For the close relationship between aphorism, wit, and brevity, see F. E. Hulme, *Proverb Lore* (London, 1902), pp. 2-6; Franz H. Mautner, "Der Aphorismus als literarische Gattung," *Zeitschrift für Asthetik und allgemeine Kunstwissenschaft*, XXVIII (1933), 132-175; *Rifoneiro portugues*, ed. Pedro Chaves (Porto, 1945), pp. 7-8; Haury, p. 180; Michel, *Rhétorique et philosophie...*, p. 279; Rüdigier, pp. 246-347; Crane, *Wit and Retoric...*, p. 8.

[60] Lobo never discusses the aphorism at length, although he constantly uses aphorisms in *Corte na aldeia*, no doubt to provide his reader with a wide sample of maxims to use in conversation. For an example of a handbook of aphorisms to be used in conversation, see Fr. Aleixo de Santo António, *Filosofia moral tirada de alguns provérbios ou adágios...* (Coimbra, 1649). The author says in his preface that his collection was compiled to lend the weight of authority to the reader's conversations: "...[para que] podesse aproveitar do rifão mandando-o à memória para que lhe tenha guardado, até que na prática e conversação; quando vier a propósito, o traga a terreiro..." (fol. 3). See below, no. 63. Regarding the role of the aphorism, Lobo says that it is a sign of acumen and a means to brevity as well as proof of a language's antiquity (pp. 26, 57). A problem which immediately suggests itself is the debt which Lobo owes to the storehouse of aphorisms which is Vasconcelos' *Eufrosina* and which Lobo himself edited in 1616.

Limiting his analysis of wit to the humorous conceit, Lívio discovers three main types each of which depends upon the ambiguity of words. The first involves replacing the most obvious meaning of a word with a less obvious significance to fit a specific context: "...mudar o sentido a uma palavra para dizer outra coisa..." (p. 222). More radical a change is required by the second type where the word or phrase undergoes a modification in accent or spelling in order to provide an added significance: "...mudar alguma letra ou acento à palavra para lhe dar outro sentido... Both types of pun are exemplified in an anecdote related by the prior concerning a young woman recently married to a wealthy old man named Oak-Grove (Carvalhal). The young wife is advised by her uncle that to ensure herself a share of her husband's estate she ought to graft a twig from another tree to the family trunk. The play centers about using a noun relating to a species of tree as a family name. A simple change of designation, then, expresses the irony that a wife's infidelity is the price which an old man pays if he is to have an heir. The witticism, however, is rendered more intricate by the prior's choice of *Cornicabra* as the other kind of tree which is to substitute for the oaks comprising the oak grove. The word not only means a kind of olive but also suggests the symbol of the cuckold, since it sounds almost the same as "corno de cabra"; i. e., goat's horn. [61]

Less salacious is a pun exemplifying the third type of conceit where the change of meaning is realized through a rapid response to an initial question: "...mudar a tenção do que as [i. e., palavras] diz..." (p. 222). [62] Lívio tells of a woman who was rewarded after six months of service to a miserly mistress with a rough hemp garment popularly known as a hair shirt ("...cilício...").

---

[61] Both Ricardo Jorge and Afonso Lopes Vieira express dismay over Lobo's pungent humor. See Jorge, pp. 125, 375, and Vieira's note in *Corte...*, p. 220. However, they are strangely unaware of the traditionally risqué quality of wit. A possible source of consolation for their modern prudery is Martial's declaration: "...lasciva est nobis paginas vita proba." See Elizabeth Hazelton Haight, *The Roman Use of Anecdotes in Cicero, Livy, and the Satirists* (N.Y., 1940), p. 124. See also George Lucky, "Vir facetus: A Renaissance Ideal," *SP*, LV (1958), 107-121; Morigi, 142-146.

[62] For the superiority of the witty response to other forms of mental agility, see Grant, p. 84.

When asked how she had been paid, she replied: "I was paid a penitent's wages — six months of bread and water and a hair shirt" (p. 222). The Doctor considers this third type of pun the most effective: "...os mais engraçados e excelentes são os de resposta..." (p. 224). His reason is that a clever repartee is the best proof of mental agility, since it entails making comic capital of the neutral words of another: "...toma entre portas o entendimentos...e tem matéria sem suspeita na pergunta...".

The Doctor draws the discussion on humor to a close by reminding his listeners that witticisms should always appear in conversation with an air of uncontrived spontaineity; i. e., one must never attempt to steer the course of a conversation so as to create an occasion for inserting a previously prepared pun.[63] A speaker is considered witty precisely because he can detect an unsuspected source of humor in an apparently prosaic topic. In retrospect his conceit seems to have been naturally suggested by the topic under discussion: "Os ditos agudos devem ser na conversação como os passamanes e guarnições nos vestidos que não pareça que cortaram a seda para êles senão que cairam bem e botaram com a cor da seda..." (p. 226). Moreover, the demands of courtesy require that even the wittiest of speakers permit the other interlocutors to make puns which he pretends to enjoy no matter how hackneyed or clumsily told they may be.[64]

In the second and third dialogues of *Corte na aldeia* the interlocutors discuss the nature of written correspondence with Leonardo providing the directions for composing a letter: "...o

---

[63] The same spontaneity is demanded by Castiglione, p. 208. But the number of examples both authors provide raises the suspicion that they intend to do quite the contrary; i.e., as in the case of aphorisms, they intend to provide the reader with witticism for use. Cf. the hundreds of puns suggested for memorization in Palmireno's *Estudioso en aldea*, pp. 199-204; and *Estudioso cortesano*, pp. 52-57. For a view which combines ready-made witticisms with a prudent judgment for effectively knowing when to insert a quip into a conversation, see Juan de Timoneda, *El patrañuelo o el sobremesa y alivio de caminantes* (Zaragoza, 1563): "...que lo [i.e., algun cuentecillo] digas al propósito de lo que trataren..." See p. 170 in the edition of Valencia, 1927. For a reference to Timoneda's work in *Corte...*, see p. 229.

[64] "...ouvir e festejar com o mesmo aplauso como se fora a primeira vez que o ouvisse..." (p. 227). For the importance of knowing how to listen as well as speak, see Woodward, *Vittorino da Feltre...*, p. 191.

que há-de ter uma carta para ser cortesã e bem escrita" (p. 29). [65] The premiss for our speaker's exposition is the identity of letters and colloquial speech insofar as both are means of communication. It follows, then, that he would advise his friends to write their letters just as they normally converse: "...devemos usar nela [i. e., a carta] o que na prática costumamos..." (p. 53). [66] Like his conversation, a gentleman's letters are characterized by the same unaffected selectivity with regard to his words: "...as palavras das cartas hão-de ser vulgares, de modo que todos as entendam... e não já populares, [nem] que sejam... palavras baixas que a cortesia não recebe..." (p. 58). The close relationship between social speech and social corespondence is indicated by the similarity of Leonardo's "new" rhetoric, developed in Dialogue IX, to his precepts in Dialogue III for every well written letter. In each case the speaker calls for uncontrived brevity, clarity, and a minimum of rhetorical flourish (p. 53). [67]

---

[65] Lobo's interest in letters is not limited to *Corte na aldeia*, since he is the collector of an anthology of letters by classical and contemporary writers. Compiled in 1612, the anthology was entitled *Cartas dos grandes do mundo* and was published under the direction of Ricardo Jorge (Coimbra, 1934). For the popularity of manuals of epistolography and collection of letters in the Renaissance, see Francisco López Estrada, *Antología de epístolas, separata de la introducción general* (Barcelona, n.d.), pp. 18-24.

[66] For letters as recorded conversation see Pinto, II, 153; della Casa, p. 195. Also see López Estrada, pp. 65-66. For the merging of the *ars dictandi* and the ars *prosandi* in the Renaissance, see Paul Abelson, *The Seven Liberal Arts* (N.Y., 1906), pp. 53-60; Curtius, pp. 72-76; Kristeller, "Humanism and Scholasticism...," p. 355; Woodword, *Wit and Retoric...*, pp. 66-67. However, just as Lobo's rhetoric is simplified in Leonardo's "new rhetoric" so too are his letters, and he cannot be included among "Renaissance teachers [who] taught that all letters... must conform to the natural divisions of an oration..." (Woodward, p. 77). Indeed in an allusion to traditional rhetoric Píndaro says: "Nunca retóricos souberam escrever cartas se as sujeitaram às leis da oração" (p. 54; cf. 59). See López Estrada, p. 57; [la carta] es la forma más mitigada del artificio literario y... la brevedad y la expresión clara eran sus mejores calidades..."

[67] Lobo's passion for unpretentious brevity would lead him to limit severely the format of an envelop (the subject of Dialogue II): "...não há *prezados, magníficos, honrados, ilustríssimos,* nem *os senhores*..." (p. 33; author's italics). Cf. "...a brevidade é necessária porque o sobrescrito... serve de notícia e não já de adulação..." (p. 36). The same simplicity is advocated in de Barros' caustic remarks regarding pompous titles on envelopes in *Ropica pnefma*, II, 51.

Despite their mutual affinity, the fact that a letter allows for more reflection in composition and interpretation than is possible with conversation tends to modify slightly Leonardo's theories concerning the colloquial use of language. Especially noticeable is the greater importance which brevity has in letters than in conversation: "...se adiantam muito as cartas da prática familiar [em] que se escrevem de cuidado, e têm mais tempo de se furtarem palavras para se subentenderem razões" (p. 52). The ideal letter is described somewhat paradoxically as one which contains more information than words: "...que se entendam dela mais coisas do que tem de palavras..." (p. 53). [68]

Lobo's host provides several techniques ("...artifícios...") for attaining maximum concision in a letter. For example, he would have his writer frequently use the zeugma thereby dispensing with wordy repetitions of complex notions. In this way a single pronoun may often substitute for a detailed antecedent: "...relativos e subsequentes... sem nomear as palavras as repetem..." (p. 53). [69] A second type of abbreviation which synthesizes a complicated situation is the adage which Leonardo regards as particularly adaptable for developing a succinct epistolary style: "...as sentenças e adágios... sem entender as cousas as declaram..." (p. 54). [70] More efficient, however, than either of the preceding

---

[68] Here Lobo comes close to defining the ideal of his time with its admiration for the extreme concision of the Latin Silver Age. See Afrânio Coutinho, *Aspectos da literatura barroca* (Rio de Janeiro, 1950), pp. 29-46; Francisco Sanmartí Boncompte, *Tácito en España* (Barcelona, 1951, pp. 27-62; Evaristo Correa-Calderón, *Baltasar Gracián, su vida y su obra* (Madrid, 1961), pp. 245-262. However, Lobo's prose is generally free of the obscurity which was often a consequence of such a style. See Jorge's introduction to *Cartas dos grandes...*, p. xiv. See also Ares Montes, pp. 86-87; Schneer, p. 148. For a dissenting criticism which sees Lobo, in at least some instances, as "...o sequaz rigoroso do cultismo..." see Crabbé Rocha, "As cartas de Rodrigues Lobo," p. 60.

[69] While not as abstruse as Crabbé Roch seems to infer, Lobo's letters are nonetheless characterized by frequent use of the zeugma, e. g., "Com os tempos contrários à navegação o foram as ocasiões ao nosso trato..." (p. 62). For the zeugma as a means to a style which is elliptical and sometimes obscure, see Edmond Courband, *Les procédés d'art de Tacite* (Paris, 1918), pp. 266-278. See also Karl Vossler, *Introducción a la literatura española del Siglo de Oro* (México, 1961), pp. 38-42.

[70] For the aphorism as susceptible of manifold interpretations, see Giovanni Maria Bertini, "Aspetti culturali del refran," *Studia philologica, Home-*

techniques is the suppression of all unnecessary adjectives. A commendable letter should contain only those qualifiers which distinguish one object from others of the same class: "Os epítetos... [que] servem para descrição e declaração das coisas..." (p. 54). Certainly it is not verbose to describe a man as wise or a woman as beautiful, since there are foolish men and plain women as well. Less permissible are adjectives which contribute no useful information to what they modify. Our speaker cites as examples qualities such as the color green when predicated of grass or warm when referring to the sun's heat. Aside from their appearance in clichés and adages, which are themselves means for attaining brevity, such adjectives are to be avoided (p. 54). A third use of the adjective involves its appearance as a decorative embellishment. However, since epithets add nothing to the factual content of a letter, they are rejected as completely superfluous ("...sobejos..."); "Os adjectivos de elegância e ornamento tenho eu que se hão de degradar das cartas missivas..." (p. 55).

Zeugmas, aphorisms, and the suppression of adjectives are all steps to verbal concision but do not ensure that careful expression of one's thoughts which is clarity. Leonardo is careful to remind his guests that a succinctly written letter is not necessarily a clear one: "...a clareza é das razões, e a brevidade é das palavras, e assim, pode a carta ser breve mas confusa, e clara sendo comprida... (p. 55). Just as in speech, therefore, clear expression requires giving to each word its proper significance with a minimum of metaphorical invention. Moreover, the greater importance which Lobo gives to brevity in writing tends to lessen even more the highly qualified use which he would make of rhetorical figures in speech. Aside from the implied metaphors of adages and idioms, our author is led by his desire for unaffected clarity to forbid all rhetorical figures in letters: "...não sofre o estilo delas [i.e., as cartas] o que em prática e em outro género de escritura não sòmente se permite, mas muitas vezes se deseja" (p. 58). [71]

---

naje ofrecido a Dámaso Alonso... (Madrid, 1960), I, 247-262. See also Courband, p. 264; Hulme, p. 9; Chaves, p. 8.

[71] The reason why letters require more reflection and clarity than ordinary speech is expressed by Antonio Guevara in his *Epístolas* (Balladolid, 1539): "Porque de una palabra inconsiderada puédome luego retractar, mas

The natural spontaneity which should characterize the choice of words and use of witticisms in conversation also determines the circumstances for composing a letter: "...as cartas mais se hão-de escrever em ocasião do que trazerem por exemplo..." (p. 59). Leonardo nevertheless complies with a request to provide samples of the three main types of letters: the simple business-like missive, the chatty note from a friend or relative, and the weighty epistle which serves an official function.[72] Each example serves to underline the speaker's rhetorical principles: "Brevidade sem enfeite, clareza sem rodeios, propriedade sem metáforas..." (p. 70). Ideally not even the most formal of diplomatic dispatches should constitute an exception: "As cartas... mais graves e levantadas não deixam de seguir a regra e preceitos das humildes..." (p. 72).[73] But Leonardo does allow for deviations from his austere precepts in such cases as writing humorous letters where an inventive wit requires greater freedom for altering the meaning of words than he would ordinarily allow.[74] Other rare exceptions include letters which involve extraordinary tact or which do not serve as a simple means of communication. For such letters it is sometimes prudent to depart from a simple style with an occasional figure from a rhetorician's manual: "...para persuadir, consolar, dar louvores, ou reprender [sic]" (p. 72). Other changes in style as language departs from colloquial speech will become apparent in our examination of the types of literary genres which are discussed in *Corte na aldeia*, the topic of the following chapter.

---

la firma de mi mano no la puedo negar...". See the edition of José María Cossío (Madrid, 1951), I, 78-79. A similar view is found in Castiglione, p. 80. Some of Guevara's examples of brevity on p. 79 are found in *Corte...*, pp. 65-66.

[72] Lobo's speaker omits love letters ("...as cartas amatórias...") with the promise, never fulfilled, to consider them at the end of his discussion. See p. 52. The practical nature of Lobo's letters is a consequence of his theory that all letters derive from the first type, the business letter; "...é para que as cartas foram primeiro inventadas..." (p. 52).

[73] Two of the diplomatic letters, one by "um Rei de Portugal antigo" the other by D. Manuel (pp. 67-68) also appear in *Cartas dos grandes...*

[74] "As cartas jocosas... têm mais campo e liberdade para se poderem usar nelas alguns termos fora das limitações das nossas regras..." (p. 70).

Chapter VII

THE TYPES OF LITERATURE IN *CORTE NA ALDEIA*

It is indicative of Lobo's interest in literary theory that the first topic discussed in *Corte na aldeia* concerns the relative merits of chivalric novels and historical chronicles. The subject is somewhat artificially suggested when Solino calls attention to Píndaro's talents for flowery compliments. [1] The host remarks that if the student were as adept at developing the stock themes of romances of chivalry, then he would surely surpass the well-known writers of the genre. [2] When Píndaro protests that he would never consider the fanciful fiction of chivalric novels a worthy subject for his talents, Leonardo observes that the student is far too harsh in his opinion. The speakers then decide to expand the question into the main topic of the first dialogue: "...cada um diga a sua opinião nos livros que mais lhe contentam e das razões que tem para os aprovar..." (p. 12).

---

[1] Literary criticism in a fictional framework is a well-worn tradition in Iberian letters. See Fidelino Figueiredo, "Uma forma híbrida de crítica," *Pyrene* (Lisbon, 1935), pp. 146-180. For the suitability of literary topics as a means for developing conversation, see Palmireno, *El estudioso cortesano* where the author gives the following advice to the student of etiquette: "...si entra conversación de libros en romance, pedirás que te defiendan a Montemayor en matar tan presto a Alcida y a Celia sin gran causa ... Como le faltó muchas veces el probábile [sic] de las narraciones en ... Celestina..." (p. 83).

[2] "...pudera pôr a um canto o Amadis, Palmeirim, Clarimundo, e ainda o mais pintado de todos que nesta matéria escreveram..." (p. 10). For a study of the importance of these and other chivalric novels to the Iberian Renaissance see Menendez y Pelayo, *Orígenes...*, I, 293-466; Henry Thomas, *Las novelas de caballería españolas y portuguesas*, tr. Esteban Pujals (Madrid, 1952).

From the outset it is agreed that only those genres should be included which satisfy the traditional criterion: i.e., "...os que são de maior gosto e utilidade... (p. 12). Consequently, the interlocutors declare unacceptable for discussion any books which violate the standard by providing only instruction such as is the case with religious works and practical manuals. Curiously, there is no corresponding prohibition of literary genres which incur the opposite extreme by affording nothing more than entertainment.[3] An example of the latter is the anecdote which, we shall see, receives a prominent place in a later dialogue. An analysis of Lobo's theories of literature as found in *Corte na aldeia* will therefore require examining far more than the first dialogue where the focus is almost entirely on the chivalric novel and the historical narrative. In the following pages, we will consider first the conflict between the proponents of the romance of chivalry and the factual chronicle and subsequently the other types of fiction which are aired in discussion and example throughout the sixteen dialogues. Final consideration will be reserved for the place of poetry.

A defense of the chivalric novel is first proposed by Leonardo who points out the usefulness of the genre as a means for developing those social virtues which we have already seen as being proper to a courtier. Careful to limit his remarks to the foremost examples ("...dos famosos autores..."), the host claims that the diligent reader of such works as *Amadis* and *Palmeirim* will find abundant examples of the proper use of language; "...mostraram... a sua boa linguagem com toda a perfeição..."[4] Also important for the socially ambitious reader is the precise

---

[3] This is a far cry from the more traditional view expressed by Arrais: "Se [o livro] ao bom viver não refere, não é... senão instrumento de inchação... vã..." (p. 3). See Toffanin's appraisal of the common Renaissance view: "...le lettre valgono solo en cuanto servono alla virtù" (p. 106).

[4] For the relevance of chivalric novels to developing a good style, see Juan de Valdés, pp. 9, 75. For the importance of *Amadis* especially in good writing and manners, see the discussions on *Trésor des Amadis* in Thomas, pp. 164-165; Magendie, p. 267. That this argument was often dismissed as a rationalization is clear from Pinto, III, 23: "Gastam os homens o tempo em os ler [i. e., livros profanos]... dão por escusa que... é pela boa linguagem que neles acham... mas debaixo daquelas suas palavras doces está às vezes muito veneno...".

instruction for mastering the details of etiquette: "...o decoro de tratar as pessoas... [o] estilo da corte para as mesuras... e cortesias, conforme as pessoas introduzidas..." (p. 11).[5] Leonardo expands the purported social utility of the novels by alluding to their wealth of factual data which the reader can incorporate into his conversations thereby presenting a well-informed appearance. But the host's praise becomes increasingly arbitrary as he claims for the novelist the erudition of the serious scholar. His reason is that a chivalric novel reflects a thorough acquaintance with a variety of geographic locations and the mores of their inhabitants.[6] The good novelist is also said to be no less conversant with the numerous details involved in horsemanship than he is with the legal principles arising from his knightly hero's regard for justice.[7]

While Lobo's host devotes most of his defense to stressing the social value of chivalric novels, he includes a word of praise for the genre's peculiar structural form. In so doing, he anticipates any criticism which may point to the numerous adventures of fictional knights as detrimental to the organic unity essential to artistic narration. Far from combining a bewildering variety of unrelated events, therefore, a representative novel is said to comprise a harmonious unity of skillfully interconnected episodes: "...[mostraram] a graça de tecer e historiar as aventuras..." (p. 11).[8] Whether alluding to the social polish to be acquired in

---

[5] See Magendie, p. 267.

[6] Far from providing such information, the typical chivalric novels shows little regard for geography and social customs. See Edwin B. Place, "'Amadis of Gaul, 'Wales,' or What", *HR*, XXIII (1955), 99-107.

[7] In defending the chivalric novel as a repository "...de todas as ciências e disciplinas..." (p. 11), Leonardo suggests Cervantes' Canon: "...hallaba en ellos una cosa buena, que era el sujeto que ofrecían para que un buen entendimento pudiesse mostrarse en ellos... ya puede mostrarse... cosmógrafo... ya inteligente en materias de estado... siendo esto hecho con apacibilidad de estilo...". See *Don Quijote*, III, 348-349.

[8] In Solino's defense, which we shall see is mainly concerned with the genre's verisimilitude and moral relevance, there is another mention of the well-wrought character of chivalric plots: "...são tão bem inventados que levam após si os olhos e os desejos dos que os lêem..." (p. 14). Both speakers provide an answer to Cervantes' Canon charge that "...ningún libro de caballerías haga un cuerpo de fábula entero... de manera que el medio corresponda al fin y el fin al principio y al medio... parece que llevan intención a formar una quimera...". See *Don Quijote*, III, 347-348. Lobo and Cervantes, the former in his defense and the latter in his criticism,

the novels or to their internal cohesion, however, Leonardo's defense is quite different from the negative opinion generally expressed by his scholarly colleagues as he himself admits: "...ainda que eu sou bacharel em linguagem me atrevo a contradizer essa opinião..." (p. 12).

The typical scholar's attack on the novel is appropriately left to Lívio who rails against the genre's lack of verisimilitude.[9] While he tentatively admits that fiction itself may appear quite possible and thus provide ethical teaching for real situations, he denies that the wildly improbable accounts of a Palmeirim can ever fulfill the didactic end of literature by setting forth models of comportment: "...a fábula é uma coisa falsa que podia contudo ser verdadeira e acontecer assim... Porém a isto não dão lugar os livros de cavalarias com esses excessos e outros encantamentos" (p. 15).[10] So sweeping is Lívio's scorn for the "...patranhas desproporcionadas..." (p. 15) of chivalric novels, that he later disregards his tolerant premise and repudiates all types of fiction. His views accordingly comprise a defense of the factual narrative as the best type of literature for any reader seeking edification no less than pleasure: "...as histórias verdadeiras servem de exemplo para imitar, de lembrança para engrandecer, e de recreação para divertir..." (p. 15).

Lívio is not the first interlocutor to express his admiration for historical works. Earlier D. Júlio had declared his preference for chronicles, especially those concerning Portuguese history, as inducements to heroic activity through exciting reading.[11] As a noble, Júlio has especially stressed such non-literary records as coats of arms and geneological tables which he found useful for

---

are both concerned with the classical criterion for artistic harmony. See Horace's *Ars poetica*, 1-5.

[9] For the scholars' attacks on the verisimilitude of the chivalric novel, see Werner Kraus, "Die Kritik des Siglo de Oro am Ritter-Scharerroman," *Gesammelte Aufsätze zur Litteratur-und Sprachwissenschaft* (Frankfurt am Main, 1949), p. 162.

[10] Cf. Valdés' criticism of *Amadis*: "...dice cosas tan a las claras mentirosas que por ninguna manera los podéis tener por verdadera...". Also see *Don Quijote*, III, 348-349.

[11] See p. 13: "Sou particularmente afeiçoado às [histórias] do Reino em que vivo e da terra onde nasci...". Cf. Cicero's *Orator*, 20: "...cognoscat... rerum gestarum... ordinem... maxime scilicet nostrae civitatis...".

tracing surnames and pedigrees.[12] The Doctor's panegyric, however, is couched in more literary terms appropiate to the issue. Thus, he attempts to show that the real hero is better suited than a fictional knight for providing example, since his actions and ideals have been proved in the realm of practical experience: "...nenhuma lição pode haver que mais recreie e aproveite que a que eu sei é verdadeira..." (p. 14).[13] In Lívio's opinion, even the novel's encyclopedic content and social polish can be readily matched by a good history: "...o trato dos homens, o comércio das províncias, donde se conserva, alcança, e sabe senão pelas histórias verdadeiras?" (p. 15). Ever mindful of the weight of tradition, Lívio climaxes his argument with an appeal to Cicero: "...Marco Túlio chamou a história mestra da vida..."[14]

The Doctor's unreserved praise is checked by Solino's reminder that facts are in themselves mute and require an imaginative retelling if they are to fire the reader's imagination and move him to emulate past example. Moreover, the ethical force of literature is not to be found in the events related but rather in

---

[12] See p. 13: "...que soubesse... o apelido que tinha, donde lhe veio, quem foram os seus passados". Júlio is obviously referring to such medieval works as the *Livro de linhagens* de Dom Pedro who stated as one of his seven reasons for compiling the chronicle: "...por saberem estes fidalgos de quais descenderam de padre e filho. ... das linhas travessas...". See Rodrigues Lapa, pp. 271-289.

[13] Since the paradigmatic view of history rested on the assumption that man's nature is unchangeable, past experience furnishes examples for future situations. See de Barros, *Ropica...:* "...o que foi, isso é, e será..." (II, 58). See also Palmireno, *El estudioso de la aldea* where the objection that history is dead is countered with: "...las causas de los afectos de nuestros ánimos y cosas naturales no se mudan... que tomes ejemplo y experiencia en cabeza agena..." (p. 244). Cf. Pinto, I, 271-272. The adaptation of classical figures to precepts of moral guidance for princes and other notables is the subject of Francisco Soares Toscano, *Paralelos de príncipes, e varões ilustres antigos, a que muitos da nossa nação portuguesa se assemelharam* (Evora, 1623), See Edward Glaser, "Quevedo versus Perez de Montalbán: The *Auto del Polifemo* and the Odyssean tradition in Golden Age Spain," HR, XXVII (1960), pp. 103-120. See p. 106, note 10. For a study of the role of history in the Renaissance as a "...universalidad de experiencia..." see Maravall, *Los orígenes...*, pp. 21-44; Carillo, pp. 200-201; Crane, pp. 180-181; Gilmore, pp. 97-98.

[14] Livio's reference is to *De oratore*, II, 9, where history is defined as "...testis temporum, lux veritatis, vita memoriae, magister vitae, nuntia vetustatis...".

the atemporal moral truths which they illustrate. The writer of a fictional account, therefore, may re-create an ideal world which, while factually false, is morally true. In such a world the imprint of a normative order is more readily discernible than in historical chronicles which merely record happenstance: "E quanto ao retrato e exemplo da vida, melhor se colhe no [i.e., retrato] que um bom entendimento traçou... que no sucesso que às vezes se alcançou por mão da ventura sem a diligência e empenho meterem nenhum cabedal" (p. 16). [15] Solino borrows from Aristotle in summarizing his position and defines a commendable fictional work as one which portrays events as they should be and not as they actually occur: "...contam-se as coisas como era bem que fossem e não como sucederam, e assim são mais aperfeiçoadas..." (p. 16). [16]

The speaker adapts his premise to chivalric novels in an effort to underline the way in which they comply with the didactic function of literature. He begins by making the somewhat dubious claim that the chivalric world is populated with heroes who are model figures. [17] Its knights are true to a code which is consistently

---

[15] See Kraus, p. 164 where the author points out how Cervantes came to realize that factual data give no comprehensive view of human experience without the aid of intelligence to organize the data into a moral order. The same realization is attributed to J. Ferreira de Vasconcelos in Asensio's introduction to the *Eufrosina*; i. e., only the imaginative author can raise what is episodic and factual to the level of "...una categoría ética...". See p. xxx.

[16] For Aristotle's distinction between history and poetry, see *Poetics*, 1451. For this passage as a justification of fiction generally in the Peninsula, see Shepard, pp. 51-62. See below, no. 25. An analysis of the Renaissance identification of moral philosophy, poetry (fiction), and rhetoric whereby the reader is expected to be moved to adopt an ethical position through fiction can be found in Donald Lemen Clark, *Rhetoric and Poetry in the Renaissance* (N. Y., 1963), pp. 120-138.

[17] "Descreve o cavaleiro como era bem que os houvesse, as damas quão castas, os reis quão justos... o trato conforme com a razão." Cf. Eslava's similar defense of chivalric novels for their moral value, p. 40. It has been proposed that Lobo intended Solino's argument to be an answer to Cervantes' criticism in *Don Quijote*, I, XLVII, XLVIII. Also see Maritornes' far different appraisal in XXXII (III, 344). See Georges Le Gentil, *La littérature portugaise* (Paris, 1951), p. 84. Ares Montes disagrees and prefers to attribute Lobo's affection for the genre to our author's generally conservative views regarding literature. See José Ares Montes, "Cervantes y la literatura portuguesa," *AC*, II (1952), p. 213. In any case, Lobo's champion of the chivalric novel's high moral tone could easily be refuted with a reference to *Amadis* where neither knight nor lady fit Solino's idealistic

in conformity with reason while their ladies are paragons of virtue, and their kings are towers of justice. Similarly, while the speaker concedes that the events described are by no means derived from actuality, he insists that they may portray a universe governed by a natural law where the proud are vanquished, the humble exalted, the weak helped, and the honor of maidens zealously guarded. Solino contends that not even young women should be prohibited from reading such works as *Palmeirim,* for they too can profit from the moral lessons which such works contain: "...muitas donzelas guardaram extremos de firmeza e fidelidade, costumadas a ler outros semelhantes nos livros de cavalarias" (p. 18). [18]

It is apparent that Solino is describing the ideal chivalric novel, for even he admits that the genre is too often represented by plots with little relation to reality. [19] As a result the reader may despair of realizing through his own behavior the moral values expressed. However, the speaker points out that, given a talented author, it is always possible to describe events in such a way that a reader be moved in his own practical behavior. Solino proves his point with two examples. One concerns an Italian couple who burst into tears as they read Ariosto's description of the death of Zerbino in *Orlando Furioso* (p. 17). [20] Even more dramatic is the

---

description. See the edition of Edwin B. Place (Madrid, 1959), I, 285. For lascivious chivalric heroes and their sensuous ladies in such works as *Amadis, Palmeirim,* and *Tirant lo Blanch,* see Justina Ruiz-de-Conde, *El amor y el matrimonio secreto en los libros de caballerías* (Madrid, 1948), pp. 135-136; 194-196; 253-254.

[18] Solino's claim is in direct conflict with Guevara's view of *Amadis, Carcel de amor,* and other profane works. See *Aviso...,* fol. 2: "...su doctrina incita la sensualidad a pecar...". Cf. Pinto, II, 34; III, 6. For the moralist attack on chivalric novels as incitements to sensuality, see Kraus, p. 154.

[19] See Menéndez y Pelayo, *Orígenes...,* I, 404-405. The Spanish critic considers Lobo's apology for the chivalric novel as "la más hábil defensa de estos libros." See *Orígenes...,* I, 414.

[20] The death of Zerbino occurs in Canto XXIV, stanzas, 77-85. The emotional response to the passage is said to be less in sympathy for Zerbino than for Isabella in whose loving arms he dies. See Momigliano, *Saggio su L'Orlando Furioso* (Bari, 1946), pp. 155-159. For similar references to the power of literature to move the imagination with consequences in the reader's daily experiences, see Mexía in his *Silva...,* fol. 17-18: [la imaginación] torna los hombres locos... los hace enfermos..." See also fol. 123. Cf. Pal-

case of the credulous soldier in a Portuguese contingent laying siege to an Indian city. The youth has ingenuously believed that the adventures of a certain chivalric novel were a factual report. Enthused by the valor of the hero, he singlehandedly stormed the citadel in the face of the enemy's redoubtable opposition. When he was finally rescued, he dismissed his friends' chiding him for his temerity by pointing to the far more hazardous exploits of the imaginary hero, his model in combat. Solino concludes with the remark that the novel's ethical effect was not an ephemeral one: "...êle dali adiante foi muito valeroso..." (p. 18). [21]

Not content with defending the chivalric novel, Solino proceeds to refute Lívio's position by underlining the defects of historical narratives. Unlike the novelist who is free to create his hero without having to consider factual proofs, the chronicler is severely limited by the demands of documentation: i.e., "...os testemunhas que ficaram da batalha..." (p. 14). However, the pedestrian details of many historical works are not always a sign of a writer's scrupulous, if unimaginative, method. Our speaker charges that most historians are not above manipulating the data in deference to extraneous factors: "...nas histórias a que chamam verdadeiras, cada um mente segundo lhe convém, ou a quem o informou, ou favoreceu para mentir..." (p. 16). [22] Solino's sharpest words are reserved for the pseudo-history which is no more factually true than an obviously fictional tale, while far more encumbered with purported details in an effort to attain credibility. The result is a hybrid which shares in the fiction of the chivalric novel while partaking in none of the latter's freedom from the confines of a real context. Rather than indulge in such literary hoaxes — "...tão grandes mentiras que lhes não levam ventagem [sic] os fingimentos de

---

mireno's *El estudioso en aldea*, p. 242; Heitor Pinto, II, 272; Francisco de Portugal, p. 96.

[21] The average reader's attraction for the genre is in part attributable to its expanding the horizons of the drab reality of everyday life to include an awareness of heroic exploits with which the reader could identify. One may mention as an example of such a reader Cervantes' innkeeper in *Don Quijote*, III, 345. See Kraus, pp. 159-160.

[22] For the cavalier attitude towards factual documentation in sixteenth- and seventeenth-century Portuguese historiography, see Saraiva, *História da cultura em Portugal*, II, 142; Hernâni Cidade, *Lições de cultura e literatura portuguesa* (Coimbra, 1958), I, 355-366.

histórias imaginadas..." — the reader would do better to devote his attention to a well constructed chivalric novel. As Solino wryly concludes: "...se [os livros de cavalarias] não são verdadeiros, não os vendem por esses..." (p. 14). [23]

Mollified by Solino's criticism, Lívio compromises by allowing for all kinds of fictional literature provided only that they present a convincing description of a moral order. But the Doctor approves of even pseudo-histories, since they too can satisfy the didactic end of literature in much the same way as Solino's ideal romances of chivalric adventures. Lívio points to Xenophon's *Cyropaedia* as a description of a Utopian polity under the guise of a biography of Cyrus the Great. A more modern example of an informative pseudo-history is Guevara's *Libro áureo de Marco Aurelio* which provides moral precepts for sixteenth-century Spain "...em nome de um emperador romano..." (p. 19). [24] The Doctor concedes that even such obvious departures from historical veracity as Aesop's fables may well provide an ethical content under the trappings of an entertaining account.

Although Lívio says little in the first dialogue regarding the relation of a fictional work to its moral content, he later indicates that imaginative narrations might sometimes be considered as allegorical presentations of moral truths. Thus, in a reference to the place of exegetics in a university curriculum, the Doctor alludes to the Bible's multi-level significance: "...os quatro principais sentidos são... literal, moral, tropológico, e anagógico..." (p. 319). [25]

---

[23] In attacking certain historians while defending chivalric novels, Solino echoes the anonymous author of *Amadis VII* (Seville, 1514): "...las crónicas pasaron no tan ciertas como leemos..." See Kraus, p. 161. The author has been identified as Feliciano de Silva. See Thomas, p. 65. Solino's demands that history be truthful are common at this time. See *Don Quijote*, IV, 85; *Persiles y Segismunda*, II, 174.

[24] For a discussion of such "historical fiction" see Maravall, "Sobre naturaleza e historia...", pp. 222-259. For the opposing views in the Renaissance historiography — modified for moral lessons or completely faithful to documented sources — see B. L. Ullman, "Leonardo Bruno and Humanist Historiography," *Medievalia et Humanistica*, IV (1936), 45-61. Cf. Florentino Zamora Lucas' article regarding Pedro Rua's criticism of Guevara's *Libro áureo...*: "El bachiller Pedro de Rua, censor de Guevara," *Archivo Ibero-Americano*, VI (1946), 405-440.

[25] That Lívio would not limit his theory to the Bible is clear from Píndaro's observation: "...a poesia tomou princípio da Divina Escritura..."

If one allows for such subtleties in scriptural interpretation, one might also argue for the didactic relevance of a given work provided a similar distinction be drawn between its literal and its moral sense. The very test of such a work's verisimilitude is its ability to impart the type of moral lessons which Solino claims to find in chivalric novels. [26] Lívio admits, then, that while the task of the historian is to relate facts, the mission of the writer of fiction is to give a convincing portrayal of allegorical truth. [27]

In concluding the debate on the chivalric novel in the form of a truce between Solino and Lívio, Lobo is apparently as aware of the shortcomings of the genre as he is of its continuing appeal. By leaving unanswered Leonardo's and Lívio's references to the trite character of chivalric themes, our author expresses his impatience with those novelists who imitated their predecessors in a servile fashion rather than attempting an original presentation of a familiar genre. Equally reprehensible are the authors whose exaggerated accounts convert heroic deeds into caricatures of bravado. However, Lobo is careful to distinguish the abuses found in some novels from what Lívio would have considered an essential characteristic of fiction, and he is no less assertive in declaring through Solino that some romances of chivalry provide

---

(p. 20). For the Bible as poetry, see María Rosa Lida de Malkiel, "La métrica de la Biblia, un motivo de Josefo y San Jerónimo en la literatura española," *Estudios Hispánicos...* Huntington, pp. 335-359. See below nos. 58-59.

[26] While often mentioned in relation to poetry, the allegorical meaning of Scripture was invoked to justify all forms of fiction. For example, Eslava argues in favor of chivalric novels with "...muchíssimos historiadores... enredaron en sus ficciones... muchas intenciones que llamamos sentidos... literal... y moral. Notad el sentido moral... y dejad el sentido literal" (p. 40). See also Mexía's *Diálogos:* "...en las fábulas que de los dioses fingieron los poetas hallaremos buenos argumentos de como son odiosos los malos y aceptos los buenos..." (p. 259). Cf. Guevara, *Reloj...*, fol. 205; Pinto, II, 101-111. See Otis H. Green, "'Fingen los poetas', Notes on the Spanish Attitude towards Mythology," *Estudios dedicados a Menéndez Pidal*, I (Madrid, 1950), 275-288. Shepard, pp. 45-62; D. L. Clark, pp. 131-135. For a study of the way all four levels of scriptural meaning were applied to poetry in Lobo's time, see Edward Glasser, "Manuel de Faria e Sousa and the Mythology of 'Os Lusíadas,'" *Miscelânea de estudos dedicados a Joaquim de Carvalho*, VI (1961), pp. 614-627.

[27] "Resta agora que o que escreve história seja verdadeiro, e não terá Solino de que reprender [sic] nela. O que compõe fábulas seja verisímil [sic], e não terei eu razão de o reprovar" (p. 19).

gripping entertainment for their readers. Furthermore, while his defense of their moral relevance is somewhat strained, he cogently shows through Leonardo the novels' social value as models of articulate expression. In short, Lobo's position cannot be defined in terms of such prerequisites as an insistence on scholarly accuracy or moral instruction. [28] On the contrary, our author avoids the polarities of any intolerant stand by praising some novels and rejecting others depending upon their ability to entertain while providing at least a modicum of didactic content.

Although the first dialogue ends with a justification of both factual and fictional literature, Lobo shows a preference for the latter in the remaining dialogues. To be sure, there are detailed discussions on the origins of noble blazons and numerous examples drawn from history, but our author's social aims tend to give more importance to the role of the pleasant story told in polite conversation. They very order of Lobo's dialogues makes apparent the close relationship between effective speech and the short story; i.e., the conversational use of language which was analyzed in the previous chapter serves as an introduction to Dialogues eleven and twelve where the topic is "...como se havia de haver o cortesão nos contos e histórias..." (p. 192). [29] Even earlier in the dialogues Lobo provides a preview of the type of story acceptable in conversation in the form of Dom Júlio's episode with the beautiful pilgrim. The interpolated account clearly reflects the influence of several forms of imaginative literature which were popular in Renaissance Portugal and which Lobo would consider acceptable for relating in polite society.

The episode is divided into two parts each with its own distinct literary flavor. The first part concerns Dom Júlio's encounter with the pilgrim and is obviously patterned after similar occurrences which abound in pastoral novels. Thus, the setting is a forest glade by the side of a pool. Despite the rigors of late

---

[28] Aside from his arbitrary claim that popular romances of chivalry provide lofty moral instruction, Lobo makes no allusion to the attempts at explicit moralizing such as are found in the chivalric novels "a lo divino". See Kraus, p. 156-158.

[29] Cf. Francisco de Portugal, p. 62: "Valer de historias muy sabidas en palacio es discreción."

November, the trees have maintained an air of vernal lushness, "...como no melhor tempo da primavera..." (p. 101). [30] In the center of a clearing, Dom Júlio espies a strange woman combing her hair in the reflection of the pool (p. 102). [31] As might be expected, her hair is blond and so long that it forms a filigree of gold which contrasts with the rough hemp of her pilgrim's garb. [32] The narrator then launches into a lengthy hyperbolic description of the stranger's beauty, drawing upon all the resources of Petrarchan imagery. Since it will be shown below that Lobo considers such imagery poetic in origin, we shall return to the description in discussing poetry in *Corte na aldeia*. More pertinent to our present purpose is the effect which such beauty has upon the young nobleman. Like any chivalric swain, he is thrown into confusion: "...fiquei tão esquecido que deixei... [o cavalo] tropeçar entre os ramos..." (p. 101). [33] When he has recovered sufficiently from his confusion to address the pilgrim he averts his eyes "...com um respeito armado de receio..." (p. 102). Júlio ends his report with a plea that his friends learn the identity of the mysterious beauty.

On the following night, (Dialogue VI), the prior announces that the pilgrim has sought his aid and told him her story. In accordance with the pastoral theme the priest sets the time of the meeting when "...o sol se ia encobrindo com as asas da noite .." (p. 117). The village prior confesses that he too was disoriented by the woman's beauty ("...fiquei enleado..."), but, unlike Júlio, he finds it impossible to describe her comeliness, "...porque a sua beleza passava os limites dos encarecimentos humanos..." (p. 117).

---

[30] For a similar setting see Jorge de Montemayor, *Los siete libros de Diana* (Valencia, 1555). See edition of E. Moreno Baez (Madrid, 1955), p. 13. Lobo himself provides a similar scene in his *Primavera*. See *Obras*, p. 127. There is no controversy in *Corte na aldeia* regarding the pastoral novel as there was regarding the chivalric novel.

[31] Cf. Montemayor, p. 15; Lobo's *Primavera*, p. 128.

[32] So too Diana has "...cabello d'oro" (p. 75). Cf. Lobo's *Primavera*, p. 136.

[33] For a similar instance see the love-struck Amadis: "...y iba atónito que no cataba sino a las cervices de su caballo..." (p. 68). For a famous example of a lover's confusion in Portuguese literature see Bernardino Ribeiro's *Menina e Moça* (Ferrara, 1554). See the edition of Dorothy E. Grockenberger (Lisbon, 1947), p. 113.

Later, while dining in the vicarage suitably accompanied by the cleric's widowed sister and two nieces, the pilgrim explains her presence in Portugal. At this point the episode's similarity to a Byzantine novel, already discernible in the figure of the pilgrim, becomes more pronounced as the heroine unfolds her tale. [34]

The only survivor of a noble Irish family, the pilgrim had spent a sad youth surrounded by obsequious relatives and ignoble suitors, all with an eye on her fortune. Proud of her lineage, the heroine refused all pretenders and attempted to win the love of a prince who lived in straitened circumstances in Dublin. However, the prince spurned her love and sailed off in command of a war fleet which was promptly captured by Turkish pirates stationed in Algiers. Hoping to gain his love by appealing to his sense of gratitude, the heroine decided to offer her fortune to ransom the noble prisoner in return for a promise of marriage. But an agreement made in captivity may seem less tolerable at home. In any case, once back in Ireland, the prince refused to honor the contract until legally sued. The pilgrim then magnanimously released her ungrateful betrothed from his pledge and, disillusioned with her lot, decided to leave Ireland for a convent in Lisbon. Her choice was prompted by the reputation of Portuguese religious life, "...onde muitas religiosas do ilustre sangue de Bretanha vivem santamente em clausura..." (p. 121). [35] After stopping at the Shrine

---

[34] Few roles were more ideal for the hero of the Byzantine novel with its varied settings than that of the pilgrim. See Wm. C. Atkinson, "The Enigma of Persiles," *BSS*, XXIV (1947), 247-248. A similar case is found in Lobo's *Peregrino*, *Obras*, p. 338. We shall see below that a pilgrim's disguise is used by the escaping lovers of one of the interpolated novellas.

[35] In his article on Cervantes' influence on Portuguese letters, Ares Montes notes the following possible traces of the Spanish master on Lobo: the discovery of the pilgrim by the pool is similar to Dorotea's appearance in *Don Quijote*, II, 335; the pilgrim's amorous disappointments are similar to Dorotea's ill treatment at the hands of Fernando prior to fleeing to the mountain; the figure of the repatriated Prince is reminiscent of Cervantes' erstwhile captive of the Turks of Algiers (*Don Quijote*, Part II, Chapters XXXIX-XLI). See Ares Montes, pp. 213-314. The author does not claim a necessary connection and admits that the similarities are general and by no means limited to Lobo and Cervantes. However, he makes no mention of the similarity of the episode of the Irish woman to Persiles e Segismunda where Auristela-Segismunda is also a pilgrim who goes from the heretical North ("...cristianos... andam mendigando la fe verdadera entre opiniones...", I, 84) to the Catholic South where she entertains plans for a religious

of Santiago de Compostela, the heroine was robbed by her retinue. Reduced to penury, she is now forced to ask the prior's aid in gaining admission to a convent. The priest ends the tale with the news that the pilgrim has been accepted by a religious order in nearby Lisbon.

Having been entertained by the story, the interlocutors proceed to extract the moral lessons of the pilgrim's account in the rest of Dialogue VI and all of Dialogue VII which are devoted to analyzing such topics as the abnegation of love and the power of greed and avarice, motivations which figure prominently in the interpolated tale. Besides providing profitable pleasure in itself, the episode also suggests other themes for additional narratives which are related to illustrate similar moral lessons. For example, in defending the pilgrim's largesse in giving her fortune for the prince's ransom, Leonardo claims that wealth is worthless unless used. To prove his point, he then tells a tale concerning an avaricious youth. Situated in Italy, the story relates that the young miser kept his riches locked in coffers out of the reach of his family. Nonetheless, his father took advantage of his absence one day to empty the chests and spend the hoard on gifts for family and friends. He then carefully refilled the chests with sand and pebbles. When the son finally noticed his loss, the father reminded him that it made little difference whether the coffers contained sand or gold if they were never opened, for only actual use could confer a value on the contents (pp. 138-139). The Doctor praises the fable's didactic aspect with "...a história [é]...maravilhosa para o nosso intento..." (p. 139). Other pointed moral lessons regarding avarice provide the substance of similar tales in Dialogue VI (pp. 153-156).

The pilgrim's episode points to a more ambitious undertaking in Dialogue X where the interlocutors discuss the nature of the short story in theory and practice. The excuse for the model tales

---

life ("Pienso acabar la vida en religión...," I, 179). Lobo's pilgrim also refers to her homeland as under the influence of a heretical power: "...com a diferença e variedade das erradas seitas da Inglaterra, vinham [os príncipes de Dublin] em total ruina e destruição..." (p. 118). Even this similarity may be a reflection of historical facts. For the large numbers of Irish Catholics who sought religious haven in the Peninsula, see M. Herrera García, *Ideas de los españolas del Siglo XVII* (Madrid, 1929), pp. 514-515.

is provided by Júlio's infatuation for the beautiful Irishwoman. Solino caustically remarks that a woman who knew blond northern princes would hardly deign to reciprocate the love of a Portuguese village noble given to extravagant gallantries. When it is objected that love can triumph over such incompatibilities and lead to a happy marriage, the speaker demurs: "Não estou bem com a ventura dos casamentos do amor." Solino's unromantic position is assailed by Feliciano and Píndaro each of whom proposes to tell a story proving that a marriage undertaken in love necessarily succeeds no matter how adverse the circumstances. The stories in Dialogue X are accordingly intended to fulfill a three-fold purpose: Besides providing the evening's entertainment, each attempts to prove the speaker's point and to facilitate a paradigm for the short story as a genre: "...servirá de exemplo... [e] o que sobre ela se disser... servirá de doutrina..." (p. 192).

The outline followed by the interlocutors is drawn in a few theoretical precepts which Lívio provides as a guide for prospective story-tellers. As a form of literature destined to be appreciated by polite society, the genre should be couched in the decorous language of Leonardo's "new rhetoric." Even so, expression must conform to content lest a lack of harmony result between the matter and the form of the narrative (p. 210). As always, the raconteur should be mindful of the dual aims of literature, supporting his didactic material with authoritative axioms while lending a light note with an occasional show of wit: "...requer uma história... sentenças com que se autorize a graça com que se conte..." (p. 210). Even more important to the short story is a well constructed plot involving credible characterization: "...relação dos acontecimentos... boa descrição das pessoas..." (p. 199). As a means for achieving such verisimilitude, the narrator should insert likely geographical and historical details into the plot. [36]

---

[36] Lobo's elements of a short story closely follow Aristotle's parts of tragedy: plot, character, spectacle, diction, thought, melody. See *Poetics*, 1450 A. For the popularity of the Aristotelian Canon in Reanissance fiction, see Crane, *Wit and Rhetoric...*, p. 66. For the special concern for a detailed setting ("circumstantiality") as a means towards achieving verisimilitude, see Howard J. Savage, "Italian Influence in English Prose Fiction," *PMLA*, XXXII (1917), pp. 9-12.

To these traditional elements of plot, character, and setting, Lívio adds the somewhat unusual condition that at least one moving speech should be included: "...uma prática por alguma das figuras que mova mais a compaixão e piedade..." (p. 199). [37] Our speaker reasons that a rhetorical lament contributes to the reader's overall pleasure, since it increases by contrast his feeling of relief when all is resolved with a happy denouement. Lívio does not explain why the ending must be happy; however, it would seem that nothing else will do in an ideal world where only the wicked are justly punished.

Lobo borrows his first example of a model short story from the novellas of Mateo Bandello thereby providing an illustration of his technique for using extraneous elements in his own work. Feliciano closely follows the Italian author with regard to basic structure although nowhere is there any reference to the source. [38] In itself the tale is a novelesque account of Adelásia, only child of the Emperor Otto III of Germany and her love for Aleramo, the son of a Saxon Duke. [39] Fearful of professing their ardor in public because of the social inequality which separates them, the pair leaves the country in the guise of pilgrims. While crossing the Tyrol, the fugitives are robbed and forced to beg their way to safety in the mountains of southern Italy where Aleramo assumes the occupation of a woodcutter.

As the years pass, the couple rears a family of seven sons who are kept in ignorance regarding their ancestry. However, the eldest, Guilhelmo, manifests patrician tastes at an early age, now buying a sword, now a falcon; and his parents fear that his

---

[37] Lobo's moving speech to arouse compassion echos Aristotle's "thought" which is said to include "...everything effected by the personages' language; their every effort to... arouse emotion (pity, fear, anger, and the like)." See *Poetics*, 1456 B.

[38] Apparently none of Lobo's critics have dwelt on the importance of Mateo Bandello to their subject and to Renaissance writers in general: see T. G. Griffith, *Bandello's Fiction* (Oxford, 1955). The novella Lobo appropriates is entitled "Istoria de l'origine dei Signori Marchese del Carreto e d'altri marchesati in Moferrato e nele Langhe." It is number twenty-seven in the edition of Bandello's *Novelle* which I have consulted. See Matteo Bandello, *Novelle*, ed. Gioanchino Brognolio (Bari, 1911), pp. 157-174.

[39] The historical veracity of Bandello's novellas is slight. See Griffith, p. 62.

extravagances may bring about their discovery. When the youth joins the imperial army, his valor brings him to the attention of his grandfather, the Emperor. Intrigued by the soldier's superior breeding, Otto sends an attendant to investigate the youth's family. The lovers, their refuge discovered, return to the court where their anxiety turns into gratitude as Otto decides to forgive his daughter's transgression. Feliciano follows the original account to the point of enumerating the Italian titles and domains which the proud Emperor bestowed on his seven stalwart grandsons (pp. 198-199).

Despite complete fidelity in relation to plot, setting, names, and exemplary character of the principal figures, Lobo introduces significant modifications in keeping with his own aims. Since the version in *Corte na aldeia* is intended for oral delivery, it is far more concise than Bandello's written eulogy dedicated to a descendent of the protagonists. [40] Consequently, our author omits such information as Otto's genealogy, the development of the love affair under the watchful eyes of a suspicious court, and the adventures of the young Guilhelmo in the imperial army. Other significant omissions are the lengthy rhetorical monologues of the distraught lovers and the figure of Rodegonda, Adelásias's nurse and reluctant intermediary with Aleramo. [41] In conformity with the more puritanical tastes of the Peninsula, Lobo is also discreetly silent about the lovers' first *rendezvous* which the Italian version describes terminating with their union: "...con piacere grandissimo d'ambe le parte amorosamente consumarono...". [42] But Lobo does not alter the original merely by his omissions. In keeping with his stipulation that a stirring address be included for pathos, he inserts a long speech from Adelásia to Guilhelmo in a situation which Bandello dismisses in a few lines.

---

[40] Bandello dedicates the novella to Paolo Marchese del Carretto to remind him of the dignity which was his birthright: "...che sia il vostro conoscendovi esser tale qual a la grandezza di vostri passati si convieni" (p. 156).

[41] See Bandello, pp. 157-518, 162-167.

[42] See Bandello, p. 165. For the deletion of sensuous passages in Peninsular translations of Italian works, see Walter Pabst, *Novellentheorie und Novellendichtung zur Geschichte ihrer Antinomie in den Romanischen Literatur* (Hamburg, 1953), pp. 102-106.

The most significant divergence between the two accounts clearly shows the arbitrary use to which a tale may be put in fulfilling a didactic purpose. Bandello had intended that his novella show the instability of wordly honor: "...perchè, un gentiluomo per desgrazza perda le sue antiche ricchezze e da grande stato caschi in bassezza...". [43] When the lovers are robbed, the Italian author observes: "...la fortuna da tanta altezza a basso tratti li aveva...". [44] Later, when the woodcutter's sons are raised to the peerage, the author ends the list of noble titles with the sobering comment that most of the families had become extinct by his time. He then summarizes the moral with: "...non essendo sotto il globo della luna cosa stabile e ferma, che ci dimostra che non debbiamo fermar i nostri pensieri ma rivoltargli tutti al cielo...". [45]

In *Corte na aldeia*, it will be remembered, the story is intended to prove that a marriage for love will triumph against all obstacles. The robbery, therefore, serves as a means for reducing Aleramo and Adelásia to a state of helplessness. Later, when Adelásia admonishes her luxury-loving son, she attributes their poverty to her willing sacrifice for love: "...teu pai e tua mãe... puderam ter lugares levantados se amor quisera..." (p. 196). Most striking is the conclusion where Lobo makes no mention of the fate of the noble families and completely ignores the conventional moral which Bandello affixed to his novella. Rather, Feliciano optimistically ends the story by attributing the glory of the families to their ancestors' unstinting love: "...a generosa descendência... ficou devendo a glória dessa nobreza ao... amor destes dois amantes, que, ainda que êle [i. e., amor] encaminhe por ásperas dificuldades estes sucessos, sempre o fim que por meio de suas obras se alcança é glorioso" (p. 199).

The same lesson provides the motive for the second model tale which is nothing more than an exercice in shaping fictional elements around the basic plot of Bandelo's novella. In fact, Píndaro expressly announces his intention to follow Feliciano's lead. ("quero contar uma história semelhante à vossa, só para me

---

[43] See Bandello's dedication to the Marchese, p. 154.
[44] See Bandello, p. 167.
[45] See Bandello, p. 174.

oproveitar do modo que nela tivestes" (p. 200) and repeats the same situation involving a princess, Eurice, who flees her emperor-father, Constantine III, to live in rustic simplicity with her lover, the young duke Manfredo. After years of seclusion as a cattle-dealer in southern Italy, Manfredo is chosen by his neighbors to represent his district in the court of Constantine. Confident that the ravages of years of hard work will provide an effective disguise, Manfredo accepts the nomination. But the remarkable resemblance of one of Manfredo's sons to the Emperor arouses the latter's suspicions.[46] Trusting that a grandfather's affection will prove stronger than a father's ire, Manfredo anticipates discovery and reveals his identity. As in the previous story, the Emperor pardons all and gives nobles titles to his grandchildren. The moral reaffirms that a marriage for love will most likely lead to happiness despite external opposition: "...testimunho verdadeiro de que os casamentos por amor nem podem ser estranhados da natureza nem desfavorecidos... da ventura" (p. 206).

Our author hints that the elaborate from of the short story which is derived from the Italianate novella is more suitable for written expression than for informal conversation. Leonardo thus comments that Feliciano's example seems excessively long since it dominates most of the soirée: "...me pareceu comprida, sendo a matéria dela muito breve..." (p. 11).[47] The student replies that greater precision is impossible if the narrator is to provide his listeners with an interesting plot. To this end, an initial problem must be portrayed in detail to elicit their curiosity which, in turn,

---

[46] The theme of the striking resemblance between the grandson and the grandfather is important to the plot of Bandello's novella. See pp. 168-169. The fact that Píndaro borrows this element while Feliciano omits it is a further indication that both interlocutors use the same source. To be sure, the topos is the anagnoresis mentioned in the *Poetics*, 1452 A-B.

[47] The only other example of a short story is found in Dialogue XIII and is told to exemplify" "...o fruto da liberalidade e da cortesia...". The plot tells of the generosity of a Portuguese captain towards a Flemish noblewoman (pp. 250-259). The theme was a common one at this time. See Herrero García, p. 452. Lobo introduces the technique of letters to accentuate the courtesy of the principles. For the importance of letters to plot in the Renaissance, see Charles E. Kany, *The Beginnings of the Epistolary Novel in France, Italy, and Spain*, University of California Publications, XXI (1937), vii-x and 1-158. See especially pp. 39-47.

is maintained by a series of inter-connected events: ["dá-se"] lugar ao ornamento e concerto das razões levando-as de maneira que vão aperfeiçando o desejo dos ouvintes..." (p. 199). A speaker is not limited to such a complex type of narration, however and may choose to entertain his friends with the far less ambitious comic anecdote ("...conto gracioso..."). Through his speaker, then, Lobo distinguishes between two types of brief, fictional narrative: the short story and the anecdote. The latter's unadorned concision and dependence on a winning delivery for its effect set it apart from the former's more elaborate structure: "...os contos não querem tanto de retórica [i. e., como as histórias] porque o principal em que consistem é a graça do que fala e no que tem de seu a cousa que se conta." [48]

While the anecdote is fully discussed in the following dialogue, Lobo provides a transition between the two types of fiction in the form of Solino's contribution to the short story. The speaker himself admits that his attempts to imitate the didactic pretensions and august personages of the preceding speakers combined with his own penchant for witty, irreverent expression will result in an account which partakes of both genres: "...farei de um peão dama e de um conto história..." (p. 207). Even before Solino speaks it is decided that his tale will be an example of what to avoid when composing a commendable short story. [49]

Presented as a refutation of the moral lesson advanced in the longer stories of Píndaro and Feliciano, Solino tells of a king and his beautiful but jealous queen. Suspicious of her husband's

---

[48] In his distinction between the two forms of fiction according to their scope, Lobo ultimately depends upon Castiglione's discussion of short and long narrative accounts. See Castiglione, pp. 200-216. For a study of the two types of narrative in Lobo see Pabst, pp. 108-110. On p. 107 Pabst mentions Lobo's possible debt to Cervantes' *Coloquio de los perros* where Berganza describes two types of short study, one ornate and the other short and told with spirit. See *Novelas Ejemplares*, ed. Rodolfo Schevill and Adolfo Bonilla (Madrid, 1925), III, 159.

[49] Thus, Lívio declares: "Ficará à vossa conta do que se há-de fugir, pois os dois amigos [Píndaro e Feliciano] nos ensinaram a acertar." (p. 207). As one who attacked the "encantamentos" of chivalric novels, Lívio would certainly find fault with Solino's reliance on magic. In portraying human actions at the mercy of superhuman forces, the account can no longer claim to provide moral instruction, the essence of literary didacticism.

fidelity, the queen enlists the aid of a sorceress who kindles her misgivings with the report of a royal mistress in the palace retinue. To combat the king's adulterous love, the sorceress concocts three different potions: one to make the monarch infatuated anew with his wife, another to give added charms to the queen, and a third to destroy the mistress's beauty. However, the sorceress miscalculates the proportions of her recipe causing the members of the alleged romantic triangle to fall critically ill. All the resources of the palace doctors are required to save them, but not before the royal couple and their servant are left totally bald. With this ludicrous turn of events, the queen realizes her folly in indulging in groundless suspicions and blames her plight on love. The speaker concludes with the burlesque moral: "...de ciúmes e casamentos por amor não escapam senão ou com as mãos nos cabelos, ou com êles pelados" (p. 209).

The highly undignified conclusion of Solino's story and the importance which magic plays in its development are merely the more obvious characteristics of what is intended to be a popular tale with negligible didactic value.[50] Throughout his narration the speaker relies on rustic turns of speech which stand in marked contrast to the formal style of the earlier speakers: "...não me escapam termos das velhas nem remendos dos descuidados..." (p. 207). For example, his opening sentence has all the homely familiarity of "Once upon a time...": "Dizem que era um rei..." (p. 208). Throughout, Solino depends upon some of the verbal crutches which he himself earlier scored as detrimental to effective expression.[51] Among such clichés are *vem* and *vai* to effect a transition between episodes, e. g., "...vem este rei casou por amores... vem, e promete à raínha... vai, e manda chamar secretamente uma feiticeira...". Solino also interrupts his account to

---

[50] Menéndez y Pelayo sees the mark of a popular tradition in Solino's story as well as in Lobo's anecdotes. See *Orígenes...*, III, 152. While not doubting the existence of an oral tradition in Spain and Portugal, Pabst disagrees and attributes the popular character of such tales to the author's intentional use of popular elements for stories in themselves as fictional as any Italianate novella. See Pabst, pp. 108-110. Indeed, Lobo's confessed used of Solino as a negative example indicates that his popular rhetoric is a literary device.

[51] See above, Chapter VI, notes 48-49.

address his listeners with "Olhai vós" or "Vede vós". A further note of informality is added by referring to the queen as "a boa da raínha" or by cleaving a sentence with "Guarde-nos Deus" (p. 208).

Owing to its lack of a literary style and the absence of a moral truth which could be realized in practice, Solino's tale cannot be considered an example of profitable pleasure and thus fails as a short story. But there can be no doubt of its success in providing simple entertainment: "...como tinha graça até os erros lhe pareciam bem..." (p. 210). The light amusement which it provides sets the tone for the anecdotes in Dialogue XI when the interlocutors gather for no other reason except to divert one another. Indeed, as a means for providing nothing more than amusement, the anecdote represents a departure from the other genres in *Corte na aldeia* which are intended, at least in theory, to provide a useful pastime.[52] The purpose of the anecdote is reflected in its simple technique: "Os contos... consistem em dizer com breves e boas palavras uma coisa sucedida graciosamente" (p. 214).[53] Of course, not all anecdotes are comical, and Lívio mentions other types which tell of ghostly tales and terrifying adventures, "...que obrigam mais a espanto que a alegria" (p. 221). Nonetheless, all are alike in lacking any didactic motive. The appearance of only

---

[52] Pabst states that the first instance in the Peninsula of a distinction between exemplary tales and merely entertaining anecdotes is to be found in Gonçalo Fernandes Trancoso, *Histórias de Proveito e de exemplo* (Lisbon, 1578). See the edition of Agostinho de Campos (Lisbon, 1921), p. xx where there is a quote from Trancoso's dedication to the queen-grandmother, D. Catarina: "...pus a imaginação a escrever contos de aventuras, histórias de proveito e exemplo...". A similar distinction is made by Mateo Alemán in *Guzmán de Alfarache* (Seville, 1599). See edition of Samuel Gili y Gaya (Madrid, 1961), V, 145: "...lo entretenía con historias y cuentos de gusto...". In vol. III, there is a mention of harmless lies ("enganos sin perjuicio") which involve "...cuentos... novelas, fábulas, y otras cosas de entretenimiento" (p. 116). This is a view clearly different from Alemán's description of his antihero's novelesque life: "Esta ficción es una breve summa / que, aunque entretenimientos nos parezca / de morales consejos está llena." See introductory sonnet to the first book of Tomo II (III, p. 63). Lobo's own use of *conto* to refer to non-didactic fiction is not consistent. For example, on p. 154 the prior relates a "conto breve" to point out the baneful effects of greed.

[53] Lobo's humorous "...una coisa sucedida..." is a development of Cicero's second kind of jest which differs from the witty comment by narrating an event (*res*). See *De oratore*, II, 59. See Pabst, p. 107; Mary Grant, p. 108.

humorous examples in *Corte na aldeia* is obviously in keeping with Lobo's general preoccupation with the light character of cordial gatherings.

The author analyzes three main types of comical anecdotes, with the most common group comprising humorous events which are the result of carelessness or absentmindedness ("...descuidos e desatentos..."). As an example, Lívio tells of a visit to a nearsighted friend. When he arrived, he found his host berating a servant for misplacing his eyeglasses. It was only when the Doctor informed his friend that he was wearing them, that the mistery of the missing spectacles was solved: "...porque tendo-os nos olhos, os não via..." (p. 215). More careless than absentminded is Leonardo's acquaintance who was involved in an illicit affair which he conducted under the cover of darkness. On one of his nocturnal visits, a clock which he was carrying loudly struck midnight to his dismay and to the scandal of his mistress's neighbors: "...às escuras manifestou a toda a vizinhança a verdade que até então escondera dos olhos e suspeitas de todos" (p. 215).

Equally effective for sparking a comic note in conversation is the second kind of anecdote which tells of humorous events brought about by simple ignorance. The speakers cite such examples as that of a man who stumbled while carrying a jar of blood. In an effort not to lose the contents he inadvertently spilled a generous amount upon himself. When his son saw his apparently wounded father, he raised a hue and cry and was promptly joined by the other members of the family. Convinced by their laments that he was in fact wounded, the foolish man fainted in terror. A less dramatic example is provided at the expense of the bumpkin who locked a key for safe keeping in the very box which it was designed to open.

Both these types of anecdotes can be told in a succinct manner with a minimum of description and background. Such, however, is not possible with the third kind of humorous tale which involves practical jokes and subterfuges ("...enganos e subtilezas"). Since they require both an explanation of the reason for the prank as well as its outcome, they involve a more ambitious telling: "...requerem mais palavras..." (p. 219). Among the examples related is one concerning a maid with an insatiable sweet tooth. Narrated by Leonardo, the story begins with the maid's frequent pilfering from her master's cupboard. [54] Concerned by the dwindling store of jams and sweet meats, the master placed some sugar-coated pastry filled with gall to dry in the sun. Unable to resist the temptation, the maid purloined a few pieces and immediately fell sick. Confident that he had found the thief at last, the master decided to punish her further by pretending that the illness was caused by a fatal toxin. However, he was unable to conceal his satisfaction and smiled broadly thus alerting her to the trap. Whereupon the crafty maid asked to be told when death would be imminent so that she might incriminate the servant who has given her the sweets in an effort to buy her complicity for past transgressions. In this way, the servant's guile foiled her master's carefully designed trick. Such a combination of prank and wit is the most effective kind of anecdote: "...levam a todos os outros em grande ventagem [sic]..." (p. 219). The reason is that the element of surprise which is basic to all anecdotes is heightened by the added unexpected turn of events: "...a regra geral é que o desatento ou a ignorância donde menos se espera tem maior graça..." (p. 22). [55]

Although he is an accomplished poet, Rodrigues Lobo does not provide examples of his lyrical talents nor discuss his poetics anywhere in *Corte na aldeia*. [56] Even the participation of Píndaro who is said to be a student of poetry results in relatively few references to poetry. To be sure, the student is the first to mention his specialty when he claims that poets are unlike other writers, since they relate neither empirical fact nor imaginative fiction. Rather, their subject is an exalted view of a higher truth analogous to the knowledge of sibyls and seers. The poet is inspired by a transcendental influence to intuit universal truths. In support of

---

[54] One is reminded of a similar initial situation in Alemán, II, 261-275.

[55] Cf. Cicero, *De oratore*, II, 63 where the would-be comic is advised: "Notissimum genus, cum aliud espectamus, aliud dicitur."

[56] A lesser poet such as Luis Milán fills his dialogues with a wide range of poetic genres. For Lobo as a poet, the major critical work is Maria de Lurdes Belchior Pontes, *O itinerário poético de Rodrigues Lobo* (Lisbon, 1959). See also S. Spina and M. A. Santilli's preface to *Apresentação da Poesia Barrôca Portuguêsa* (São Paulo, 1967), pp. 23-48.

his assertion, the speaker [57] appeals to several authorities: "E Platão quando dêles escreve, lhes chama divinos intérpretes dos deuses, possuídos de espíritos celestes... Orígines afirma que a poesia é uma virtude espiritual que inspira em os poetas e lhes enche o ânimo e o entendimento de uma força divina..." (p. 20). [58] As an intuition of universal truth, the poetic vision is the source of any system which purports to explain physical reality in terms of all-encompassing principles. Accordingly, in his curriculum for the Renaissance university, Lívio describes poetry as the foundation of philosophy and all non-revealed religious beliefs: "...e bastava, para o grande valor [da poesia] ser conhecido, ter nela o fundamento toda a filosofia... e fundamento das deidades, que os antigos ritos da gentilidade veneravam" (p. 314). [59] Both Píndaro and Lívio present their idealist view of poetic inspiration in an academic fashion which does not allow for a dialogic development. However, their summary statements are apparently held by the author himself since they underly the only detailed analysis of an aspect of poetry in *Corte na aldeia*.

---

[57] "...entre os seus estudos se empregava algumas vezes nos da poesia..." (p. 6).

[58] "The speaker is probably referring to *Phaedrus*, 245 A, where Plato defines possession by the Muses as a kind of madness. For the idealist view of poetry as an inspired source of universal truth, see Gilbert Murray, *The Classical Tradition in Poetry* (N. Y., 1957), pp. 217-219. Píndaro's reference to Origen is intriguing, since the neo-Platonism of the third-century theologian rendered him suspect to the Thomistic rationalism of the Counter-Reformation. See Lorenzo Giusso, *Origine e il Rinascimento* (Rome, 1957), pp. 56-67. Moreover, Píndaro's reference presumes the identification of poetry and scripture, since Origen applied his theory of the inspired writer only to the composition of the Sacred Books. See Henry Crouzel, *Origène et la "Connaissance Mystique"* (Louvain, 1961), pp. 286-293. For the "higher knowledge" (*secretio enarratio*) possessed by the gnostic see Origen, *Homélies sur le Cantique des Cantiques*, tr. O. Rousseau, OSB (Paris, 1953), pp. 23-25. For the resurgence of Origen in the Renaissance through the neo-Platonism of Ficino, Pico della Mirandola, and others despite ecclesiastical opposition, see Giusso, pp. 44-46; E. Wind, "The Revival of Origen," *Studies in Art and Literature for Belle da Costa Greene*, ed. D. E. Miner (Princeton, 1954), pp. 412-424.

[59] Cf. Píneda's identification of poetry, philosophy, and theology (I, 72); Cervantes, *El licenciado Vidriera* in *Novelas...*, II, *Don Quijote*, V, 29. For a discussion of the identification of poetry and philosophy in the Renaissance and its origin in Aristotle, see Shepard, pp. 38-41; D. L. Clark, pp. 133-137.

The poetic topic Lobo analyzes occurs in Dialogue V and concerns the hyperbolic descriptions of ideal beauty which are common among the poets of the Petrarchan school. As with so many other subjects which we have discussed, the occasion is provided by D. Júlio's pastoral encounter with the Irish Pilgrim. When the young noble attempts to describe the beauty of the mysterious woman, he draws heavily upon the familiar clichés of literary endearments saying that her eyes are diamond stars with emerald pupils, while her lips are a cut ruby enclosing a string of pearls. These treasures rest on a crystal neck finely etched with the red and blue quartzlike tracings of her veins. The speaker continues the jeweled imagery by describing the rough collar of her pilgrim's robe with a term proper to the art of setting precious stones: "...a coluna... se engastava no áspero burel da esclavina..." (p. 101-102). Hair of gold and a snow-like complexion complete the stylized verbal portrait.[60]

The swain's description evokes an unsympathetic response from the three senior members of the gathering who generally find fault with the hyperbole and trite nature of lyrical endearments. Showing an historian's insistence on factual data Lívio chides the young noble for giving an impressionistic account of his own feelings while pretending to describe the pilgrim's physical appearance: "São mais pinturas vossas que gentilezas suas porque não há mulher na obra da naturaleza tão perfeita..." (pp. 104-105). For the Doctor, the description is one more example of the hackneyed, etherealized picture drawn by rapt lovers for whom all that glitters is quite literally gold. In support of this criticism, Solino charges that the group's poet, Píndaro, would have invoked even more extreme examples of over-worked images: "...se uma coisa destas aparecera a... Píndaro, que... poesias apareceram... que alabastros, marfins, mármores, cristais, topázios, jacintos, esmeraldas...

---

[60] The Petrarchan canon admitted few variations. For examples see Montemayor, p. 75; cf. Camões' sonnets in *Obras*, I, pp. 222, 304. For a discussion of such conceits in Lobo's "O Poeta por antonomasia" see Camilo Guerrieri Crocetti, *La lirica de Camões* (Genova, 1938), pp. 50-55. Lobo used the same elements in his pastoral novels. For examples see *Obras*..., pp. 136, 148, 372.

arcanjos, querubim, dominações, e potestades..." (p. 104). [61] Finally, Leonardo concurs with his colleagues and suggests that hyperbolic figures be more realistic and as varied as the feelings which prompt them (p. 106).

An apology for the traditional forms of endearment is jointly undertaken by Píndaro and Feliciano. The latter begins his explanation by countering Leonardo's demand that each instance of poetic rapture be uniquely described. The speaker points out that the very nature of endearments limits their field of comparison to those objects which are commonly considered symbols of worth. If, then, the same metaphors are frequently used, the reason is that there are not enough kinds of precious objects to enable a lover to be completely original in his choice. Therefore, while there can be no doubt that each lover feels his love to be completely unprecedented, the language in which he is obliged to express his experience is part of the common patrimony of a symbolic correlation which has long established gold as a standard for valuable yellow objects and snow as a measure of whiteness. Demands for originality in hyperbolic panegyrics should accordingly be tempered with the realization that "Para louvar não há tantos caminhos como para ter afeição" (p. 106). [62]

Although appeals to the limitations of figurative language may help to understand the reasons for the clichés of literary lovers, the speaker must still account for their hyperbolic character which Lívio had described as smacking of the supernatural ("...retrato tão sobrenatural..."). Feliciano now repairs to Renaissance neo-Platonism as he attributes love's exaggerated metaphors to an

---

[61] For a similar criticism of Petrarchan commonplaces, see Cervantes, *El licenciado...*, pp. 48-49.

[62] See Stegnano Picchio, pp. 9-10 for the lexical poverty of Petrarchan poetry as a direct result of a limited number of symbolic correlations. Lobo is not unaware of other metaphors; rather, he doubts that lesser objects could convey the poet's esteem of his lady. Indeed, Solino reverses his earlier position and agrees that it would hardly do to coin new figures such as "fresh as an apple orchard," "clear as spring water," "slim as a beech tree," "pretty as a garden" for describing a damsel's fragance, complexion, trim figure, or general appearance. Furthermore, lovers are not alone in using traditional figures. Solino points out that for doting mothers every male baby is a little prince while babies of both sexes are invariably diamonds, carnations, or roses.

attempt at describing the spiritual ascent implied by ideal love. The Platonic lover in quest of an object of perfect beauty to describe the source of his inspiration progresses from the relative permanence of precious gems to a transcendental realm where perfection is immaterial and therefore eternal: "...de não imaginar na terra... cousa que se iguale ao objeto de sua afeição, dá em... a comparar aos espíritos que não alcança com o entendimento, subindo pelas hierarquias mais levantadas..." (pp. 105-106). [63] The lover's enraptured descriptions constitute the essence of poetic expression: "...os motes avisados... os versos excelentes... tudo é doutrina tirada das escolas do amor..." (p. 114). Feliciano concludes his explanation of literary hyperboles by adding that their origin in a spiritual experience renders them incomprehensible to those who have never felt the need to utter them. As a result, only lovers can evaluate the merits of figurative endearments: "...o juizo deste acerto se não deve fazer por homens livres desta paixão amorosa..." (p. 114). [64]

Feliciano's thesis that poetic expression is derived from the experience of lovers is opposed by Píndaro who reverses the sequence; i. e., while concurring that the hyperbolic character of endearments may be justified with regard to their origin, the poet traces their use by lovers to a poetic source: "Os encarecimentos que usam os amantes menos são seus que adquiridos dos famosos poetas que lhes ensinaram deixando-os em suas obras" (p. 107). He bases his argument on his earlier definition of the poet as a divinely inspired seer of universal harmony. In describing his vision, the poet employs an unusual means of expression whose other-wordly flavor is adopted by mystics and lovers: "...como a frase poética é mais excelente e elevada [é] escolhida das sibilas

---

[63] For a description of the Platonic lover's ascent see Castiglione, pp. 504-514. See Camões' Ode, "Pode um desejo imenso..." in *Obras,* II, 137. For the "spontaneous" relation between Petrarchan canon and Platonic love, see Toffanin, pp. 28-29.
[64] Feliciano's warning recalls Ausias March: "...quien lo [i.e., el amor] padece entiende la substancia, juzgallo sin sentirlo es ignorancia..." See Ausias March, *Las Obras,* tr. Jorge de Montemayor (Valencia, 1560). See edition of Madrid, 1947, p. 30. See also, p. 286.

e oráculos... também fizeram os amantes a mesma eleição..." (p. 108). [65]

Any attempt to arbitrate the issue of priority regarding the origins of hyperbolic figures would be bootless, since both Platonic lover and philosopher-poet appeal to a type of spiritual experience — the lover in his ascent to a vision of eternal beauty and the poet to a contemplation of cosmic harmony. When Píndaro refers to the poet as someone possessed by celestial spirits and Feliciano says that the lover is in a state of ecstasy, both are describing a similar phenomenon. [66] In view of the Late Renaissance notion of love as the animating force of the universe, one might say that Feliciano's lover and Píndaro's poet are really the same, for the ideal beauty glimpsed by the former in his mistress is the universal harmony descerned by the latter in the sublunary regions. [67] That is, both mistress and nature are ciphers of the absolute perfection whose vision enthrals the beholder. [68] For this reason, Lívio accepts the arguments of both speakers and concedes that all exaggerated endearments are attempts to capture in exalted language the fleeting glimpse of the divine: "...raios derivados da beleza divina..." (p. 109). [69]

---

[65] For a study relating the lover's mystical ascent and the hyperbole of poetic expression, see Lowry Nelson Jr., "The Rhetoric of Ineffability: Toward a Definition of Mystical Poetry," *CL*, VIII (1956), 323-336.

[66] "...[os poetas são] possuídos de espíritos celestes..." (p. 20) and "...os que amam [vivem] em certo modo fora de si..." (p. 109).

[67] In his eclogue "A quem darei queixumes namorados...," Camões says "Bem vês que por amor se move tudo / ... / o animal mais simples... / o de mais levantado pensamento..." See *Obras*, II, 74-75. The most ambitious explanation of the universe as bound by love is Leon Ebreo's *Dialoghi d'amore* (Rome, 1535). See the translation of Inca Garcilaso de la Vega (Montilla, 1586): "...amor es el vínculo del mundo inferior con la divindad." See the edition of Buenos Aires, 1947, p. 239. For the importance of Ebreo to the Renaissance in Portugal see Hernâni Cidade, *O conceito da Poesia como expressão da cultura* (Coimbra, 1957), pp. 80-86. See also Nesca A. Robb, *Neo-Platonism of the Italian Renaissance* (London, 1935), pp. 19ff; Paul Oscar Kristeller, *The Philosophy of Marcilio Ficino* (New York, 1943), pp. 112 ff.

[68] See Ebreo: "...podremos subir del conocimiento de la hermosura corpórea al conocimiento de la hermosura del ánima del mundo, y de ella... al de la summa hermosura del primer entendimiento divino..." (p. 285). Cf. Camões' sonnet, "Dizei Senhora, da Beleza ideia..." in *Obras*, I, 269.

[69] Lívio's words recall Camões': "...os olhos amantes... vêem logo a graça pura / a luz alta e serena / que é raio da Divina Formosura..." See

Lovers and poets alone, therefore, are exempt from the prosaic demands of normal language: "Sòmente na licença poética podem entrar os desvarios... por serem muito iguais o furor poético e o amoroso" (p. 109). [70] Leonardo's summation of the discussion settles the issue provoked by Júlio's description: "...o alhearem-se de si os amantes... [é] como os poetas com o furor divino..." (p. 113).

In our survey of Lobo's literary theories we have seen that our author defends different genres at different times. Thus, his interlocutors decide that such fictional forms as romances of chivalry and Italianate novellas can both satisfy the traditional criterion of profitable pleasure, though in a manner different from the well-written historical chronicle. We have also seen that Lobo departs altogether from the demands of didactic content in the case of the anecdote whose only reason for being is to provide amusement with accounts of human foibles. Finally, it has been shown that the most conventional hyperboles of lyrical poetry acquire new significance against a background of Renaissance neo-Platonism. Nowhere does Lobo indicate that he would consider one genre inherently superior to another. Each type of literature is valuable whether quickening the reader's pulse with the adventures of Amadis, stirring his compassion with tales of forlorn lovers, or appealing to his patriotism with the history of his country's glories.

Far from deciding in favor of a specific genre, it seems that Lobo would consider the ideal form of literature to be a combination of all genres thereby providing a maximum of entertainment while enlarging the reader's awareness of the different facets of human experience. This can be seen in the very beginning of *Corte*

Obras, II, 138. Cf. Pinto, I, 34: "Deus é uma unidade simplíssima, um acto puríssimo, que está em todas as cousas, do qual procedem os raios da formosura das criaturas." See Kristeller, *The philosophy...*, p. 253.

[70] For the restrictions regarding poetic license, see Cicero, *De oratore*, II, 14: "Poetas omnino quasi alia quadam linguam... locutus, non conor attingere...". Thus Barros warns his son that "duma maneira falam os poetas, e doutra os oradores...". See *Diálogo da Linguagem*, p. 77. Cf. the censor's license to Francisco de Portugal's *Arte...* where the quasi-religious hyperboles of endearment are admitted with the reason: "são... adorações que as licenças da poesia e os conceitos do amor inventaram."

na aldeia where Lobo refers explicitly to his dialogues as an example of the best vehicle for combining a diversified literary diet combining topics suitable for both formal and informal gatherings: "...os melhores [livros] são os livros que tratem... de matérias políticas e engraçadas, de corte e de aldeia, e de qualquer sujeito aprazível... cuja variedade e doutrina é uma lição mui saborosa... e esta [variedade] é mais certa e mais própria nos diálogos..." (pp. 21-22). [71] Lobo is fully aware that the greatest obstacle to gaining a reader's continued interest is tedium. Here again the dialogue's diversity with regard both to content and to perspective is a virtue, for it implies the brevity of many parts which can be conveniently encompassed in a work of modest size like *Corte na aldeia*. Diversity and brevity, therefore, are both invoked at the very end of the last dialogue in another, indirect reference to the advantages of the dialogue form. [72]

---

[71] Lobo would apparently agree with Lope de Vega's verses from "Arte nuevo": "...la variedad deleita mucho... buen ejemplo nos da naturaleza / que por tal variedad tiene belleza." See R. Menéndez Pidal, "Lope de Vega, El 'Arte nuevo' y la nueva biografía," *RFE*, XXII (1935), 337-398. See pp. 348-350. For another view of variety as an artistic norm found in nature, see Edward C. Riley, "Episodio, novela, y aventura en *Don Quijote*," *AC*, V (1955), pp. 209-231.

[72] Our author gives the accolade of a literature of diversion to those works which are conveniently divided into parts, chapters, "...e outras divisões" (p. 328). There is no doubt that Lobo would include dialogues among the "other divisions." Similarly, in his only reference to drama, Lobo imputes the popularity of comedies to their diversity and variety. See p. 328.

CHAPTER VIII

CONCLUSION

In our analysis of the estructure and major themes of *Corte na aldeia* our intention has been to evaluate Rodrigues Lobo's work in light of the Peninsular dialogue tradition. We have found that his speakers show a wide range of interests reminiscent of the encyclopedic works of such earlier writers as Pinto and Pineda, while their debates remind one of the animated conversations of Valdés and de Barros. Moreover, in a manner rarely equalled by his predecessors, Lobo succeeds in exhausting the discursive possibilities of his chosen genre. Without frequent clashes between such well informed interlocutors as Solino and Lívio, our author would have been hard put to combine the multiplicity of perspectives and subjects which comprise his sixteen dialogues. As was pointed out in the previous chapter, the speakers' discussion of the dialogue's literary merits merely makes explicit the organic unity between form and content which is the most salient characteristic of *Corte na aldeia*.[1]

Lobo's effective fusion of intriguing themes and graceful presentation is also made possible by his pursuit of profitable pleasure as the writer's ideal goal. Hinting at the two-fold aim in the very title of the work, the author-narrator holds the reader's interest by assigning diversified roles to his interlocutors and allowing them to take turns in dominating the conversations. Sometimes

---

[1] In criticizing the work within the work itself, Lobo brings to mind the evaluation of Part One of *Don Quijote* which is found in Part Two, II-III.

declaiming and often disputing and lecturing, the speakers are therefore not cast into a master-disciple relationship with a single interlocutor acting as a spokesman for the author. Leonardo's lead in guiding a discussion depends upon Lívio's erudition, and the two are frequently no match for Solino humorous criticism. Less vocal to be sure, are the younger speakers Píndaro and Júlio who nevertheless provide pertinent comments on literature, national history, and protocol. Complementing the original group are the courtier-priest and the student Feliciano. Only Alberto remains somewhat marginal to the discussions, since he is summoned to speak on two occasions and then merely to provide a soldier's point of view.

The extent to which Lobo depends upon the joint efforts of all the interlocutors is amply demonstrated in his views regarding courtesy and the courtier. In his analysis of the complex topic, which is first suggested by the nobleman Júlio and then defined by the prior, there is scarcely a nod given to the traditional prerequisite of a noble birth. Rather, the priest identifies the ideal courtier with anyone who has mastered the habit of polite behavior. Tracing all ceremony to its origin in religious observance, the speaker describes courtesy as a feigned humility whereby one may seek acceptance in a society rigidly ruled by an elaborate etiquette. Not only in there no attempt to affix a moral significance to the subject, but it is frankly admitted that polite behavior is a façade which may or may not indicate a sincerely humble person. Accordingly, Solino and Feliciano describe courteous phrases as completely formalistic with the result that they should not be interpreted literally. However, that genteel society is not content merely with a repertory of conventional phrases and gestures is shown in Leonardo's insistence on the need for a rich vocabulary as a means towards giving an impression of worldly sophistication.

The author further addresses himself to the topic in the course of three discussions. Each exchange considers a specific career which has traditionally offered opportunities for acquiring the disciplined comportment and detailed knowledge necessary for social success. Since the speakers limit themselves to the external aspects of etiquette, there is constantly present a suspicion of hypocrisy which sheds an unfavorable light on their observations. Thus, even while directing the student to a royal court — the first "career" — where he can observe genteel manners, Leonardo includes as models of polished behavior not only high-minded aides and gallant swains but also scheming grandees and opportunistic sycophants.

A similar clash between theoretical advantages and real deficiencies is found in Alberto's description of a military career. Disciplined by an uncompromising code, the soldier may attain a kind of nobility through heroism while developing a cosmopolitan outlook from his far-flung campaigns. An ambiguity arises, however, when the speaker points to duels both as a means for steeling character as well as a barbaric recourse for settling personal differences. When Solino portrays the typical soldier as an ill-paid mercenary obliged to pillage in order to live, it becomes quite clear that Alberto's ideal type, if he ever existed, was not generally to be found in the armies of Lobo's day. Again, Lívio's apology for the sophistication of the scholar is countered by his admission that an academic formation often involves little more than memorizing the various nomenclatures proper to the university curriculum. With Solino's references to the schoolmaster's social awkwardness and the pedant's affectations, it is once again clear that a traditional career, while still an asset for a would-be gentleman, can no longer be embraced without reservations.

To what advantage Lobo unites theme and structure is also apparent in his analysis of the nature of the vernacular and its proper uses in society. To be sure, the theoretical treatment of the second major topic does not allow for the shifting perspectives of the first with its awareness of changing social realities. [2] Nonetheless, the subject bears on an essential characteristic of dialogue, for it is prompted by the interlocutors' interest in the proper development of their conversations. Regarding the nature of their language, the speakers are in complete accord as they echo the

---

[2] The ambiguity of Lobo's views regarding such questions as the role of courtiers, soldiers, and scholars has been attributed in part to the collapse of the earlier hierarquized social order following the Portuguese Age of Expansion and the subsequent loss of national autonomy. See Lopes Vieira's introduction to *Corte na aldeia*, p. xviii.

apologies commonly expressed by Portuguese grammarians and philologists of the Renaissance. There is hardly a spirited debate as Lívio arbitrarily claims for their language a euphony and lexical wealth which can be equalled by no other tongue, ancient or modern. Perhaps the only significant departure from earlier and contemporary panegyrics is the author's extreme linguistic conservatism which leads him to ban all neologisms. A criterion for linguistic propriety is consequently found in the speech of women, since the latter are but rarely subject to foreign or classical influences.

Lobo divides the proper use of language into two parts, one dealing with the choice of words and the second with the physical aspects conducive to their effective expression. Of the major themes Lobo's rhetoric is the least dialogically discussed, since it consists of little more than a simplified version of classical treatises on the subject.[3] In Leonardo's five directives for the gentleman, the speaker's regard for the Renaissance ideal of unaffected elegance is unmistakable. With rare exceptions the lexicon of the well bred speaker is current and used with semantic propriety, avoiding the extremes of prolixity and brevity. Above all, discretion must be observed in selecting one's topics. Similarly, the classical regard for a golden mean is the basis of Lívio's seven precepts for public speaking. Conversing in modulated tones, the polite speaker accompanies his words with measured gestures. Careful not to dominate the conversation or in any way make his presence annoying, he avoids clichés. He also takes pains not to interrupt others nor indulge in immoderate hilarity.

As always, the speakers's views are subject to prudent modifications in certain circumstances. For example, the insistence on semantic propriety is waived for the sake of humor which is a necessary adjunct of polite conversation. Wit is therefore discussed in detail as an ingenious manipulation of verbal ambiguities. Although our author provides numerous instances of puns from all the interlocutors, Lívio reminds his friends that joking is the spice of social gatherings and therefore is to be used sparingly.

---

[3] Schneer traces the similarity of both Lobo's and Castiglione's rhetorical theories to their heavy dependence on Cicero's *De oratore*. See Schneer, pp. 138-139.

A similar departure from linguistic simplicity is found in Leonardo's discussion of epistolography where the change is in favor of a greater concision than is possible in speech. However, even while proposing such stylistic devices as the zeugma, aphorism, and the supression of adjectives, the speaker reminds his friends that simple elegance remains the ideal. It is, therefore, in Lobo's disapproval of the extreme artificial concision so dear to the canons of his day that our author sounds an original note in his rhetorical theories. [4]

With the third major topic, the types of literature, our study of *Corte na aldeia* comes full circle, for it is precisely in the dialogue's adaptability as a means for including many themes and points of view that our author finds its literary value. Interlocutary exchanges is put to full use in discussing the multifaceted nature of literary theory with its references to the various kinds of writing. Each speaker is called upon to defend his favorite genre with the only premise being the hoary injunction that literature should inform as well as entertain. For Leonardo the choice falls to the chivalric novel which he finds suited to expanding the reader's general knowledge while improving his use of language. A chivalric hero is also a model of gallantry, and his adventures, if properly narrated, provide a good example of a well structured plot. Solino further develops Leonardo's apology by claiming to find no less moral truth in a knight's purported respect for ethical norms than in a historical figure's heroic feats. With fiction and fact thus defined as basic literary categories, it is decided that one cannot serve as a norm for evaluating the other. While both entertain, each provides the reader with its own form of truth; i. e., history relates actual occurrences and fiction presents moral principles in imaginary accounts.

The preoccupation with literature's didactic purpose becomes less marked as Lobo turns to other popular forms of fiction. In the extra-dialogic episode involving Júlio's encounter with the Irish pilgrim, our author not only finds a nexus for many of

---

[4] Such originality is relative only to the prevailing literary trends of his era. In itself, Lobo's insistence on clarity and simplicity is a consequence of his preference for the stylists of the Latin Golden Age as opposed to the writers of the Silver Period. See Chapter VI, note 68.

the remaining ideological debates, but also an opportunity for presenting the stock themes of pastoral and Byzantine novels. The interlude consequently involves such familiar figures as the mysterious beauty by a forest pool, the lovestruck cavalier, the wandering pilgrim, the Christian captured by Turks, and the disenchanted maiden seeking solace in the religious life. A less ambitious example of narrative fiction is the Italianate short story with its carefully constructed plot, detailed characterization, and decorous language. It was noted in our study that by making no mention of the Italian source of the stories which Feliciano and Píndaro narrate, Lobo can modify the original moral in adapting the account to his own purpose. Later, in turning to the anecdote as a second type of brief narrative, our author completely abandons the pretense of didactic relevance, thereby leaving the raconteur free simply to narrate an interesting event.

Lobo avails himself of the meandering plot of dialogue to complete his enumeration of the types of literature with a few scant remarks regarding poetry as an expression of metaphysical truth. The only debate suggested by the subject concerns the Petrarchan endearments found in lyrical poetry. Even here, however, there is a conflict of perspectives as the older speakers score romantic metaphors as hackneyed and ethereal. An attempt at justification is made by the youths Píndaro and Feliciano who appeal to neo-Platonic interpretations of love and poetic creation. Nonetheless, the reader is left with the impression that the problem is not really resolved. In this way, Lobo once again appears to transmit traditional views from an earlier period while subjecting them to the hesitant criticism of a more modern age.[5] It is precisely such parrying with accepted values which represents the very essence of the dialectic process.

---

[5] Lobo's combination of classical learning and a tendency to criticize tradition from a more modern point of view prompted Jorge to speculate on what might have been the course of our author's development had he not met such an early death. See Jorge, p. 350.

BIBLIOGRAPHY

ABELSON, PAUL. *The Seven Liberal Arts.* New York, 1906.
ABREU E MELO, LUIS. *Avisos para palacio,* tr. E. Díaz Garsifa. Madrid, 1761.
ADLER, MORTIMER. *Dialectic.* New York, 1927.
ALCIATI, ANDRAE. *Emblemata.* Lugdum Badtavarum, 1593.
ALMEIDA, FORTUNATO. *Historia de Portugal.* 4 vols. Coimbra, 1826.
ALONSO, AMADO. *Español, idioma nacional.* Buenos Aires, 1938.
ÁLVARES DE ORIENTE, FERNÃO. *Lusitânia transformada.* Lisbon, 1781.
ANDRIEU, L. *Le dialogue antique, structure et présentation.* Paris, 1954.
ANSELMO, ANTÓNIO J. *Bibliografia das obras impressas em Portugal no século XVI.* Lisbon, 1926.
ARES MONTES, JOSÉ. "Cervantes y la literatura portuguesa," *AC,* II (1952), 193-230.
―――. *Góngora y la poesía portuguesa del siglo XVII.* Madrid, 1956.
ARISTOTLE. *Poetics.*
―――. *Categories.*
―――. *Nicomachean Ethics.*
ARRAIS, AMADOR. *Diálogos.* Coimbra, 1602.
―――, ed. Fidelino Figueiredo. Lisbon, 1944. Pp. ix-liii.
ASENSIO, EUGENIO. "España en la época filipina," *REF,* XXXIII (1949), 66-109.
―――."La lengua compañera del imperio," *RFE,* XLIII (1960), 399-413.
―――. "Juan de Valdés contra Delicado, fondo de una polémica," *Studia Philologica; Homenaje Ofrecido a Dámaso Alonso...* Madrid, 1960. I, 101-113.
ATKINSON, WILLIAM C. "The Enigma of the Persiles," *BSS,* XXIV (1947), 242-253.
AULUS GELLIUS. *Noctium atticarum liberi virginti,* ed. H. M. Hornsby. 3. vols. London, 1936.
BANDELLO, MATEO. *Novelle,* ed. Gioachim Brognoligo. 5 vols. Bari, 1911.
BARROS, JOÃO DE. *Diálogo da viciosa vergonha.* Lisbon, 1540.
―――. *Diálogo evangélico sobre os artigos da Fé contra o Talmud dos judeus,* ed. I. S. Révah. Lisbon, 1950.
―――. *Ropica Pnefma II,* ed. I. S. Révah, Lisbon, 1955.
―――. *Diálogo em louvor da nossa linguagem,* ed. L. Stegnano Picchio. Modena, 1955.
BATAILLON, MARCEL. *Erasme en Espagne.* Paris, 1937.
―――. "Pérégrinations espagnoles du Juif Errant," *BH,* XLIII (1941), 81-122.

BATAILLON, MARCEL. "Melancolía renacentista o melancolía judía?" *Estudios hispànicos, Homenaje a Archer M. Huntington*. Wellesley, Massachusetts, 1952, Pp. 39-50.
———. *Etudes sur le Portugal au temps de l'humanisme* (Coimbra, 1952).
———. *La Celestina selon Fernando de Rojas*. Paris, 1961.
BEARDSLEY, THEODORE S. "The First Catalogue of Hispano-Classical Translations; Tomas Tamayo de Vargas' 'A los aficionados a la lengua española,' *HR*, XXXII (1964), 287-304.
BEAU, ALBIN EDUARD. *Die Entwicklung des Portuguieschen Nationalbewusteins*. Hamburg, 1945.
———. "A valorização do idioma nacional no pensamento do humanismo português," *Estudos*. Coimbra, 1959. 349-370.
———. "Sobre el bilingüismo en Gil Vicente," *Studia Philologica; Homenaje Ofrecido a Dámaso Alonso...* Madrid, 1960. I, 217-225.
BELCHIOR PONTES, MARIA DE LURDES. *Itinerário poético de Rodrigues Lobo*. Lisbon, 1959.
BERTINI, GIOVANNI M. "Aspetti culturali del refran," *Studia Philologica; Homenaje Ofrecido a Dámaso Alonso...* Madrid, 1960. I, 247-262.
BLANCHARD, PIERRE. "Studiosité et curiosité, le vrai savoir d'après St. Thomas d'Aquin," *Revue Thomiste*, LIII (1953), 551-562.
BLANCO-GONZÁLEZ, BERNARDO. *Del Cortesano al Discreto, Examen de una Decadencia*. I. Madrid, 1962.
BUCETA, ERASMO. "La tendencia a identificar el español con el latín," *Homenaje a Menéndez Pidal*. Madrid, 1925. I, 85-105.
CAMÕES, LUIS DE. *Lírica de Camões*, ed. J. M. Rodrigues and A. Lopes Vieira. Coimbra, 1932.
———. *Obras*, ed. Hernani Cidade. 5 vols. Lisbon, 1962.
CARO BAROJA, JULIO. *Los judíos en España moderna y contemporánea*. 3 vols. Madrid, 1961.
CARVALHO DIAS, JOAQUIM. "Frei Heitor Pinto (novas achegas para a sua biografia)," *Boletim da biblioteca da Universidade de Coimbra*, XXI (1953), 1-181.
CASA, GIOVANNI DELLA. *Il Galateo*, ed. G. Tinivella. Milan, 1954.
CASTIGLIONI, BALTASAR. *El Cortesano*, tr. Juan Boscán, ed. D. Antonio María Fabié. Madrid, 1873.
CERVANTES, SAAVEDRA. *Persiles y Segismunda*, ed. Rodolfo Schevill and Adolfo Bonilla. 2 vols. Madrid, 1916.
———. *Novelas ejemplares*, ed. Schevill and Bonilla. 3 vols. Madrid, 1927.
———. *Don Quijote*, ed. F. Rodríguez Marín. 10 vols. Madrid, 1947.
CHAVES, PEDRO. *Rifoneiro português*. Porto, 1945.
CICERO. *De amicitia*, ed. J. B. Reid. Boston, 1882.
———. *De oratore*, ed. M. E. Courband. Paris, 1922.
———. *Orator*, ed. Henri Bornecque. Paris, 1921.
———. *De inventione*, ed. H. M. Hubbell. Cambridge, 1949.
CIDADE, HERNANI. *A literatura autonomista sob os Felipes*. Lisbon, n.d.
———. "João de Barros, o que pensa da língua portuguesa, como a escreve," *BF*, XI (1950), 281-303.
———. *O Conceito da poesia como expressão da cultura*. Coimbra, 1957.
———. *Lições de cultura e literatura portuguesa*. 2 vols. Coimbra, 1959.
CLARK, DONALD L. *Rhetoric and Poetry in the Renaissance*. New York, 1963.
CORNFORD, FRANCIS M. *Plato's Theory of Knowledge*. New York, 1957.

CORREA-CALDERÓN, F. "Guevara y su invectiva contra el mundo," *Escorial*, XII (1943), 41-68.
———. *Baltasar Gracián, su vida y su obra*. Madrid, 1961.
CORTAZAR, CELINA. "'El Galateo español' y su retrato en el 'Arancel de necedades'," *HR*, XXX (1962), 317-321.
COSTA E SILVA, JOSÉ. *Ensaio biográfico-crítico sobre os melhores poetas portugueses*. 5 vols. Lisbon, 1853.
COURBAND, EDMOND. *Les procédés d'art de Tacite*. Paris, 1918.
COUTINHO, AFRANIO. *Aspectos da literatura barrôca*. Rio de Janeiro, 1950.
COUTO, DIOGO DO. *O soldado prático*, ed. M. Rodrigues Lapa. Lisbon, 1954.
CRABBÉ ROCHA, ANDRÉE. "As cartas de Francisco Rodrigues Lobo," *Colóquio*, XXIX (1964), 58-60.
GRANE, THOMAS F. *Italian Social Customs of the Sixteenth Century*. New Haven, 1920.
CRANE, WILLIAM. *Wit and Rhetoric in the Renaissance*. New York, 1932.
CROCE, BENEDETTO. "La teoria del dialogo secundo il Tasso," *La Critica*, XIII (1942), 143-147.
CROCETTI, C. B. *La lirica de Camões*. Genova, 1938.
CROISET, ALFRED AND MAURICE. *Histoire de la littérature grec*. 5 vols. Paris, 1895.
CROUZEL, HENRI. *Origène et la "Connaissance Mystique."* Louvain, 1961.
CURTIUS, ERNST R. *European Literature and the Latin Middle Ages*, tr. Willard R. Trask. New York, 1953.
DANIELOU, JEAN. *Platonisme et théologie mystique, essai sur la doctrine spirituelle de Saint Grégoire de Nysse*. Paris, 1944.
DELGADO, SEBASTIÃO. *Glossário luso-asiático*. 2 vols. Coimbra, 1919.
DELEBEQUE, EDOURD. *Essai sur la vie de Xénophon*. Paris, 1957.
DÍAZ-PAJA, GUILLERMO. *El Estilo de S. Ignacio de Loyola y otras páginas*. Barcelona, 1956.
DICKINSON, G. L. *Plato and his Dialogues*. London, 1931.
DUARTE, CARLOS. *A graça portuguesa*. Lisbon, 1923.
ELSDON, JAMES H. "On the Life and Works of the Spanish Humanist, Antonio de Torquemada," *University of California Studies in Language and Literature*, XX (1937), 127-183.
ESLAVA, ANTONIO DE. *Noches de invierno*. Barcelona, 1609.
ERASMUS, DESIDERIUS. *Querella pacis*, tr. Elise C. Bagdat, Paris, 1924.
———. *Praise of Folly*. Ann Arbor, 1960.
FELIX LOPES, P. "Traduções manuscritas portuguesas de F. António de Guevara," *Archivo Ibero-Americano*, XXIII (1946), 605-607.
FERREIRA, CARLOS ALBERTO. "Francisco Rodrigues Lobo — Fontes inéditas para o estudo de sua vida e obra," *Biblos*, XIX (1943), 229-317.
FIGUEIREDO, FIDELINO. *Pyrene*. Lisbon, 1935.
FLORA, FRANCESCO. *Storia della letteratura italiana*. 3 vols. Verona, 1947.
FRANCISCO DE PORTUGAL. *Arte de Galantaría*. Lisbon, 1670.
FRIEDLANDER, PAUL. *Plato, I: An Introduction*. New York, 1958.
GALINO CARRILLO, MARÍA ÁNGELES. *Los tratados sobre educación de príncipes (Siglos XVI y XVII)*. Madrid, 1948.
GARCILASO DE LA VEGA. *Obras*, ed. T. Navarro Tomás. Madrid, 1958.
GIANNI, A. "Cárcel de Amor y el Cortegiano," *RH*, XLVI (1919), 547-568.
GILMAN, STEPHEN. *The Art of the Celestina*. Madison, Wisconsin, 1956.
GILMORE, MYRON. *Humanists and Jurists*. Cambridge, Massachusetts, 1963.
GIUSSO, LORENZO. *Origene e il Rinascimento*. Rome, 1957.

GLASER, EDWARD. "Referencias anti-semitas en la literatura peninsular de la Edad de Oro," *NRFE*, VIII (1954), 39-62.
——. "El lusitanismo de Lope de Vega," *BRAE*, XXXIV (1954), 387-412.
——. "Miguel da Silveira's *El Macabeo*," *Bulletin des études portugaises*, XIX (1955), 5-49.
——. "Miguel Faria e Sousa and the Mythology of 'Os Lusíadas'," *Miscelânea de estudos dedicados a Joaquim de Carvalho*, VI (1961), 614-627.
——. "On Portuguese 'Sprachbetrachtung' of the Seventeenth Century," *Studia Philologica; Homenaje Ofrecido a Dámaso Alonso*. Madrid, 1961. II, 115-126.
——. "Fr. Heitor Pinto's *Imagem da vida cristã*," *Aufsatze zur Portuguiesischen Kulturgeschichte*, III, (1962), 47-90.
——. "The Odyssean Adventures in Gabriel Pereira de Castro's *Ulysseia*," *BEP*, XXIV (1963), 25-75.
——. "Introducción" and editing of Fray Héctor Pinto, *Imagen de la Vida Cristiana*, anonymous Spanish translator (Barcelona, 1967), pp. 1-167.
GOLDSCHMIDT, VICTOR. *Les dialogues de Platon — Structure et méthode dialectique*. Paris, 1958.
GONÇALVES, F. R. "História da filologia portuguesa. Os filólogos portugueses do Século XVI," *BF*, IV (1936), 1-13.
GRACIÁN, BALTASAR. *Obras completas*, ed. Arturo de Hoyo. Madrid, 1960.
GRACIÁN, DANTISCO, LUIS. *Galateo español*. Barcelona, 1796.
GRANT, MARY A. "The Ancient Theories of the Laughable," *University of Wisconsin Studies in Language and Literature*, XXI (1924), 7-166.
GRAY, HANNAH H. "Renaissance Humanism: The Pursuit of Eloquence," *Journal of the History of Ideas*, XXIV (1960), 497-514.
GREEN, OTIS H. "On the attitude towards the *vulgo* in the Spanish Siglo de Oro," *Studies in the Renaissance*, IV (1957), 190-200.
——. "'Fingen los poetas,' notes on the Spanish attitude towards Pagan Mythology," *Estudios dedicados a Menéndez Pidal*. Madrid, 1950.
GRIFFITH, T. G. *Bandello's Fiction*. Oxford, 1958.
GUAZZO, STEFANO. *La civile conversatione*. Venice, 1579.
GUEVARA, ANTONIO DE. *Reloj de príncipes o libro áureo de Marco Aurelio*. Valladolid, 1529.
——. *Aviso de privados y doctrina de cortesanos*. Valladolid, 1539.
——. *Menosprecio de corte y alabanza de aldea*, ed. Martínez de Burgos. Madrid, 1952.
——. *Epístolas familiares*, ed. J. M. Cossío. 2 vols. Madrid, 1952.
HADAS, MOSES. *A History of Greek Literature*. New York, 1950.
——. *A History of Latin Literature*. New York, 1952.
——. *Ancilla to Classical Reading*. New York, 1954.
HAFTER MONROE, Z. "Lobo's *Corte na aldeia* (1619) in a Spanish Disguise (1755)," *Romanische Forschungen*, LXXXI (1969), 567-570.
——. *Gracián and Perfection. Spanish Moralists of the Seventeenth Century* (Cambridge, Mass., 1966).
HAIGHT, ELIZABETH H. *The Roman Use of Anecdotes in Cicero, Livy, and the Satirists*. New York, 1940.
HAMILTON, RITA. "Villalon et Castiglione," *BH*, LIV (1952), 200-202.
HAURY, AUGUST. *L'ironie et l'humor chez Cicéron*. Leiden, 1955.
HEBREO, LEON. *Diálogos de amor*, tr. Inca Garcilaso de la Vega. Buenos Aires, 1947.

HERCULANO DE CARVALHO, A. "Um tipo literário e humano do barroco, o 'cortesano discreto'," *Boletim da biblioteca da Universidade de Coimbra*, XXVI (1963), 3-43.
HERRERA GARCÍA, M. *Ideas de los españoles del siglo XVII*. Madrid, 1929.
HIRZEL, RUDOLF. *Der Dialog, ein literar-historischer Versuch*. 2 vols. Hildessheim, 1963.
HORACE. *The Complete Works*, ed. C. E. Bennett. New York, 1954.
HULL, VERNON. *Renaissance Literary Criticism — A Study of its Social Content*. Gloucester, 1959.
HULME, F. E. *Proverb Lore*. London, 1902.
JANKÉLÉVITCH, VLADIMIR. "Apparence et manière," *Homenaje a Gracián*. Zaragoza, 1958. Pp. 119-129.
JORGE, RICARDO. *Francisco Rodrigues Lobo, estudo biográfico e crítico*. Coimbra, 1920.
KANY, CHARLES. *The Beginnings of the Epistolary Novel in France, Italy, Spain*. University of California Publications, XXI (1917), vii-x and 1-158.
KAYSER, WOLFGANG. *Interpretación y análisis de la obra literaria*, tr. D. Mouton and J. Yebra. Madrid, 1961.
KRAUS, WERNER. "Die Kritik des Siglo de Oro am Ritter — und Schäferroman," *Gesammelte Aufsätze zur Litteratur - und Sprachwissenschaft*. Frankfurt am Main, 1949. Pp. 152-175.
KREBS, ERNEST. "Il Cortegiano en España," *BAAL*, VIII, 93-116; IX, 125-142, 517-543.
KRISTELLER, PAUL O. *The Philosophy of Marcilio Ficino*. New York, 1943.
———. "Humanism and Scholasticism in the Italian Renaissance," *Humanitas*, X (1950), 988-1015.
———. "The Modern System of the Arts: A Study in the History of Aesthetics," *Journal of the History of Ideas*, XII (1951), 496-527.
LABANDE-JEANROY, THÉRÈSE. *La question de la langue en Italie*. Strasbourg, 1925.
LAPA, RODRIGUES, M. *Lições de literatura portuguesa, época medieval*. Coimbra, 1964.
LAPESA, RAFAEL. *Historia de la lengua española*. Madrid, 1962.
LEÃO, GASPAR DE. *Desengano de Perdidos*, ed. Eugenio Asensio. Coimbra, 1958.
LE GENTIL, GEORGES. *La littérature portugaise*. Paris, 1951.
LEVI, ALBERT W. *Literature, Philosophy, and the Imagination*, Bloomington, Indiana, 1962.
LIDA, ROSA MARÍA. "Fray Antonio de Guevara, Edad Media y Siglo de Oro español," *NRFH*, VII (1945), 346-388.
———. "La métrica de la Biblia, un motivo de Josefo y San Jerónimo en la literatura española," *Estudios... Huntington*, 335-359.
———. *La originalidad artística de la Celestina*. Buenos Aires, 1962.
LIEVSAY, JOHN L. *Stefano Guazzo and the English Renaissance*. Chapel Hill, 1961.
LOOS, ERIC. "Baltasar Castiglione's *Libro del Cortegiano*," *Analecta Romana*, II, (1955), 1-235.
LÓPEZ ESTRADA, FRANCISCO. *Antología de epístolas, separata de la introducción general*. Barcelona, n.d.
LUCK, GEORGE. "Vir facetus: A Renaissance Ideal," *SP*, LV (1958), 107-121.
MACHADO BARBOSA, DIOGO. *Biblioteca lusitana, histórica, crítica, e cronológica*. 4 vols. Lisbon, 1752.

MAGENDIE, MAURICE. *La politesse mondaine et les théories de l'honnetété en France au XVIIe siècle de 1600 à 1660.* Paris, n.d.
MARAVALL, JOSÉ ANTONIO. *Los orígenes del empirismo en el pensamiento político español del siglo XVII.* Granada, 1947.
———. "La cortesía como saber en la Edad Media: *Cuadernos Hispano Americanos.* LDXXXVI (1965) 528-538.
MARCH, AUSIAS. *Las obras,* tr. Jorge de Montemayor, ed. F. Carreres de Calatayud. Madrid, 1947.
MATOS, LUIS DE. *A corte literária dos Duques de Bragança no renascimento.* Lisbon, 1956.
MATULKA, BARBARA. *The Novels of Juan de Flores and their European Diffusion.* New York, 1931.
MAUTNER, FRANZ H. "Der Aphorismus als literarische Gattung," *Zeitschrift fur Aesthetik und allgemeine Kunstwissenschaft,* XXVII (1933), 132-175.
M. E. M. "Leaves from the Portuguese Olive — No. VI: Rodrigues Lobo," *Dublin University Magazine,* LVI (1856), 46-74.
MENÉNDEZ Y PELAYO, MARCELINO. *Historia de las ideas estéticas en España,* ed. Enrique Sánchez Reyes. 5 vols. Santander, 1947.
———. *Orígenes de la novela,* E. Sánchez Reyes. 4 vols. Santander, 1947.
MENÉNDEZ PIDAL, RAMÓN. "Lope de Vega, *El arte nuevo y la nueva biografía,*" *RFE,* XXII (1935), 347-398.
METTE, HANS JOAQUIM. "Curiositas," *Festschrift Bruno Snell.* München, 1956, pp. 227-235.
MEXÍA, PERO. *Silva de varia lección.* Anvers, 1544.
———. *Diálogos.* Seville, 1747.
MCKEON, RICHARD. "Renaissance and Method," *Columbia University Studies in the History of Ideas.* New York, 1935. II, 36-114.
MICHAELIS DE VASCONCELOS, CAROLINA. "O Judeu Errante em Portugal," *Revista Lusitana,* I (1888), 34-44. II (1890), 74-76.
MICHEL, ALAIN. *Rétorique et philosophie chez Cicéron.* Paris, 1960.
———. *Le "Dialogue des orateurs" de Tacite et la philosophie de Cicéron.* Paris, 1962.
MILÁN, LUIS. *El Cortesano,* ed. F. del V. and J. S. R. Madrid, 1874.
MONSIGLIANO, ATTILIO. *Saggio su L'Orlando furioso.* Bari, 1946.
MONTEMAYOR, JORGE. *Los siete libros de Diana,* ed. E. Moreno Báez. Madrid, 1955.
MORAIS, FRANCISCO DE. *Palmeirim de Inglaterra,* ed. S. T. Ferreira. 3 vols. Lisbon, 1786.
MORIGI, GIOVANNA WYSS. *Contributo allo studio del dialogo all'epoca del Umanesimo e del Rinascimento.* Monza, 1950.
MORREALE, MARGUERITA. "El tratado de Juan de Lucena sobre la felicidad," *NRFH,* IX (1955), 1-21.
———. "El mundo del Cortesano," *RFE,* XLII (1958), 229-260.
———. *Castiglione y Boscán: El ideal cortesano en el renacimiento español,* *BRAE,* Anejo I (1962).
———. "Una obra de cortesía en tono menor, el *Galateo español* de Lucas Gracián Dantisco", *BRAE,* XVII (1962), 47-89.
MURILLO, LUIS ANDRÉ. "The Spanish Prose Dialogue," Harvard University (unpublished dissertation, 1953).
———. "Diálogo y dialéctica en el Siglo XVI español," *RUBA,* IV (1959), 51-59.

MURRAY, GILBERT. *The Classical Tradition in Poetry*. New York, 1957.
NELSON, IVER N. "The Contribution of Pineda's *Agricultura cristiana* to the *Diccionario Histórico*," *HR*, XII (1944), 158-167; XVII (1949), 137-146.
NELSON, LOWRY. "The Rhetoric of Ineffability: Toward a Definition of Mystical Poetry," *CL*, VIII (1956), 323-336.
NUNES, JOSÉ JOAQUIM. *Compêndio de gramática histórica portuguesa*. Lisbon, 1956.
OATES, WHITNEY J. "Horace and the Doctrine of the Mean," *Classical Studies Presented to Edward Capps*. Princeton, 1936, pp. 260-267.
OLBRECHTS-TYTECA, R. *Traité de l'argumentation*. 2 vols. Paris, 1958.
OLIVEIRA MARTINS, J. *História de Portugal*. 2 vols. Lisbon, 1908.
ORIGEN. *Homélies sur le Cantique des Cantiques*, tr. O. Rousseau, OSB. Paris, 1953.
ORNSTEIN, J. "La misogenía y el profeminismo en la literatura castellana," *RFE*, III (1961), 219-276.
OSÓRIO, JERONIMO. *De regis institutionis disciplina*, tr. A. J. Cruz Figueiredo. Coimbra, n. d.
PALLAVICINO, SFORZA. *Trattato dello stile e del dialogo*. Venice, 1698.
PALMIRENO, LORENZO. *El estudioso en aldea*. Valencia, 1568.
———. *El estudioso cortesano*. Valencia, 1573.
PABST, WALTER. *Novellentheorie und Novellendichtung zur Geschichte ihrer Antinomie in den romanischen Literatur*. Hamburg, 1953.
PEDRO, PRINCE OF PORTUGAL. *O livro da virtuosa benfeitoria*, ed. Joaquim Costa. Porto, 1940.
PEIXOTO, AFRANIO. "A paixão de Camões," *Arquivo camoniano*. Rio de Janeiro, 1943, pp. 232-267.
PERELMAN, CHAIM. *Rhétorique et Philosophie*. Paris, 1952.
———. *Traité et l'argumentation*. 2 vols. Paris, 1958.
PERES, DAMIÃO, Ed. *História de Portugal*. 8 vols. Barcelos, 1928.
PFANDL, LUDWIG. *Historia de la literatura nacional española del Siglo de Oro*, tr. J. R. Balaguer. Barcelona, 1952.
PINEDA, JUAN. *Agricultura cristiana*. BAE, CLXI-CLXIII.
PINHEIRO CHAGAS, M. *História de Portugal*. 12 vols. Lisbon, n. d.
PINTO, HEITOR. *Imagem da vida cristã*, ed. M. Alves Correia. 4 vols. Lisbon, 1957.
PLACE, ARTHUR S. "Things without Honor," *CP*, XXI (1926), 27-42.
PLATO. *Dialogues*, tr. D. Jewett. 5 vols. Oxford, 1892.
PORQUERAS MAYO, A. "Función del 'Vulgo' en la preceptiva dramática de la Edad de Oro," *RFE*, L (1967), 123-143 (in collaboration with F. Sánchez-Escribano).
PRADO DE COELHO, JACINTO (ed). *Dicionário de Literatura*. 2 vols (Porto, 1970-71).
QUINTILIAN. *Institutio oratoria*, tr. and ed. John S. Watson. 3 vols. London, 1873.
RENNERT, HUGO A. *The Spanish Pastoral Romance*, Philadelphia, 1912.
RÉVAH, I. S. "Les Marranes," *Bulletin des Etudes Juives*, CXVII (1958), 29-77.
———. "João de Barros," *Revista do Livro*, III (1958), 61-72.
REYES, ALFONSO. "De un autor censurado en el *Quijote*," *CA*, VI (1947), 188-224.

RIBEIRO, BERNARDIN. *Menina e moça*, ed. Dorothy Grokenberger. Lisbon, 1947.
RICE, EUGENE F. *The Renaissance Idea of Wisdom*. Cambridge, Massachusetts, 1958.
RILEY, EDWARD C. "Episodio, novela, y aventura en Don Quijote," *AC*, V (1955), 209-231.
ROBB, NESCA A. *Neo-Platonism of the Italian Renaissance*. London, 1935.
RODRIGUES LOBO, FRANCISCO. *Corte na aldeia e noites de inverno*. Lisbon, 1619.
——. *Corte na aldeia...*, ed. A. Lopes Vieira. Lisbon, 1959.
——. *Corte en aldea y noches de invierno*, tr. Morales. Montilla, 1623.
——. *Obras políticas, morais, e métricas do insigne português Francisco Rodrigues Lobo natural de Leiria*. Lisbon, 1723.
——. *Éclogas*, ed. José Pereira Tavares. Coimbra, 1928.
——. *Cartas dos grandes do mundo*, ed. Ricardo Jorge. Coimbra, 1934.
ROMERO-NAVARRO, M. "La defensa de la lengua española en el Siglo XV," *BH*, XXXI (1929), 204-255.
RUDIGERS, HORST. "Pura et illustris brevitas," *Festschrift fur Erich Rothacker*, ed. Gerhard Funkes. Bonn, 1958, pp. 345-372.
SÁ DE MIRANDA, FRANCISCO. *Obras*, ed. M. Rodrigues Lapa. 2 vols. Lisbon, 1960.
SABBADINI, REMIGIO. *Storia del Ciceronianismo*. Torino, 1886.
SALAS BARADILLO, GERÓNIMO. *El caballero perfecto*, ed. Pauline Marshall *University of Colorado Studies in Language and Literature*, II (1949), i-li and 1-95.
SANCEAU, ELAINE. *D. João de Castro, Knight of the Renaissance*, London, n. d.
SÁNCHEZ ESCRIBANO, F. "Santillana y la colección de *Refranes*, Medina del Campo," *HR*, X (1942), 354-358.
SANMARTÍ BONCOMPTE, FRANCISCO. *Tácito en España*. Barcelona, 1951.
SANTO ANTÓNIO, ALEIXO DE. *Filosofia moral tirada de alguns provérbios ou adágios...* Coimbra, 1640.
SARAIVA, JOSÉ A. *História da literatura portuguesa*. Porto, n. d.
——. *História da cultura em Portugal*. 3 vols. Lisbon, 1953.
SAVAGE, HOWARD J. "Italian Influences in English Prose Fiction," *PMLA*, XXXII (1917), 1-21.
SCHNEER, WALTER J. "Two Courtiers: Castiglione and Rodrigues Lobo," *CL*, XIII (1961), 138-153.
SCUDIERI, JOLE. "Premessa allo studio linguistico del *Agricultura cristiana* di Fr. Juan de Pineda," *Cultura neolatina*, XX (1960), 253-259.
SENA, JORGE DE. *Uma canção de Camões*. Lisbon, 1966.
SEVERIM DE FARIA, MANUEL. *Discursos políticos*. Lisbon, 1624.
SHEPARD, SANFORD. *El Pinciano y las teorías literarias del Siglo de Oro*. Madrid, 1962.
SILVA, INOCENCIO FRANCISCO DA. *Dicionário bibliográfico português*. 22 vols. Lisbon, 1859.
SINCLAIR, THOMAS ALAN. *A History of Classical Greek Literature*. New York, 1935.
SPINA, SEGISMUNDO, ed. *Apresentação da Poesia Barrôca Portuguêsa*. Sao Paulo, 1967.

Spitzer, Leo. *Classical and Christian Ideas of World Harmony. Prolegomena to an Interpretation of one Word, 'Stimmung.'* Baltimore, 1963.
Tarrant, Dorothy. "Plato as Dramatist." *Journal of Hellenic Studies*. LV (1955), 82-89.
Taylor, Alfred. *Plato, the Man and His Work*. New York, 1958.
Thomas, H. *Las novelas de caballerías españolas y portuguesas*, tr. Esteban Pujals. Madrid, 1952.
Thomas, F.-J. *A Short History of Philosophy*, tr. E. A. Maziarz. New York, 1955.
Timoneda, Juan de. *El patrañuelo o el sobremesa y alivio de caminantes*, e. V. Blasco Ibáñez. Valencia, 1927.
Toffani, Giuseppi. *El cortegiano nella trattatistica del rinascimento*. Naples, n. d.
Torquemada, Antonio de. *Jardín de flores curiosas*. Salamanca, 1570.
Trancoso, Gonçalo Fernandes. *Histórias de proveito e exemplo*, ed. Agostinho de Campos. Lisbon, 1921.
Valdés, Juan de. *Diálogo de la lingua*, ed. José F. Montesinos, Madrid, 1928.
Vasconcelos, Jorge Ferreira. *Comédia de Eufrosina*, ed. Eugenio Asensio, 1951.
Vega Carpio, Lope Felix de. "Descripción de la Tapada," *BAE*, XXXVIII, 455-458.
Vicente Gil. *Obras*, ed. Marques Braga. 6 vols. Lisbon, 1952.
Vossa, Juan Baptista. *Sossia perseguida*. Madrid, 1621.
Vossler, Karl. *Introducción a la literatura española del Siglo de Oro*. México, 1961.
Weinberg, Bernard. *A History of Literary Criticism in the Italian Renaissance*. 2 vols. Chicago, 1961.
Wilamowitz-Moellendorf, Ulrich von. "Erkenne dich selbst," *Reden und Vortrage*. Berlin, 1929.
Wilkins, Eliza. *The Delphic Maxim in Literature*. Chicago, 1929.
Wind, E. "The Revival of Origen," *Studies in Art Literature for Belle du Costa Grene*, ed. D. E. Miner (Princeton, 1954), pp. 412-424.
Woodward, William H. *Vittorino da Feltre and Other Humanist Educators*. Cambridge, Massachusetts, 1912.
———. *Studies in Education during the Age of the Renaissance*. Cambridge, Massachusetts, 1924.
Xenophon, *Works*, tr. H. G. Dilkyns, London, 1892.
Zanta, Léontine. *La rénaissance du Stoicisme au XVI siècle*. Paris, 1914.

www.ingramcontent.com/pod-product-compliance
Lightning Source LLC
Chambersburg PA
CBHW022022220426
43663CB00007B/1178